THE PRIMARY CORE NATIONAL CURRICULUM
Second Edition

The Primary Core National Curriculum

Policy into Practice

Second Edition

Edited by

David Coulby and Stephen Ward

CASSELL

This book is dedicated to Jacquie and Heather

Cassell
Wellington House
125 Strand
London WC2R 0BB

127 West 24th Street
New York
NY 10011

British Library Cataloguing-in-Publication Data
A catalogue record for this book is available from the British Library.

ISBN 0-304-33804-4

Typeset by York House Typographic Ltd, London
Printed and bound in Great Britain by Redwood Books Trowbridge, Wiltshire

Contents

Notes on Contributors   vi
Preface to the Second Edition   viii
Abbreviations   x

1   The Construction and Implementation of the Primary Core Curriculum
    David Coulby   1

2   English in the National Curriculum
    Howard Gibson   15

3   Mathematics in the National Curriculum
    Mike Spooner   38

4   Science in the National Curriculum
    Ron Ritchie   53

5   Thematic Approaches to the Core National Curriculum
    Stephen Ward   71

6   Implementing English in the National Curriculum
    Sally Yates   96

7   Implementing Mathematics in the National Curriculum
    Ruth Barrington   120

8   Implementing Science in the National Curriculum
    Diane Ward   143

9   Information Technology in the National Curriculum
    David Clemson   158

Index   180

Notes on Contributors

Ruth Barrington is a Senior Lecturer in Primary Mathematics at Bath College of Higher Education. Prior to this she taught in Sandwell Local Education Authority as a primary school teacher and as a mathematics support teacher.

David Clemson taught in primary schools in Wolverhampton where he later became a primary advisory teacher. Since 1987 he has been Senior Lecturer in Information Technology and Primary Professional Studies at Bath College of Higher Education. During this period he has worked closely with NCET in developing teacher support materials: *Getting Started with Information Handling* and *Making Sense of Information*. He is also a member of the DFEE Primary GEST-IT steering committee. He is particularly interested in the development of pupils autonomous use of IT applications through the principles of child-centred primary practice.

David Coulby is Dean of the Faculty of Education and Human Sciences at Bath College of Higher Education. His most recent book is (with Crispin Jones) *Postmodernism and European Education Systems*.

Howard Gibson taught at the University of Hull and in primary schools and worked as an advisory teacher for English in East Sussex. He is a Senior Lecturer in Language in Primary Education at Bath College of Higher Education. His research interests include the study of texts and the use of non-Standard English.

Ron Ritchie is Head of Department for Professional Development at Bath College of Higher Education where he is responsible for in-service courses and consultancy activities. Prior to working in higher education he was an advisory teacher for science in Avon. He has taught in secondary and primary schools. He is the author of numerous books and articles on the teaching of science and technology, including *Primary Science: Making it Work* (with Chris Ollerenshaw, 1993) and *Primary Design and Technology: a Process for Learning* (1995).

Mike Spooner is a Senior Lecturer in Primary Mathematics at Bath College of Higher Education where he teaches on undergraduate and in-service programmes. Before joining the staff at the college he worked as a primary school teacher in England and overseas and latterly as an advisory teacher in Avon.

Diane Ward joined the staff of Bath College of Higher Education in 1991 as Senior Lecturer in Primary Science. She taught in schools in the UK and in Kenya before becoming an advisory teacher in primary science for Avon Local Education Authority.

Stephen Ward taught in primary and secondary schools and in a language centre in Leeds before joining Bath College of Higher Education. He has run the In-service Programme for Teachers at the college and is now the co-ordinator of the Primary Undergraduate Initial Teacher Training Course. Other publications include (with Jo Glover) *Teaching Music in the Primary School.*

Sally Yates taught in primary schools in Inner London before becoming an advisory teacher for language. She is currently Senior Lecturer and Curriculum Co-ordinator for Language at Bath College of Higher Education. She teaches on undergraduate, postgraduate and in-service courses. Her main research interests are in the teaching and development of reading and children's literature.

Preface to the Second Edition

The evolution of the National Curriculum for England and Wales has been complex and controversial. The first edition of this book appeared in 1990 shortly after the introduction of the core subjects – English, mathematics and science – in schools. Since then the other subjects have appeared and there have been six years of teachers' efforts to implement the orders. As was predicted in Chapter 1 of the first edition, the statutory curriculum proved to be overloaded and the ambitious standardized assessment schedule impossible to implement. The much publicized conflict between politicians and professionals came to a head in 1993 with the government's capitulation over testing, the agreement to slim down the statutory curriculum and the return of some control of the curriculum to teachers. One result of this process of reduction has been a return to the salience of the core subjects, which makes a second edition of this book timely.

The first edition told of the development of English, mathematics and science in the National Curriculum: the controversies and the conflicts which had occurred in devising the content of each subject. Suggestions for the implementation of the core subjects were also given, together with a discussion of curriculum integration.

In this edition, Chapter 1 reviews the years of conflict between politicians and professionals and sets the scene for the next three chapters. These take up the stories of each of the subjects, examining the twists and turns of proposals, orders and revisions, and show how the original debates of 1989 have been followed through. Chapter 5 continues the discussion of the integration of the core curriculum in the light of current thinking about primary teaching methods.

A second result of the thinning of the National Curriculum documents in 1995 was the lack of the type of non-statutory guidance which accompanied the orders in 1989. This makes the need for guidance on implementation of the curriculum orders even more important. Chapters 6, 7 and 8 review the ways in which teachers are implementing the statutory orders for English, mathematics and science. These are not comprehensive guides on how to teach each of the subjects. Instead, they offer examples of the policies and practice which schools have employed, the way they have formed and managed curriculum policies and the role of subject co-ordinators together. There is also commentary on the development of teaching methods.

Since 1989 the role of information technology (IT) has become even more urgent in primary schools and can now be said to be a *core subject*: 'As in all key stages, basic skills in information technology should form part of the core' (Dearing, 1993, p.30, para. 3.20). For this reason an additional chapter on information technology in the primary curriculum has been included in the present volume. It stresses the need for skills in information technology and provides a perspective on the curriculum for the twenty-first century.

ACKNOWLEDGEMENTS

Thanks are due to the many primary teachers who supported us in the production of this book by offering examples of their classroom practice and by sharing with us their ideas about the implementation of the National Curriculum.

In particular the authors and editors are grateful to colleagues in the following schools which are mentioned in the text:

Abbotswood Infants School, Yate, near Bristol
Bleakhouse Junior School, Oldbury, Warley, West Midlands
Henleaze Junior School, Bristol
Moorlands Infants School, Bath
Shield Road Primary School, Bristol
Walwayne Court Primary School, Trowbridge
Widcombe Infants School, Bath

We are also grateful to our students on initial teacher education and professional development courses for their support in discussing ideas and practice.

REFERENCES

Coulby, D. and Ward, S. (1990) *The Primary Core National Curriculum: Policy into Practice.* London: Cassell.
Dearing, R. (1993) *The National Curriculum and its Assessment: An Interim Report.* London: SCAA.

Abbreviations

APU	Assessment of Performance Unit
ASE	Association for Science Education
AT	attainment target
CIP	Classroom Interaction Project
CLIS	Children Learning in Science (project)
CTC	City Technology College
DES	Department of Education and Science
DFEE	Department for Education and Employment
ESG	education support grant
INSET	in-service education of teachers
IPSE	Initiatives in Primary Science: an Evaluation
IT	information technology
LEA	Local Education Authority
NCC	National Curriculum Council
NSG	non-statutory guidance
OFSTED	Office for Standards in Education
PC	profile component
SAT	standard assessment task
SCAA	Schools Curriculum and Assessment Authority
SCDC	School Curriculum Development Committee
SE	Standard English
SEAC	School Examinations and Assessment Council
SPACE	Science Processes and Concept Exploration
TA	teacher assessment
TGAT	Task Group on Assessment and Testing

Chapter 1

The Construction and Implementation of the Primary Core Curriculum

David Coulby

THE ORIGINAL NATIONAL CURRICULUM AND THE REVISED NATIONAL CURRICULUM

When the first edition of this book was published, the National Curriculum in primary schools consisted only of the core. The rest of the National Curriculum was still being developed. Now much of the rest of the curriculum has been slimmed down. The emphasis is back on the core curriculum. This is the area which, although revised, has had by far the least reduction in importance. It is, critically, the area where national assessment and/or tests will continue to be conducted. Once again, in primary schools, the emphasis is overwhelmingly on the core curriculum.

This book sets out to clarify the three core subjects of the National Curriculum – English, mathematics and science – as they will apply in primary schools following the Dearing revision which was finalized in 1995 for implementation in primary schools in the same year. Following the decision to make information technology a distinct and compulsory strand of the National Curriculum, it contains a chapter on the way in which this will link with the core subjects. In order to provide background on the evolution and revision of the primary core curriculum, the book explains the debates which took place at the time that the three subjects were being finalized in 1989 and revised in 1994. It then goes on to consider how the best of primary practice can be developed within the revised National Curriculum and indeed how the national framework can provide opportunities for further improvement. Crucial to this, the book emphasizes the part which primary teachers and headteachers have themselves already played and have yet to play in the formulation of the revised National Curriculum. Without this active engagement on the part of the practitioners the national framework will still not become a successful aspect of primary school practice.

It is necessary at the outset to distinguish two core curriculum initiatives in primary schools. The first, preparation for which began in 1987, was gradually implemented following the passing of the 1988 Education Act. This was part of the grand curriculum edifice created by the Act which consisted of all pupils between the ages of 5 and 16 across England and Wales following the same highly specified syllabus which would occupy almost all their time in school. This grand curriculum was to be accompanied by regular detailed testing and by meticulous record-keeping and reporting. This edifice started to crumble long before its construction was completed and, following a sequence of modifications and exemptions which cumulated in the Dearing Review, a second, much slimmed-down National Curriculum was evolved in 1994 for implementation from 1995 onwards (DFE, 1995a; DFE, 1995b). This chapter continually distinguishes between the original National Curriculum and the revised National Curriculum.

Obviously the introduction of the revised National Curriculum provides the ideal opportunity for publishing a second edition of this book. Not only has the primary core curriculum itself been changed, but developments in primary curriculum planning and in primary teaching which have taken place since the publication of the first edition can also be incorporated. However, there are some elements which have not changed. Firstly, the core curriculum is the least slimmed-down and hence the least changed component of the primary curriculum. Secondly, the critique which the first edition made of the practicality of implementing the original National Curriculum proved to be a very accurate forecast of the difficulties against which it subsequently faltered. The editors were not alone in making such predictions, of course, but the nature of the commentary of the first edition has proved to be a sound touchstone against which to assess the revised National Curriculum. Thirdly, the political debates which surrounded the formation of the original National Curriculum were couched in the terms which still dominate in conflict over the revised National Curriculum. The emphasis of the book remains on the possibilities which the core National Curriculum provides to primary schools and teachers to develop sound curriculum planning and practice.

These possibilities lie in at least two directions. Firstly, the removal of much of the content from the rest of the curriculum returns to teachers the flexibility to design their curriculum more according to their pupils' needs and interests and their own expertise. In this respect, the removal of much of the overcrowding will also mean that the core curriculum can itself be adequately taught without the interference of time pressures. Secondly, the core provides a range of subjects and topics which themselves lead into other curricular areas, thus allowing for a less fragmented and distracted curriculum.

THE NATIONAL CURRICULUM AND THE 1988 EDUCATION ACT

In approaching the revised National Curriculum in this way, the book sees it as a major opportunity to be grasped by primary schools. However, the National Curriculum cannot be understood apart from the wider legislation within which it is embedded. Certainly it cannot be separated from the 1988 Education Act, of which it actually forms so small a portion. There has been a tendency to treat the National Curriculum as an isolated topic, as if it existed in a legislative vacuum (for instance, Emerson and Goddard, 1989; Pring, 1989). The wider legislative context and, in particular, the assessment arrangements are actually fundamental to understanding both the National Curriculum and its political purposes.

One of the main purposes of the 1988 Act was to increase differentiation between schools and to encourage competition between them (for a further discussion of the issues raised in this section see Bash and Coulby, 1989; Coulby and Bash, 1991). Differentiation at secondary level was increased by the foundation of City Technology Colleges and the establishment of grant-maintained status for schools. This introduced the opportunity to 'opt out' of Local Education Authority (LEA) control and receive funding directly from the then Department of Education and Science (DES), now Department for Education and Employment (DFEE). For both primary and secondary schools competition was increased through the introduction of open enrolment. This meant that schools could enrol pupils beyond the numerical limits which had previously been established by LEAs. The funding of schools is based on a formula whereby the more pupils who are enrolled, the larger the budget of the school. Popular schools could and did increase their rolls and sprout mobile classrooms in their playgrounds. The rolls of less popular schools commensurately fell and in some cases their future viability has come into question. At the same time, the introduction of devolved resources and local management of primary schools provided both the mechanisms and the ethos to increase competitiveness between schools. Headteachers, having found themselves and their governors responsible for the school's budget, realized that they might be faced with making teachers redundant or making other undesirable cuts in resources if they did not recruit sufficient pupils. In order to avoid this they began, openly or covertly, to compete for pupils.

The encouragement of competitiveness rests on the philosophy that by competing individuals and institutions make themselves strong and effective. It is considered necessary to reward the effective and to penalize the less effective. In the case of primary schools, the effective ones will be rewarded with more pupils and resources and the less effective ones will receive fewer pupils and less resources and so ultimately close, to make way completely for their more successful rivals. The issue at this stage is neither with the moral or economic rightness of this philosophy, nor with its appropriateness for application to schools; rather it is with the role of the National Curriculum in the implementation of this wave of educational change.

In this respect it is necessary to consider on what basis the schools have been competing. To a certain extent the terms of the competition are those of parental gossip and rumour, often enough fed by the tidiness of school uniforms, the success of football teams and the demeanour of pupils on their way to and from school. The National Curriculum and its associated assessment arrangements have provided much more public and apparently objective terms for the competition than were previously available. For secondary schools this has resulted in national league tables which are now published on an annual basis. Testing at 7 and 11 provides the basis on which parents may judge primary schools (even though for some schools the 7-year-old results may not have been officially published). The National Curriculum is inseparable from its assessment arrangements because these provide the politically necessary criteria on which competition between schools, between teachers and between pupils can be introduced with the appearance of legitimacy.

This book is by no means an unremitting critique of the National Curriculum. On the contrary, the authors regard it as an important opportunity for primary schools. However, in examining and developing the opportunities, the wider framework of political change, within which the National Curriculum rests, must not be forgotten.

THE POLITICS OF THE NATIONAL PRIMARY CORE CURRICULUM

The general principles behind the introduction of the National Curriculum as it was originally proposed (DES and Welsh Office, 1987) met with a good deal of political and professional approval. These principles included the advantages of continuity within and between schools and the establishment of a clear curricular entitlement for all children. Opposition to the introduction of the National Curriculum tended to focus on the testing arrangements or on the exclusion of particular subjects from the statutory curriculum. Concern was, however, expressed at the way in which the compulsory curriculum of state schools was to be determined (Simon, 1988; White, 1988). The concern was that the knowledge now to be taught in schools was to be decided finally not by subject experts nor by teachers but by politicians. From the outset the National Curriculum was a site of conflict between politicians and professionals for the control of school knowledge.

The 1988 Act clearly and deliberately gave the power to determine what is taught, in both the core and foundation subjects, to the Secretaries of State for Education and for Wales. In practice the decisions are taken by the Secretary of State for Education. It is important to stress that there is nothing intrinsically undemocratic about this. On the contrary, controversial subjects are decided in a democracy by means of the decisions of properly elected representatives. There is little doubt that during the 1970s and 1980s the school curriculum had become an area of political interest and controversy (Coulby, 1989a). It is apparently appropriate, then, that it should have been placed in the hands of elected representatives rather than left with teachers or experts, neither of whom have any democratic mandate.

It could be objected that local democratically elected representatives – via LEAs – might have been better placed to ensure that a common curriculum was also responsive to particular needs and interests of different areas. But this would, even if not to a necessarily damaging extent, impair the attractive notion of a national curriculum. However, given that fee-paying schools and City Technology Colleges, not to mention Scotland and Northern Ireland, are exempt from the compulsory National Curriculum, the case for total Westminster control is considerably weakened. Furthermore, in a general election, it is more than possible that the content of the primary school curriculum might be less influential on people's voting decisions than, say, promises about income tax or defence policy. In a local election, by contrast, educational issues are more likely to have a greater influence on the way in which people vote. Certainly, the earlier attempts, in the late 1970s and early 1980s, which had been made by LEAs to co-ordinate the curricula within their schools had resulted in a haphazard pattern which was far from a structured national curriculum. But this should perhaps have pointed to the difficulties and dangers facing anyone attempting to impose a single national scheme. Either way the formation of a credible national curriculum was going to take more time than politicians were prepared to allow. A piecemeal curriculum developed by LEAs would have been slow and not necessarily consistent and system-atic but it might have carried wider teacher and parent consent. The original central National Curriculum collapsed under its own weight and time and credibility were wasted in the process.

The issue of a national curriculum was not seen as an exclusively right-wing concern in 1987. Indeed, prior to the 1988 Act, a core curriculum had been a component of the progressive educational agenda. However, with a school curriculum controlled by Westminster party politicians, there was the risk that there would be major changes in what is meant to be taught in schools each time the government, or indeed the Secretary of State for Education and Science, changed. This risk was well borne out by the tinkering and interference that took place, under Baker, Clark and Patten, between 1988 and 1994. There was further the risk that the school curriculum would be constructed in a way which is politically partisan. In short, the passing of the 1988 Act made possible the introduction of deliberate political bias into the school curriculum (Coulby, 1989b). There were many who feared at the time that this was actually the intention of the National Curriculum clauses of that Act (White, 1988). From the outset, the National Curriculum placed heavy stress on the basic three Rs and explicitly excluded, for instance, all forms of social science. These fears were strengthened by the 1988 Act's stipulation that compulsory religious education should be of a 'mainly Christian' character, as it seemed like a manifestation of the traditionally Anglican aspect of Toryism. It was anticipated that the National Curriculum which was to be drawn up would be a Conservative curriculum, traditionalist, formal, unintegrated and nationalist.

The Secretaries of State certainly have had the power to ensure that this is the case. They were able to appoint the members of the working groups established in 1987 and 1988 to draw up the syllabus for each subject as well as the members of the National Curriculum Council (NCC) itself. The NCC was, with the Schools Examination and Assessment Council (SEAC), one of the two predecessors of the Schools Curriculum and Assessment Authority (SCAA), founded from their effective merger. At the time of the initial NCC appointments the newspapers reported clear political vetoing of appointees, coming, it was rumoured, from the then Prime Minister herself. Further, the roles of the NCC and SEAC were anyway only advisory. SCAA remains an advisory body, like its predecessors a classic quango. The Secretaries of State were free to ignore their recommendations, and in some cases did just that. Where this did not happen strict political guidance was given to the NCC as to how it should modify the final reports of the working groups. Similarly, firm initial and supplementary guidance was given to all the working groups by the Secretary of State for Education and Science.

After the passing of the 1988 Education Act, then, there was an expectation that the schools were about to have thrust on them a controversial and politicized National Curriculum. Were these expectations justified by the way in which the core primary curriculum was, in the event, drawn up, implemented, modified and subsequently radically revised?

THE CONSTRUCTION AND DESTRUCTION OF THE ORIGINAL NATIONAL CORE CURRICULUM

The three core curriculum subjects, mathematics, science and English, were the first to be finalized. The main mechanisms for their establishment were three working groups, one for each subject. It is worth considering these working groups in some detail since they had such influence on both the original and the revised National Curriculum. It is helpful to observe their impact on the National Curriculum in terms of membership, structure and time-scale. The working groups were appointed by the then Secretary of

State, Baker. Their membership had no mandate from the teaching profession, from LEAs, from learned associations of subject specialists or from university departments. They were not in any sense meant to be seen to be representative. However, their membership was widely drawn and did, indeed, include recognized national subject experts, practising teachers (though no primary teachers on the mathematics group) and representatives of LEAs and teacher-training institutions. There were also members from industry and commerce – that is, from one side of industry and commerce; there were no members chosen for their work in the trade union movement. The membership of the groups, then, was safely, if not provocatively, right wing, but with good representation from specialists and professionals. This pattern was repeated in appointments made to the NCC and to SEAC. It has again been replicated for the new quango, SCAA.

The minutes of these original working groups have not been made public nor have those of the conversations between the various chairs and the Secretary of State. These working groups were actually having the definitive conversations about the content of school knowledge in England and Wales and their minutes would certainly make interesting reading. A group of people was gathered together to decide what should be the content of major subjects in both primary and secondary schools. Their debates might well have reflected familiar conflicts within each subject area, but the resolution of those debates constituted an unprecedented step towards the finalization of school knowledge. The absurdity of such proceedings should not distract from their significance.

There were surprisingly few leaks from the groups and it would be interesting to know, further, the mode of procedure of the working groups and especially whether they actually split up into subgroups to determine the particular details (profile components – PCs) of the core curriculum. If this were the procedure it might explain the resulting proliferation of PCs and attainment targets (ATs). It could well be that the chairs of each of the working groups, beset with demands for the inclusion of material from a range of subgroups, took the easy route and simply included everything.

But perhaps there is no need to look further than the tight time-scales to explain the proliferation of the material. The working groups were composed in the main of people who already had busy jobs; they were attempting to finalize the National Curriculum in a matter of months, and doing it in their spare time. In order to prevent proliferation, the groups would have had to have honed down their early work, looking for overlaps and seeking the most parsimonious formats; they would, further, have had to do this across all the groups to avoid overlap and duplication. This work, to judge by the results, was not done. It could not have been done in the time allowed by the Secretaries of State. They, of course, were in a hurry to have some results to show in order to prove their effectiveness to their party and to the electorate. The upshot was that an overcrowded National Curriculum was hurriedly introduced into primary schools after tokenistic consultation and inadequate preparation. It was only after this first National Curriculum had collapsed on its introduction to secondary schools that a more rigorous review of the whole curriculum was undertaken and a full process of consultation with the teaching profession initiated, as then Secretary of State Patten belatedly brought in Lord Dearing in a doomed attempt to save his own political career.

The major structural decision about the groups, and the one which had most impact on the subsequent shape of the National Curriculum, was one over which the members had little influence. That was the decision to have subject groups at all. As Chapter 5 makes clear, a more sensible procedure for primary education might have been to have constructed the National Curriculum by age phase. The decision to have subject-based groups meant that an unintegrated and secondary-oriented National Curriculum was predetermined. (See Chapter 5 for a further discussion of this.) The subject-based nature of the groups also accounts for some of the syllabus overload of the original National Curriculum. Working in isolation and committed to their own particular subjects, the members of the working groups were not able to leave out any area of knowledge with the certainty that another group would cover it. The principle became to include everything and, at best, to cross-reference it to the recommendations of other groups.

The ways in which the three core areas of the National Curriculum were constructed were subtly and importantly different, although each followed the same broad pattern. The substance of the debates involved in this construction is outlined and discussed for each subject in the three succeeding chapters. These chapters also examine the ways in which the revised core curriculum differs from that originally implemented. At this stage, it is the differences in the process which need to be clarified, since the finalization of each of the core subjects provides an insight into that conflict between political and professional pressure which so readily emerged.

A Mathematics Working Group was established but its *Interim Report* (Mathematics Working Group, 1987) met with the displeasure of the then Secretary of State, Baker. The chair resigned and the group produced a final report (DES and Welsh Office, 1988a) which went to the NCC with a commentary from the Secretary of State. The NCC carried out a consultation exercise, the results of which it explicitly ignored, preferring to follow the precepts of the Secretary of State. Baker consulted rapidly on the NCC advice, published draft orders with no important changes, again consulted rapidly and produced final orders which once more were not significantly changed.

The Science Working Group's *Interim Report* (Science Working Group, 1987) had a more favourable reception from the Secretary of State and they were able to continue under the same chair to produce their final report (DES and Welsh Office, 1988b). Again stern advice from the Secretaries of State (playing down the ATs for exploration and investigation and for communication and science in action) accompanied the final report on its way to the NCC. Again the NCC explicitly chose to heed this advice rather than the overwhelming results of their consultation. More consultation led to draft orders and yet more consultation to final orders without there being any major change of substance.

Whilst the 1987 Education Bill was still before Parliament a Committee of Inquiry into the Teaching of English Language had been established. The reasons for this were the orchestration of traditionalist fears over changes in the language curriculum which had supposedly resulted in matters such as grammar and spelling being neglected in both primary and secondary schools (see Chapter 2). Given that this committee, chaired by Kingman, was already in operation, it was thought inappropriate to establish a working group. The Kingman Report (DES, 1988) made recommendations which could be interpreted as a reassertion of the importance of grammar in the English curriculum. When a delighted Baker affirmed that the Kingman Report should form the basis for the deliberations of the English Working Group, and announced that the group would be chaired by a member of the Kingman Committee and prominent Black

Paperist, Brian Cox, fears about the politicization of the school curriculum were at their height.

Because of the scramble to have the primary core curriculum up and running in September 1989, the English Working Group published its recommendations for ages 5 to 11 (DES and Welsh Office, 1988c) in advance of completing its work on the secondary phase (DES and Welsh Office, 1989). The final reports did not in the event echo the traditionalist concerns of Kingman, advocating instead the adoption of much of the best of current progressive primary practice in the language area, including speaking and listening and the recognition of the importance of non-standard forms of English and of the strengths of bilingual pupils. With the September 1989 deadline for the introduction of the core curriculum to 5-year-olds ever nearer, the NCC followed up with ATs and programmes of study for the first key stage only (NCC, 1989). In this case the NCC's changes apparently showed them to be more right wing than the government. It was reported in the press at the time that Cox and his entire group had threatened to resign, leaving their secondary work uncompleted, because of the changes made by the NCC (Nash, 89). In the event, Baker sided with Cox and the final orders actually saw the reinstatement of the more liberal and professionally acceptable consensus advocated by the working group. Retrospectively this might be seen as the first victory for the professionals, particularly important as it was in the key subject of English, which later provided the decisive battleground. Nevertheless, the English curriculum remained subject to conflict. It was the one area of the core curriculum which the government was already revising before the establishment of the Dearing Review.

The Science and Mathematics working groups were the first to be established along with a third general group, the Task Group on Assessment and Testing (TGAT). The reports of this group (TGAT, 1987; TGAT, 1988) were highly influential on all subsequent thinking on the National Curriculum and its main recommendations were not completely abandoned even in the Dearing revision. However, following the Dearing revision, their influence on the shape and scale of the National Curriculum is far less tight. At the time of their publication the recommendations of TGAT served to reassure many in the profession that national assessment need not be a reversion to crude eleven-plus style testing. The first report emphasized the formative aspects of assessment. A range of assessment approaches, consistent with normal classroom activities and delivered and marked by teachers, was advocated as against short sharp standardized tests.

In a sense the TGAT reports can be seen as an attempt to professionalize the political demand for testing. As indicated in the first section of this chapter, the importance of testing in the 1988 Act is far from confined to ensuring the effective implementation of the National Curriculum. The tests were intended as the mechanisms for the introduction of competitiveness into state schooling. The TGAT reports, stressing the positive values of assessment and ignoring the probable negative effects, inevitably came as a relief to professionals. However, if the relief was any more than short-lived it was the product of wishful thinking. It was the framework of ATs, key stages and the 10-level scale established by TGAT which was to assist the working groups in their proliferation of curricular material.

The predictions of a politicized National Curriculum were, to a limited extent, proved, as subject material was argued among sponsored and selected professionals and between professionals and politicians. Whilst the Secretaries of State clearly had the loudest voices throughout this process, the inclinations of the profession and of the subject specialists were far from unheard. The content of the core curriculum was recognizably the product of the right in British politics, but, except perhaps for the exclusion of multicultural and equal opportunities aspects, it was not blatantly politicized. In some cases, notably English, political intention did seem to have been suborned by professional determination. This conflict between political intention and professional resistance is one of the main elements in the implementation – and even in the actual formation – of the National Curriculum.

The original testing arrangements proved even less pervious to professional argument. The proliferation of ATs meant that a considerable amount of teacher time was being spent on setting, marking and moderating the tests as well as on completing the demanding forms and records which were associated with the assessment of the original National Curriculum (DES, 1989). So demanding did this work become that the time needed to assess the National Curriculum was seriously undermining the time available to teach it.

It became increasingly evident that the shift to national testing at four ages was a leap in the dark. It was not something that had in any way been previously attempted. The mechanisms put into place were highly bureaucratic. It became clear that where there was a difference between a teacher assessment and the result of a national test, it was the latter which was to be deemed correct (Halsey, 1989). The principles of teacher-directed assessment within the normal activities of the school day, apparently embodied in the TGAT reports, seemed gradually to be being abandoned.

The original National Curriculum was implemented in schools beginning with the youngest children. It was first seen in practice in infant classes and then with juniors. Against the difficulties of rapid introduction, little preparation, curriculum overload and extensive testing, primary schools struggled in the period following 1988. Whilst the difficulties of implementation became apparent and were increasingly being emphasized by teacher and specialist groups, it was only when the original National Curriculum was visited on secondary schools that it finally hit the political rocks. The testing arrangements announced for Key Stage 3 in 1993 met considerable opposition. In particular the English tests were strongly opposed by the English secondary teachers. This group was well organized through the National Association of Teachers of English and their well reasoned opposition to the tests received wide professional support.

In the face of this opposition, the then Secretary of State, Patten, was prepared to make few concessions. The record of the implementation of the National Curriculum up to this point seemed to indicate that the Secretary of State could do as he wished and take no account of professional opinion. Opposition to the Key Stage 3 tests, however, was but one manifestation of deep seated professional suspicion of the whole national testing and league table publishing enterprise. Even the heads of fee-paying schools voiced their criticism of the testing arrangements. The opposition was taken up by the teachers' trade unions. Cleverly, the trade unions did not voice political opposition to the testing, they merely concentrated on the increased workload which the testing procedures implied for their members. This view was taken clearly and strongly by the National Association of Schoolmasters/Union of Women Teachers. The trade unions took national ballots and received a mandate for teachers boycotting the tests, not only at Key Stage 3 but in primary schools as well. Wandsworth LEA, acting as a cat's-paw for the government, took the National Association of Schoolmasters/Union of Women Teachers to court on the basis that the boycott meant that teachers in schools were not doing the job for which the LEA employed them. By concentrating on the workload issue the union won the court case and the way was clear for widespread boycotting of the National Curriculum testing both in secondary and primary schools.

In the face of this boycott, Patten's first response was not to conciliate but to try to compel headteachers and governors to insist that teachers complied with the testing arrangements. When this approach failed and the 1992 tests were almost completely disregarded, Patten shifted to a more conciliatory position. In April 1993 he set up a review of the whole National Curriculum, under the chair of Sir Ron Dearing, with exceptionally wide terms of reference to evaluate the entire construction and implementation of the National Curriculum. The interim report of the Dearing Committee (Dearing, 1993a) was published in the summer of 1993. It recommended a complete revision of the National Curriculum: the whole framework was to be substantially reduced; its compulsory nature in secondary schools was to be further eroded; its testing arrangements were to be considerably slimmed down and teacher assessment was to be the only form of testing for non-core subjects at primary phase and to have equal weighting with the national tests in all subjects at both phases. With Patten absent from his office with illness and his career sailing towards the same rocks as the original National Curriculum, a bemused government immediately accepted the entire Dearing proposals (DFE, 1993). The National Curriculum as envisaged by Baker in the 1988 Education Act was abandoned in the course of one summer vacation. Dearing was encouraged to develop his work further, which he did by an unprecedentedly wide consultation exercise. In contrast to the original round, teachers in particular were consulted in meticulous detail. Not only were their views sought, they were actually listened to and proved influential on the Dearing final report (Dearing, 1993b).

The following chapters in this section of the book spell out the changes to the primary core that were entailed in the revised National Curriculum. The next section of the book explores ways in which the revised core can be implemented in primary schools. This chapter concludes with an evaluation of the changes which have taken place in the primary core curriculum over the last eight years.

THE CONTRIBUTION OF THE NATIONAL CORE CURRICULUM TO PRIMARY PRACTICE

The original National Curriculum could have represented a major improvement in primary schools. However, given the curricular overload and the rigid testing arrangements, together with the whole competitive philosophy behind the publication of results, it was frequently seen as a retrogressive and harmful measure. It is unfortunately not possible to separate the testing difficulty from the curriculum initiative. It is worth considering what differences the National Curriculum made to primary schools, including the assessment and testing.

The first significant difference from previous practice is that there is now far more consistency between schools and, in some cases, within schools, than was the case prior to the introduction of the National Curriculum. Teachers entering a primary school for their first year's teaching will be able to have firm and reasonable expectations about what their pupils will have covered. Similarly, parents transferring their child between primary schools will be able to have the expectation that the child will fit fairly readily into the new curriculum without leaving any large gaps and without undue repetition (OFSTED, 1995).

Further, this consistent curriculum embodied much of what was good primary practice in some schools. A lot more of it represented high aspirations for primary schools. In terms of wide and deep coverage of a whole range of appropriate and necessary themes, the original primary national core curriculum represented, on paper, a potential improvement for a great many schools. That these aspirations proved to be too broad in the event does not necessarily undermine them. The Dearing Review, whilst it substantially slimmed down the primary curriculum, did not impair the height of these aspirations in the core subjects. Assuming that these aspirations are realizable (a large assumption), then the curriculum in most primary schools is likely to improve following the introduction of the revised National Curriculum. The original National Curriculum undeniably provided some of the foundation for this improvement.

In most schools there has been a dramatic increase in the amount of time that is devoted to scientific activity. As Chapter 4 makes clear, the development of science was an important component of emerging positive primary practice. However, progress was undoubtedly slow. In placing science as one of the three compulsory core subjects, the National Curriculum made probably its major positive initiative in the primary phase of schooling.

Whether the revised National Curriculum can succeed where the original faltered may yet depend on the assessment arrangements and the amount of credibility and commitment these induce in the teaching profession. Even after the Dearing Review, concern remains over the whole area of assessment. The commitment to systematic testing and the publication of results is the flaw which undermines the National Curriculum edifice. Assessment has always been an important component of successful teaching. Formative assessment allows teachers to know what pupils have learned, what remains to be learned, and how this learning might best be brought about. Without such regular, indeed routine, assessment, teaching could hardly be carried out in an effective way. However, this is very different from the systematic, age-specific, national testing now in place. Although results at 7 may remain confidential to the parents, conversations among them as well as among the children will inevitably lead to the open discussion of patterns of academic stratification. Furthermore, successive Secretaries of State have explicitly encouraged primary schools to go ahead with the publication of results at age 7. Those children who are not succeeding with the National Curriculum will be officially recognized at an early age. Few aspects of this recognition will be to their advantage: public labelling may be added to frustration in diminishing their commitment to the official curriculum of the school and in leading them to look for other ways of proving their remarkability. Public 'failure' at 7 or 11 will all too easily lead to lower aspirations for particular pupils. Children, parents and teachers may reduce their expectations as a result of the official national status given to this testing.

The assessment provisions of the National Curriculum are designed to encourage competition between schools, between teachers within schools and implicitly between pupils as well. Not only are there unfortunate casualties of these competitions but the whole National Curriculum initiative is still confused with the ideology of competitiveness. The danger is that what the National Curriculum teaches above all else is competitiveness for its own sake. The rigid assessment and publication stipulations may actually undermine many of the positive consequences which could flow from a national primary curriculum.

On the other hand, the introduction of the National Curriculum has certainly led to significant improvements in the reporting processes of primary schools. Previously reporting between classes, between schools and particularly to parents had been haphazard, dependent on school or LEA initiative. Whilst the reporting procedures associated with the national curriculum may have originally been bureaucratic and politically motivated, they did lead to a clear and systematic improvement in lines and modes of reporting. This change has been rapid and dramatic. Primary schools now take it as a matter of course that parents should receive regular reports on their children's academic progress.

A further difficulty for the National Curriculum in primary schools is that it is perceived and described in terms of subjects. In many ways the National Curriculum framework is that of the previously almost totally discarded grammar school curriculum (Aldrich, 1988). The curriculum is structured in terms of subject disciplines which themselves follow an exceedingly traditional pattern of content selection. At secondary level subjects such as life skills or economic and political awareness were excluded; for primary schools the opportunities for social studies work were diminished since these did not form an explicit part of the National Curriculum. It is unlikely that the time freed up by the Dearing Review will be widely used to revive these subjects, since teachers are increasingly framing their own vision of what constitutes primary school knowledge within the subject terms of the National Curriculum. In the process of attrition of the original National Curriculum, from interim reports through to final orders, most mentions of equal opportunities and multicultural education were lost in the published documents. The loss of a multicultural approach to the curriculum is regrettable since it risks a narrow and one-sided view of knowledge as well as failing to reflect the diversity of the cities of England and Wales. Although not overtly political, the selection of subjects, and the processes whereby they are introduced, risk the establishment of a bland, unquestioning, uncritical curriculum at primary as well as secondary level.

The National Curriculum which has been discussed so far was actually something which until September 1989 only existed in documents. Even after that only a few subjects were being taught to relatively few children. The National Curriculum was an ideal which politicians and civil servants hoped to put into practice. Although it may not be easy to draw up a National Curriculum which commands any kind of consensus, it is an appreciably easier task than monitoring what happens in classrooms and ensuring that the curriculum is actually delivered day in, day out, in all the primary schools of England and Wales. In the first edition of this book the question was asked as to whether it would be possible to implement the National Curriculum. The three factors which the book saw as being central to the answer to this question were influential in the eventual faltering of the original National Curriculum. They remain central to the success of the Dearing revision. These three factors are: firstly, the amount of time in the school day; secondly, the skills that primary teachers have across the National

Curriculum; thirdly, the commitment of primary teachers to developing the skills and materials which might allow the National Curriculum to be a success.

The first factor concerns curriculum overload. The first edition lamented this and explained how it had appeared in the original National Curriculum. Overload was one of the key reasons for pressure to set up and implement the Dearing review. Now that the review is finalized it is hoped that this difficulty has in large measure been overcome. It should be noted that the result of the slimming down has been to give even more prominence to the core elements of the primary National Curriculum. It is here that there has been the least cutting and it is here that the political and perhaps professional impetus remains strong.

The second factor concerns teacher skills and, at the time of the introduction of the primary core curriculum, it was open to doubt as to whether primary teachers had the skills to teach all the subjects. With regard to science in particular the reservations were profound. Few primary teachers had covered science in great detail in their own education and their actual knowledge of scientific content and methodology was in many cases quite scant. While Chapter 4 reports the improvement in primary teachers' confidence in teaching science that has come about since 1988, there remain gaps in teachers' knowledge in this area in particular. There remains a need for a widespread and in-depth INSET project right across England and Wales if teachers are to be in a position successfully to teach the primary core. This of course would be an exceedingly costly endeavour. Current reduction in centrally funded INSET, combined with devolution of funding to primary schools with palpably inadequate resources, will by no means meet this need.

The commitment of primary teachers is obviously a related issue. Many still have reservations about the National Curriculum enterprise, particularly as it refers to the testing arrangements for primary children. In the first edition it was predicted that:

> If they then find themselves being expected to implement this curriculum without adequate training and materials, they may well collectively or individually, openly or tacitly, be resistant to the profound changes which are implied. . . . Passing an Act at Westminster and giving teachers a collection of loose-leaf binders does not automatically nor immediately change what they teach on Monday mornings.

Teacher resistance has now resulted in the wholesale revision of the National Curriculum. The edifice envisaged and brought about by the 1988 Education Act has now crumbled. The more modest and flexible curriculum which has taken its place, due to widespread and prolonged consultation with teachers, now commands much wider and deeper respect. It remains the case that without properly trained, confident and committed teachers the National Curriculum will remain a documentary exercise.

The National primary core Curriculum remains only part formed. Drawing up the documentation, even that which resulted from the radical Dearing Review, was the easy part of the process. Changing practice in primary schools is a more daunting task. In this part of the task the influence of the Secretaries of State and SCAA will be as nothing beside the individual and collective endeavours of primary teachers themselves. Their much larger and more difficult part of the task is now being undertaken for a second time. In introducing the revised National Curriculum to headteachers, Secretary of State Shephard took pride in the fact that it would give 'teachers more professional freedom' (Shephard, 1995, p. 3). Teachers have now demonstrated that professional consent is an essential element of a national curriculum. The implementation of the resulting revision is the point at which primary practitioners will again play their crucial role in the creation of the National Curriculum. With a political promise of five years' stability, a more realistic workload and a wider consensus, it may be that the second primary National Curriculum will last longer than the first.

REFERENCES

Aldrich, R. (1988) The National Curriculum: an historical perspective. In Lawton, D. and Chitty, C. (eds) (1988) *The National Curriculum*. London: Institute of Education.

Bash, L. and Coulby, D. (1989) *The Education Reform Act: Competition and Control*. London: Cassell.

Coulby, D. (1989a) From educational partnership to central control. In Bash and Coulby *The Education Reform Act*.

Coulby, D. (1989b) The National Curriculum. In Bash and Coulby *The Education Reform Act*. (1989).

Coulby, D. and Bash, L. (1991) *Contradiction and Conflict: The 1988 Education Act in Action*. London: Cassell.

Dearing, R. (1993a) *The National Curriculum and its Assessment: Interim Report*. York/London: National Curriculum Council/Schools Examination and Assessment Council.

Dearing, R. (1993b) *The National Curriculum and its Assessment: Final Report*. London: Schools Curriculum and Assessment Authority.

DES (1988) *Report of the Committee of Inquiry into the Teaching of English*. London: HMSO.

DES (1989) *The Education (School Curriculum and Related Information) Regulations 1989* (Circular 14/89). London: DES.

DES and Welsh Office (1987) *The National Curriculum 5–16: A Consultation Document*. London: DES.

DES and Welsh Office (1988a) *Mathematics for Ages 5 to 16*. London: DES and Welsh Office.

DES and Welsh Office (1988b) *Science for Ages 5 to 16*. London: DES and Welsh Office.

DES and Welsh Office (1988c) *English for Ages 5 to 11*. London: DES and Welsh Office.

DES and Welsh Office (1989) *English for Ages 5 to 16*. London: DES and Welsh Office.

Department for Education (DFE) (1993) *Final Report on the National Curriculum and its Assessment: The Government's Response*. London: Department for Education.

DFE (1995a) *Key Stage 1 and 2 of the National Curriculum*. London: HMSO.

DFE (1995b) *The National Curriculum*. London: HMSO.

Emerson, C. and Goddard, I. (1989) *All About the National Curriculum*. London: Heinemann.

Halsey, P. (1989) *National Curriculum Assessment and Testing* (letter to Secretary of State, Baker, 13 July 1989). London: SEAC.

Mathematics Working Group (1987) *Interim Report*. London: DES.

Nash, I. (1989) Cox 'threatened to resign'. *The Times Education Supplement*, 21 April 1989, p. A1.

NCC (1989) *English 5-11*. York: NCC.

OFSTED (1995) *The Annual Report of Her Majesty's Chief Inspector of Schools. Part 1: Standards and Quality in Education*. London: HMSO.

Pring, R. (1989) *The New Curriculum*. London: Cassell.

Science Working Group (1987) *Interim Report*. London: DES.

Shephard, G. (1995) The National Curriculum (letter to headteachers in England). London: Department for Education.

Simon, B. (1988) *Bending the Rules: The Baker 'Reform' of Education*. London: Lawrence and Wishart.

Task Group on Assessment and Testing (TGAT) (1987) *A Report*. London: DES.

TGAT (1988) *Three Supplementary Reports*. London: DES.

White, J. (1988) An unconstitutional National Curriculum. In Lawton, D. and Chitty, C. (eds) (1988) *The National Curriculum*. London: Institute of Education.

Chapter 2

English in the National Curriculum

Howard Gibson

A CASE FOR REVISING THE ORDER?

In autumn 1989 the National Curriculum for English at Key Stage 1 was implemented, followed in the spring of 1990 by the programmes of study and ATs for Key Stage 2 (DES, 1990a). The 'Cox Order' as it became known, after Professor Brian Cox who chaired the working party, was the outcome of a considerable struggle both at an academic and political level about how children in primary schools should best be taught English. The debates ranged across many areas of conflict that often rekindled the contested domains of previous eras and that had their roots in earlier national reports like Kingman (DES, 1988a), Bullock (DES, 1975) and Newbolt (Board of Education, 1921). And yet, although it was acknowledged that English had *always* lived on contested ground, what the Cox Order managed to do was provide a degree of consensus across many disparate elements of the teaching profession. Despite areas of enduring controversy – assessment, bilingual provision, models of writing development, the status of media studies, as well as the sheer workload – the order was viewed by many as managing to bridge discordant opinions and resolve many competing voices on language and literacy development. Thus what could easily have emerged as a conspicuously partisan and unworkable view of English teaching was generally welcomed by the profession. As *The Times Educational Supplement* at the time put it: 'Cox committee spells out a new consensus' (*TES*, 18 Nov. 1988).

In July 1992 the National Curriculum Council published *The Case for Revising the Order* (NCC, 1992). Having weighed 'the case for and against change' it concluded that five areas of the Cox Order were in need of substantial revision:

1. the importance of phonic instruction in initial reading was said to be inadequate;
2. considerably more emphasis needed to be placed on children speaking Standard English;
3. there was a need for a canon of 'great literature' and for an English order to spell out what was the best in 'our literary heritage';

4.   too much value had been placed on the composing aspects of writing so that 'basic' competencies in spelling and grammar were said to be suffering; and
5.   the three ATs for writing, spelling and handwriting needed to be amalgamated.

The rationale for these 'revisions' provoked much acrimonious debate between May 1992 and January 1995 when the new order was published. This sections look at one specific aspect of the 'revision' and investigates the case made for augmenting the provision for phonics in the programme of study for reading. The second examines the nature of the 'revision' within a broader political context and tries to account for the considerable professional opposition to the changes. The third and final sections look at language as a connotive device and explores what is meant by 'the basics' in English, whether there is a link between the quest for more 'Standard English' and moral standards, and what part national identity and Englishness might play in the construction of a National Curriculum for English.

One of the principal reasons for the call for 'revision' was the apparent lack of explicitness of phonic skills in the Cox Order and an overreliance on 'real books', instead of reading schemes, in primary schools:

> It is ... important that the Order is balanced in the emphasis which it gives to different methods of teaching children to read ... At present, the General Provisions for Key Stage 1 identify one teaching method ... but make no reference to the potential contribution of reading schemes. Balance is important ... The programmes of study for AT2 currently make only one reference to phonics ... The teaching of phonics and the use of reading schemes should ... be given greater prominence in the Order if it is to promote a balanced approach to the teaching of reading.
> (NCC, 1992, para. 20)

Much of this concern had been stimulated by a Croydon psychologist called Martin Turner, whose publication, *Sponsored Reading Failure* (Turner, 1990), led to an outcry in the press at the alleged decline in reading standards in the early 1990s: 'Psychologists alarmed by fall in reading scores' (*TES*, 29 June 1990a, p. 1); 'Children's reading ability plummets' (*Guardian*, 29 June 1990); 'Tests reveal fall in standard of pupils' reading' (*Daily Telegraph*, 29 June 1990). Turner's booklet, with a foreword by the Campaign for Real Education (CRE) member Stuart Sexton, presented no convincing evidence about the reasons for the decline nor revealed the methods used to teach the children tested. He had combined the reading scores from different tests so that his data, for many, seemed to lack validity. But even if his data had been persuasive he threw all caution to the wind when he blamed 'unstructured methods of teaching reading' and the 'real books movement' as the cause of the decline in standards. For Turner poor teaching methods – and by implication poor teachers – had *sponsored* the failure, for as the press saw it: 'Either the curriculum or teaching methods must be responsible' (*TES*, 29 June 1990a).

But even *if* there had been a decline in reading standards, neither Turner's polemic nor the press at the time were willing to conceive of possible factors other than 'real books' – the teachers strike of 1985, the introduction of the National Curriculum in 1988/89, the underresourcing of primary schools, socio-economic pressures outside schools influencing attainment within and so on. Her Majesty's Inspectors (HMI) report, *The Teaching and Learning of Reading in Primary Schools* (DES, 1990b), released in January 1991, was the first to challenge and destroy one of Turner's principal assumptions. They reported that 'phonics skills were taught almost univer-sally' and that there was a 'clear and balanced approach' in the vast majority of primary schools. The report confirmed that 'there was no evidence to show that a single method was overwhelming the teaching of reading', and that the great majority of teachers – almost 85 per cent – used a blend of methods to teach initial reading skills.

HMI had concluded, however, that in about 20 per cent of schools 'the work in reading was judged to be poor and required urgent attention'. They added that 'serious as that level of poor teaching and learning is, the broad picture has changed little since the findings of the 1978 HMI National Primary Survey' (DES, 1978). In other words, despite another frenzied and distorted coverage by the media at the publication of HMI's report – ' "Pupils not taught to read properly" shock' (*Daily Mirror*, 10 Jan. 1991); '5% of children aged 11, "hardly able to read" ' (*Daily Telegraph*, 10 Jan. 1991); 'Clarke "deplores" reading standards' (*The Times*, 10 Jan. 1991); 'Can't read, can't learn' (*Guardian*, 10 Jan. 1991); 'Reports fuel debate on poor reading' (*Guardian*, 10 Jan. 1991) – HMI had in fact concluded that there was no general pattern of declining standards (DES, 1990b, p. 6ii). What they *were* critical of was the way primary schools developed reading in Key Stage 2, where the question of phonic methodology was an irrelevance for most pupils:

> In broad terms the work in Key Stage 2 was not as satisfactory as that in Key Stage 1. Most of the schools needed to review their reading programmes to ensure that the careful attention given to younger readers does not peter out too quickly and that the more advanced reading skills and the extended range of reading required towards the end of Key Stage 2 are being widely secured.
> (DES, 1990b, para. 79)

The House of Commons' Education, Science and Arts Committee in 1991 confirmed HMI's findings in *Standards of Reading in Primary Schools* (House of Commons, 1991). Having reviewed evidence presented by Turner and his associates, the committee concluded that there was no reason to believe that, if there has been any general decline in standards, 'real books' methods alone had caused it.

In June 1991 a Buckinghamshire psychologist published the results of a ten-year survey of primary children's reading attainment (Lake, 1991). In many respects Lake was an interesting match for Turner for both were senior psychologists able to access the reading scores of pupils in their respective Local Education Authorities (LEAs). One of the areas of divergence in their reading of available evidence, however, was Lake's suspicion of the assumption that if standards had fallen the decline could be axiomatically attributed to changes in the methods or materials used to teach initial reading. In contrast to Turner, where the blame was put squarely on teachers and schools for failing to use schemes and instruct children in phonics, Lake came to the conclusion that in his LEA there had been a small decline in reading standards between 1985 and 1990; however, this decline could be attributed to socio-economic factors beyond the school gate: 'one may infer that, during the last five or six years, there had been a slight but measurable deterioration in the quality of background experiences of the less able readers – who also, it will be recalled, tend to come from the less privileged areas' (Lake, 1991, p. 12). Lake then extrapolated that, although he assessed only a small downturn in reading attainment in his somewhat 'stable and privileged' authority, the differences one would expect to find between an area such as his own and a less affluent catchment would be quite great:

The conclusions of this investigation, which involved reading scores from thousands of children throughout a whole area and over a substantial period of time, appear to exonerate the teachers from the kind of accusations which have been levelled of late at the teaching profession. *It certainly looks as though any deterioration in reading is more connected with worsening background factors than with faulty teaching.*
(Lake, 1991, p. 13, my emphasis)

At first sight Lake's study seemed to conflict with one aspect of HMI's findings. HMI had also observed that although the socio-economic background of pupils might lead to a lessening of reading attainment, they had concluded that the effects of disadvantage could be 'mitigated' by the tight management and organization of reading within a school:

Of the 20% of schools where reading was less than satisfactory, two-thirds were in areas suffering various degrees of disadvantage. However, the wider picture was mixed; schools serving disadvantaged areas also featured significantly among those whose standards of teaching and learning were high. Plainly, the policies and practices of these schools were powerful in mitigating the effects of disadvantage.
(DES, 1990b, para. 60)

Kenneth Clarke, then Secretary of State for Education, was delighted and circulated his demand that:

We must reject the mistaken notion that children from deprived backgrounds are bound to do badly at school ... I am writing again to chairmen [*sic*] of education authorities asking them to take an active and critical interest in raising standards of reading. ... It has little or nothing to do with social deprivation or levels of public spending ... Early reading failure ... is the surest foundation of all-round under-achievement in late life. We have got to get these basics right and I am determined ...
(DES, 1992, p. 1)

Despite HMI's (DES, 1990b, para. 60) observation of the possibilities of 'mitigation' by good management, Mr Clarke's attempt to draw fire from the link between reading and poverty ignored both Lake's research evidence that often instability of staffing – and therefore instability of reading policy and practices – was more prevalent in poorer catchments. Moreover, it could not anticipate a study by the National Foundation for Educational Research published later in the year.

Gorman and Fernandes *Reading in Recession* (1992) was an unruffled clarification of the correlation between reading standards and social deprivation. Gorman started by reminding his reader of the well-established links between reading attainment and 'background variables' (Tizard and Hughes, 1984; Wells, 1986), such as whether 'the child was living with both natural parents', the degree of 'parental interest' in the child's educational progress and 'patterns of employment' within the family. Given this evidence about the effects of aspects of family life on children's attainments in language and literacy, Gorman considered it necessary to consider which factors might have particular relevance to the reading attainment of pupils. He suggested that in the late 1980s/early 1990s three associated sets of variables were relevant in affecting the home life and pre-school environment of the children. They were:

(i) Changing patterns of family life ... (and) evidence of financial disadvantage in such families. ...

(ii) Changes in patterns of employment, most notably the rise in absolute levels of unemployment among men and the increase in the proportion of married women, with children under five, who have paid employment. ...

(iii) The corresponding growth in the number of establishments providing substitute-care for children under five … There is research available to show that 'the quality of the day care environment appears to have a profound effect upon language development'. … According to Moss (1991) there are aspects of day care that mark Britain out from most other countries. … These are: low level of public sector involvement; the concentration on part-time places; the poor pay and conditions of most of the workers; and large variations in provision between local authorities.
(Gorman and Fernandes, 1992, pp. 15–16)

Thus far this chapter has focused on evidence concerning beginning reading that might lead one to question the assumption made in *The Case for Revising the Order* (NCC, 1992) that primary teachers lacked methodological 'rigour' (p. 11) and a 'clear and balanced framework' (p. 9) and that standards in consequence were in decline. What has been demonstrated is that, with a sensitive assessment of the evidence, one might conclude that any decline in standards was rooted in factors outside schools and not teaching methods within: in what children brought to school with them rather than in any 'trendy' changes to policy and practice. For the evidence confirms that phonics skills were taught almost universally in primary schools; that more than 95 per cent of schools used graded reading schemes; that it was not in Key Stage 1 that reading was problematic but in Key Stage 2 where phonics were less relevant for most pupils; that standards in reading were not in decline universally but on a par with those in 1978; and that where there was cause for alarm there were signs that it could be largely attributable to – in Gorman's terms – the recession.

THE POLITICS OF 'REVISION'

In short, the evidence would suggest that there was no obvious *educational* need to redefine the established English order regarding policies and practices of beginning reading. Indeed, in other ways not only was the need for change being questioned but, equally importantly, the *motives* of those making the case for 'revision' as well. In answering *The Case for Revision* the Curriculum Council for Wales pronounced that they found no substantial or convincing evidence to support such changes (*TES*, 5 Feb. 1993). On the issue of Standard English and the need for a literary canon there was a 'considerable difference of emphasis' in Wales that threatened to end in an embarrassing separation of provision for English by the two nations, as one member declared upon her resignation from the NCC (Clanchy, 1993b; see also *TES*, 16 April 1993; *TES*, 25 March 1994b). The two most prestigious professional associations for English teachers, the National Association for the Teaching of English (NATE) and National Association for Advisors of English (NAAE), argued passionately against the wisdom of the 'revision'. Their joint survey, *The National Curriculum in English: Success or Failure?* (NATE/NAAE, 1992), assessed the way 16 LEAs had implemented the English order and had concluded that on many fronts standards were rising, that teachers' planning was better, that their understanding of how children learn to read had improved and that any call to rewrite the order would deeply damage teachers' morale and that it would be more likely to lower standards than to raise them (Johnson, 1992b).

Prominent academics concerned with language and literacy were also vociferous in questioning the case made for revising the order. Hilary Hester, as editor of *Language Matters*, advised her readers that 'the proposals for the revision of the English Orders offer a curriculum that is narrow, prescriptive and socially divisive' (Hester, 1992/1993, p. 1). Myra Barrs (Director of the Centre for Language in Primary Education), Henrietta Dombey (Professor of Primary Literacy, University of Brighton), Graham Frater (HM Staff Inspector for English) and John Johnson (Director of National Oracy Project) combined to write an article in which they concluded that 'the only justification for changing the English curriculum is ideological' (Barrs *et al*, 1993, p. 3). Gunter Kress, Professor of Education at the University of London Institute, complained of 'the extreme politicization of the curriculum' (Kress, 1994, p.2). Brian Cox, chair of the former English working party and Professor of Language and Literacy at Manchester University, argued passionately that 'the proposed revisions must be totally rejected' (1992/1993) and that the considerable successes of the current Order were being 'jeopardised' (1992c).

Other educationalists too, outside the sphere of language and literacy, were also in open conflict with the apparent 'politicization' of the curriculum. Duncan Graham, as Chair and Chief Executive of the National Curriculum Council, wrote in the *Observer*:

> The National Curriculum is good news. For the first time we have a broadly acceptable indication of entitlement, of benchmarks and of standards. ... We need to protect it from those who seem to fear its success, and from those who recognise a good thing when they see it and want to make it their curriculum rather than the nation's.
> (in Johnson, 1992b, pp. 10-11)

Eric Bolton, the former Chief HMI, said at the Council of Local Education Authorities conference:

> There is no crime in listening to your political friends. But a wise government listens more widely than that and especially to those with no political axe to grind. It is not auspicious that the formal channels of advice about education to the government appear either to be muzzled (e.g. HMI), or packed with people likely to say whatever the government wants to hear – the National Curriculum Council (NCC) and Schools Examination and Assessment Council.
> (in Johnson, 1992b, p. 10)

Professor Paul Black, former Chair of the Task Group on Assessment and Testing (TGAT) (see Chapter 1) and Vice-Chair of the NCC, said at the British Association for the Advancement of Science conference:

> Those who gave dire warnings that the Education Reform Act would be an instrument for direct government control, in which the opinions of ministers would be insulated from professional opinion and expertise, have been proved correct. Of course, it may be that the bulk of that opinion and expertise is deeply in error. In the pressure groups' rhetoric, the so-called educational establishment has been relegated to the status of bogeyman, and the terms 'expert', 'academic', 'researcher', have been turned into terms of abuse. As an expert academic researcher who saw the Act as a force for good, and who has given much of his time trying to help its development, I am disappointed and fearful at the outcomes.
> (in Johnson, 1992b, pp. 9–10)

There was, then, a substantial body of professional opinion suggesting that not only change to the National Curriculum in general but the case for 'revising' the English order in particular was ideologically driven. Looking in retrospect at the construction and motion of this educational/political machinery it is possible to discern four components:

1. the construction of a crisis in an aspect of English teaching;
2. the promotion of this construction in the media;
3. securing desired advice through the patronage of one section of professional opinion at the expense of another by means of quangos (quasi-autonomous non-governmental organizations); and
4. the employment of an inflected lexicon that cleverly created and exploited a popular demand for 'a return to basics', 'traditional values', 'proper English' and the like.

The first three points are relevant here and the fourth is discussed in a broader context in the third and final sections.

Crises in education are not new – or rather, crises in the *media* are not – for one legitimate strategy that pressure groups employ to enact an agenda is to encourage dissension, articulate conflict and publicize alternatives as a way of engineering change. Indeed, the existence of influential and organized lobbyists with access to the media has been an integral and enduring part of the structure of political life in the UK (see Cameron and Bourne, 1988, pp. 147–60). In recent years the initiative in education has tended to come from right-wing groups as a cause/response to a 'crisis' in the teaching of this or that, or to a 'crisis' in the very fabric of the teaching profession itself:

CLASS WAR RETURNS TO BRITAIN'S SCHOOLS: MARXIST TEACHERS AIM-ING TO WRECK EDUCATION PLANS
A startling dossier revealing how the Left is seeking to dominate State school English teaching has been handed to The Mail on Sunday. It discloses that an innocently-named teaching association has drawn up a highly political agenda to challenge how the Government plans to improve standards in our 26,000 schools. .... Last night Education Minister John Patten said he was alarmed by the dossier's contents and said: 'I hope that all teachers will join with me in truly condemning any moves to bring politics into the teaching of English – which is, after all, one of the essential basics.' And Dr John Marks, a key Government adviser on education, explained: 'The teaching of English has become the main ideological weapon for those who want to politicise education in a Left-wing direction. English is to the school curriculum today what sociology was in the universities and polytechnics during the attempted Marxist takeover of higher education in the Sixties.'
(*Mail on Sunday*, 31 Jan. 1993)

There have been many specific 'crises' in English of late. The media relished Prince Charles's outspokenness on the quality of English teaching in June 1989, and of the defects of 'fashionable theorists who undermine Britain' in May 1994 – 'English is taught so bloody badly, that's the problem' – that rebounded somewhat painfully when it was revealed that his office staff, the quality of whom had stimulated his grievance, had in the main attended public schools (see *Guardian*, 29 June 1989, p. 4). In June 1989 there was a 'crisis' of standards in grammar that prompted Oxford University dons to consider 'running remedial English classes' for students below par: 'The decline of the teaching of formal grammar has had quite a bad effect,' reported Professor John Carey; 'I blame the schools,' said Professor Jack Pole (*THES*, 9 June 1989, p. 1). In November 1991, as part of the wider 'crisis' in reading standards, the media relished the suggestion that student teachers emerging from colleges and universities were not properly equipped to teach reading: 'We have to restore confidence in the teacher training system' (see Jones, 1991, p. 22; see also *TES*, 1 Nov. 1991, p. 13). Turner's 1990 polemic, about the decline in reading standards, has already been interpreted in this chapter as an exemplary and unsubstantiated 'crisis' and attributable to the right-wing Campaign for Real Education. Similarly, John Marenbon's influential 'English our English: the new orthodoxy examined' (1987) was illustrative of the work of the Centre for Policy Studies, a right-wing think-tank formed under Margaret Thatcher, which established the notion of a 'crisis' in the teaching of Standard English and national heritage in our schools.

Quangos are one mechanism by which a 'crisis' is articulated, power invested and a policy 'revision' secured. They are not an exclusive feature of the political left or right in Britain and neither are they a modern phenomenon. Brian Doyle in *English and Englishness* (1989) for example, talks of the 1921 Newbolt Committee (Board of Education, 1921), set up to advise on the post-war reconstruction of English teaching, being an outgrowth of the English Association that was developing as an increasingly vociferous pressure group at the time:

> Indeed, one way of viewing the Newbolt Report is as the outcome of a bestowal by the state upon a civil association of the right to report and make recommendations on public policy. Furthermore, the Report represents a familiar tactic through which influential groups are recruited in the voluntary service of state interests and policies ... In both cases the combined efforts of state functionaries, professionals, and selected volunteers from the 'community' were instrumental in shaping quasi-state institutions.
> (Doyle, 1989, p.42)

Doyle rightly questions the misnomer of the Newbolt quango being in any sense 'autonomous', for like all quangos it was an outgrowth of the state, in this case the Board of Education.

The mechanism for appointing members to such 'quasi-state' bodies in the last decade – such as the Further Education Funding Council, The Higher Education Funding Council for England and Wales, The Funding Agency for Schools, The Teacher Training Agency, Schools Examination Assessment Council, National Curriculum Council, Schools Curriculum and Assessment Authority, the City Technology Trust and so on (see *TES*, 22 April 1994b, pp. 12–13) – have been the subject of much recent protestation regarding questions of secrecy and 'sleaze' (see *TES*, 28 Oct. 1994). Research by Stuart Weir of the University of Essex has intimated a link between membership, patronage and nepotism: 'It is easy to get on a quango. You work in business, donate to the Tory party and identify very closely with government policy' (in *TES*, 4 Nov. 1994a; *TES*, 20 May 1994b). The House of Commons too has shown an increasing concern for 'quangocracy' on both sides of the floor. Michael Meacher from the Labour benches has denounced them: 'Quangos are virtually impervious to democratic influence, are by nature secretive, and packed by nomenclature like a one-party state' (Meacher, 1994). And Alan Howarth, the Conservative MP for Stratford, has declared:

> Quangos lack codes of practice and rules of conduct. Local government has declined. This has been an aberration of the Conservative party over the past 15 years. It has neglected local government, even reduced the role of local government – decentralising responsibility to quangos while outflanking and atrophying local government. That's bad for our political culture.
> (*TES*, 28 Oct. 1994, p. 6)

The extent to which the 'earnest packing of bodies to ensure ministers were not given advice they found awkward' (*TES*, 22 April 1994a) is impossible to prove beyond doubt because of the very secrecy of quangos. What can be said is that concerning the English curriculum the appointment of Dr John Marenbon as Chair of the Schools Examination and Assessment Council's English committee was not a universally popular appointment among the teaching profession. As an English don at Trinity College, Cambridge, he had set out in 'English our English' (1987) to admonish what he called the 'new orthodoxy' in English teaching and carried with him – if not the acclaim of the English profession – a set of 'traditional values' and a canon of 'traditional authors for pupils' (see *TES*, 4 Nov. 1994b). His views strongly influenced both the National Curriculum Council's reading lists and the SEAC English anthology that arrived in schools in January 1993 to form the basis of tests at Key Stage 3. As custodian of what might be described as a more modern orthodoxy of the right, and husband to the voluble Dr Sheila Lawlor, Deputy Director of the Centre for Policy Studies, Hollindale has suggested: 'For English teachers who wish to know why their job has been officially disconnected from reality, *English our English* is a key text' (Hollindale, 1993, p. 8). An interesting postscript to Marenbon's appointment to SEAC is that he eventually resigned, for although he openly endorsed the government's view that a 'simple test' in English was desirable, the quest for which led to the greatest dispute of the whole curriculum and to the mass boycott of testing in 1993, he declared the task set by the government to be impossible (see *TES*, 4 Nov. 1994b).

Lord Griffiths of Fforsetfach, a former head of Margaret Thatcher's policy unit, was made chair of the Schools Examination and Assessment Council (see *TES*, 4 Nov. 1994a; and *TES*, 4 Nov. 1994b). David Pascall, a keen moralist and reformer of young children speaking non-Standard English, was also a member of Mrs Thatcher's policy unit and became Chair of the National Curriculum Council. Dr John Marks, a prominent English aficionado and celebrated member of the Campaign for Real Education, was originally appointed to the National Curriculum Council, moved to School Examination and Assessment Council and later became a member of School Curriculum and Assessment Authority (SCAA). If one reads between the lines of the *Mail on Sunday*'s article above one may discover his ideological predisposition as well as his political acumen: 'The teaching of English has been the main ideological weapon for those wanting to politicise education in a Left-wing direction' (*Mail on Sunday*, 31 Jan. 1993). Martin Turner, as discussed earlier in this chapter, can be viewed as a polemicist stimulating the 'reading standards' debate. In 1994 he was appointed Director of the Dyslexia Institute and a member of the English group serving SCAA (see *TES*, 22 April 1994b).

It has been suggested that quangos thrive on secrecy. And yet what they cannot legislate against is internal dissension and rupture. Throughout the process of responding to the 'revision' of the English order there has been a wealth of informative disclosures by various members of working groups. In March 1993 Joan Clanchy, a headteacher at North London Collegiate School, resigned from the NCC after serving only 18 months declaring:

> It is well known that some members of the council are members of right-wing think tanks. I have never objected to that. ... But I did object as a council member to only being given Centre for Policy Studies pamphlets to read by way of homework. ... This year we were sent copies of Dr John Marks' *Value for Money in Education* and he addressed us on it,

again without a counterview being aired. We were sent Stuart Deuchar's pamphlet on history in the Campaign for Real Education series, but not Chris Husband's rebuttal of it. We were not sent copies of Professor Eric Bolton's and Professor Paul Black's pamphlets on *Putting the Record Straight*. 'Plain' men and women making their minds up on momentous matters should have a more balanced reading list.
(Clanchy, 1993a)

In May, two months later, *English in the National Curriculum: Draft Proposals* (SCAA, 1994) was released. In June Annabelle Dixon, deputy head of Holdbrook Primary School in Waltham Cross and member of the SCAA Key Stage 1 advisory group, exposed the group's lack of influence and talked of 'the realism of the situation':

English was somehow 'off-limits'. . . . The new draft Order . . . has so much in it that is . . . related to curious and unsubstantiated bias. . . . It is, patently, one of culpable ignorance, combined with a wilfulness based on prejudice – why else the bias against bilingualism?
(Dixon, 1994, p.11)

In July 1994 Gillian Johnson, deputy headteacher of Tweedale Infants School, Carshalton, and member of the English Advisory Group wrote:

What earned wide support for Cox was a basic philosophy which respected children as learners and trod a sensible path between valuing and working with what the child brought to literacy and the need to teach basic skills. By contrast, the present proposals often focus upon a teaching programme at the expense of the need of the learner.
(Johnson, 1994, pp. 2–3)

Her paper showed that although many members of the advisory group believed that there was a link between children's 'talk and thinking', it was a view of learning included only after 'strong representations' and then merely cursorily. With regard to their insistence on the inclusion of 'picture clues' in developing young children's reading Johnson reported: 'In the course of the work of the Advisory Group, no arguments for their inclusion would be countenanced by SCAA officials' (Johnson, 1994, p. 2– 3).

Dr Alastair West, Vice-Chair of National Association for the Teaching of English and a member of the English advisory group to SCAA, detailed in 'The unacceptable face of change' how his group's proposals had been altered between submission and publication:

The group recommended that this be 'Language Study and Standard English' in order to emphasise the importance of Standard English within the context of a broader programme of language study. The terms have been reversed. . . . at every Key Stage, the bullet points referring to Standard English have been moved from the bottom to the top of the lists. In Key Stage 1, deft surgery has removed the bracketed sections in the following sentences:

- Pupils *(may be speakers of more than one variety of English and)* should develop confidence in their ability to adapt what they say to their listeners and the circumstances.
- Pupils' understanding of English *(both Standard and other varieties)* should be enhanced through their reading.

In Key Stage 2, the requirement to *'consider some of the differences in vocabulary and grammar between Standard and non-Standard varieties of English'* has been deleted. No longer do pupils have to *'understand the importance, in more formal contexts, of consistent use of verb tenses and subject-verb agreement; acceptable standard forms of the negative; correct use of plurals and pronouns'*. Instead, they simply 'learn characteristic features of Standard English, including the consistent use of verb tenses etc'. In Key Stages 3 and 4, the linguistic police round up any remaining doubts or suggestions that anything other than

spoken Standard English is acceptable. Consider this sentence, which used to read: 'Pupils should be taught to adjust their talk to suit the circumstances so that they are confident in formal and informal situations.' Now read the same sentence, inserting the phrase *'users of Standard English'* after the word 'confident'. ... Such editing is reminiscent of the bad old days when direct political intervention was said to be at its height and which the review was to bring to an end. ... I often felt that I glimpsed the group's most prominent member only rarely. ... *The rejection of so many of the subject group's recommendations indicates that Brian Cox's fears about the backward looking politicisation of English remain well founded.*
(West, 1994, p. 20, my emphasis)

REVISING ENGLISH OR REVISING *THE* ENGLISH?

West's revelation illustrates not merely the politicization of the English curriculum. It also makes questionable the notion that the Dearing Review *merely* cut verbiage and 'streamlined' the existing order. What West has shown is that the questions of inclusion or omission are factors that indicate preference and that this is significant even at the level of sentence grammar. There are three interrelated points here. The first is that any 'streamlining' of complex notions associated with language, literacy and learning can lead to a backgrounding of theory and an ambiguity regarding underlying assumptions. Much of the earlier Department of Education and Science documentation relating to the Cox proposals contained detailed referenced chapters that sought to 'set out some principles which underlie the construction of attainment targets and programmes of study' (DES, Nov. 1988b, para. 10.1). This has now gone and gives the new order the feel of a traditional syllabus where space cannot be found for the discussion of aims, objectives and reasons. The second point is that a 'streamlining' of the order was bound to be a revision by omission. The decommissioning of drama, media studies and knowledge about language in the draft order (SCAA, 1994) – and their niggardly reinstatement in the new order (DFE, 1995) – can be read either as a legislative step towards more teacherly discretion on such issues, or as a statement about what is thought to be most 'basic' within the English curriculum. Dombey (1992/1993), for example, has shown that what the draft order chose to remove from the Cox programme of study for reading – the notion that print carries meaning, that children should learn to read beyond the mere literal comprehension of texts, that interest and enjoyment are vital factors, that children should approach reading not as interpreters or obedient collectors of information for someone else but as questioners and responders, and so on – is crucial in illustrating the philosophical preferences of a 'back to basics' approach to language and literacy that underpin a revision by omission.

And third, unlike other curriculum areas, the 'revision' of English was not based upon the existing order. For some it was a fundamental attempt to move away from the assumptions and philosophy of learning contained within Cox:

> Unlike the proposed revisions in other curriculum areas, the draft proposals for English are not based upon the present Orders, with which teachers are familiar, but on the consultation report on English issued in September 1993 by the National Curriculum Council. This must be regarded as a strange decision ... the English Advisory Group had to begin from a set of proposals which were untried and very different in approach from those of Professor Cox.
> (Johnson, 1994, p.2)

For Johnson the very description of the new order as a 'revision' is a misnomer. Indeed, this section argues that the very language used to effect the 'revision' is indicative of a deeper ideological battle concerning the teaching of English. Vocabulary is never 'neutral', for all lexical selection brings with it connotation and nuance, subtlety and shade, and reveals – or attempts to conceal – cultural, moral or political preferences. From the naming of children, to a football commentary that resonates with the inflections of war – *shooting, strikers, attacking* – there is abundant evidence that words chosen to describe or name are not culturally naïve or historically innocent. In recent educational debates the media's recurrent use of trigger devices – *a more balanced approach, raising standards, the return to traditional values, our literary heritage, proper English, more precision, a clearer definition* and so on – have had the function of distancing the 'revision' from what was apparently a less rigorous and more permissive order, and have served to mask issues of commitment and preference (see Laar, 1993).

Thus the notion of a 'revision' is not simply a misnomer. Like 'streamlining' and 'getting back to basics', it is part of a lexicon laden with inflected meaning and semantic ambiguity. For 'revision' connotes amending, making pure, refining, putting right or completing, and 'streamlining' implies the need to straighten out, correct or rectify previous errors. Both terms have frequently been coupled with the desire to recapture 'traditional' values that have been lost. The Women Writers Society, for example, have uncovered: 'overwhelming support for traditional teaching methods. ... Our members are a real cross-section of the English public. What they want is to go back to basics – back to the good old days when children learned the alphabet and rhymes' (*TES*, 11 March 1994a, p. 5). Such lexical gaming is rhetorical and unreliable however, for the call for a return to a 'traditional' approach to reading is easily countered by summoning alternative 'traditional' approaches – E. H. Huey espoused a somewhat 'modern' apprenticeship model at the start of the century when he recommended that the secret of it all lies in parents' reading aloud to and with the child (Huey, 1908). Furthermore, because 'traditional' can have unintended inflections, it can also be used disparagingly to signify nostalgia and the unhealthy 'warm glow' of what one did at school (see Carter, 1991; Barrs *et al.*, 1993; Dombey, 1992/1993; Harding, 1994). Again, the call for more 'balance' in initial reading strategies has been part of the current rhetorical lexicon. Presumably because no one would wish their view to be considered *unbalanced* – and because 'balance' brings with it connotations of moderation and reflection and implies a position that is considered and stable – it has been employed equally by antagonists with very different views, as well as ideologues of the centre (see Balance, 1992; Turner, 1990; NCC, 1992; NATE, 1992; Seaton, 1992).

The matter of lexical selection and inflection has been considered at some length because it is more significant in the debate about English teaching than in other curriculum areas. Because the word itself – *English* – also serves as a proper noun, discussion about the 'revision' of the English curriculum has carried with it a debate about *Englishness*, about what it is to *be* English and has generated resonances that imply the need to 'revise' *the* English. Furthermore, because English is coupled with a National Curriculum, the juxtaposition of *English* with *nation* has also produced a semantic equation that has brimmed with connotation (see Carter, 1992; 1993). Two discourses in particular, the need for an English literary canon and the issue of teaching Standard English in school, have shown that current discussions about language and literacy have often alluded to broader issues, to questions of cultural identity and the nation. The issue is not new. The Newbolt Report (Board of Education, 1921) made the connection between English teaching and social policy quite explicitly. The report, *The Teaching of English in England*, was published at a time of perceived social deterioration with the aim of reuniting 'a divided Nation'. Its purpose was to address the role of English teaching *within* the wider remit of post-war social and economic reconstruction:

> An education fundamentally English would, we believe, at any rate bridge, if not close, this chasm of separation. The English people might learn as a whole to read their own language, first with respect, and then with a genuine feeling of pride and affection. More than any mere symbol it is actually a part of England: to maltreat it or deliberately to debase it would be seen to be an outrage; to become sensible of its significance and splendour would be to step upon a higher level. ... Such a feeling for our own native language would be a bond of union between classes, and would beget the right kind of national pride. Even more certainly should pride and joy in the national literature serve as such a bond.
>
> (Newbolt, 1921, p. 22)

George Sampson, a prominent member of the Newbolt Committee, published *English for the English: A Chapter on National Education* also in 1921. He too addressed the effects of economic recession and unemployment upon the problem of 'class antagonism', which he described as 'dangerously keen' and showing 'no sign of losing its edge', by declaring a point of unity, an 'English for England'. As with Newbolt, proper English teaching would 'mitigate antagonism and remove misunderstanding' for surely, implored Sampson, 'if there is a unity called England there should a unity called English!' (Sampson, 1921; p.67; see also Newbolt, 1921, para. 14/20). This *cultural* agenda, the goal of setting the nation to rights, was then to focus upon raising the cohesiveness of *the* English through English. Newbolt and Sampson concluded that this should be enacted in schools in two ways: first by directing the nation's children towards 'our literary heritage', the storehouse of great English literature, and second by teachers striving to eradicate the 'distressing' sound of non-Standard English in their pupils. The two issues – the canon and Standard English – were said to be 'so inextricably connected as to form the only basis possible for *a national education*' (Newbolt, 1921, p. 14, my emphasis). Both have featured as important aspects of the 'revision' of the National Curriculum for English in the 1990s too.

The first, the need for a literary canon, was one proposal that met with substantial disapproval from the profession. Arguments against legislating for nationally prescribed lists revolved around two related questions – 'Why *these* texts?' and '*Whose* canon?.' Many authors selected for Key Stages 1 and 2 wished to disclaim their own privileged status (see Brown *et al.*, 1994) while others found no agreement regarding which texts should feature on such lists (see *TES*, 25 March 1994a; *TES*, 8 April 1994). Others argued that the educational context of a literary list was self-contradictory, for in disregarding notions of 'conversation' (Rosen, 1992/1993, pp. 7-8) and 'discourse' (Hollindale, 1993, p. 8) a canon seemed to assume the prior achievement of a community with shared goals and values; in other words, a canon seemed to endorse a reverence for received wisdom, fixed in time and non-negotiable, and was thus thought to be epistemologically inappropriate in institutions of learning. Moreover, by defining literature in such a high cultural manner, by removing the defence and rejection of it not only from the sphere of scholarly endeavour but also from reference to historical and cultural contexts, some suggested that what was proposed was a domain that was being intentionally raised above the history of 'common' culture. The Kingman Committee (DES, 1988a, see Chapter 1) had laid the ground work for the 'revision' by referring to a canon that self-evidently constituted 'the powerful and splendid history of the best that has been thought and said in our language'. The committee concluded that 'too rigid a concern with what is *relevant* to the lives of young people seems to us to pose the danger of impoverishing not only the young people, but the culture itself' (DES, 1988a, para. 22; see also Newbolt, 1921, 16/24). Unusually, in a 'note of reservation' appended to the proposals, a member of the committee logged an objection:

> what English is on the curriculum *for*, is not really explored here with any rigour, but simply asserted in very general (and traditional) terms. When this point was raised in committee, it was decided that any more radical enquiry into the purposes for English would be a distraction. I believe, on the contrary, that it was central to the Committee's concerns.
> (DES, 1988a, p. 77)

While Professor Widdowson's concern was not explored by Kingman, others have suggested that what a canon is *for* – in Kingman, in Newbolt and in the 'revision' – is the promotion of a particular set of literary conventions that can be linked to a very *specific* sense of Englishness (see Doyle, 1989, p. 51). For what may appear to some as self-evident recommendations concerning literary quality, appear to others as cultural intervention into popular linguistic practices and, moreover, are linked to an attempt to generate individual attachments to a *particular* sense of national identity. A canon, defined by that which it has chosen to exclude, is, in this sense, about the transmission of *specific* aspects of 'our' – to use Kingman's term – cultural heritage. Exclusivity in the 'revision' has been discovered in the predominance of texts written by dead, middle-class males (see *TES*, 23 April 1993), and in the *opposition* of work from 'other traditions' to a white-English literary heritage (see Rosen, 1992/1993; Anderson, 1994). Where alternatives to the vision of national identity are being assumed – a vision of 'our' heritage that is other than plural, diverse and culturally heterogeneous – it is only by focusing upon the ambitions of those wishing to institute a canon that one can comprehend the ideological significance of the demand for its periodic rival. As Knight (1994b) would have it, only by interpreting the loss of beliefs associated with the idea of a canon can one account for recent attempts to reinstate it. Under pressure from the teaching profession the new English order (DFE, 1995) has chosen to omit the prescription of particular authors at Key Stages 1 and 2, although at stages 3/4 the lists remain. In 1987 Kenneth Baker, then Secretary of State for Education and Science, made explicit the role a national curriculum might play in national reconstruction. He expresses a sentiment reminiscent of issues significant in 1921 – see above – and that perhaps helps focus our attention upon the ideological backdrop to the recent debate: 'I see the National Curriculum as a way of increasing our social coherence. ... The cohesive role of the National Curriculum will provide our society with a greater sense of identity' (in Carter, 1993, p.8).

The use of English teaching as a focus for national identity – or 'social coherence' – is found also in the second issue, the demand to increase the provision for Standard English. Whereas the 'revision' proposed that Key Stage 1 pupils should be taught to use the vocabulary and grammar of spoken Standard English (SCAA, 1994), the new orders (DFE, 1995) refer to the value of non-Standard English but only to bind it to the higher purpose of developing competence in the standard language: 'The richness of dialects and other languages can make an important contribution to pupils' knowledge and understanding of Standard English' (DFE, 1995, p. 2). The way elements of the press reported the 'revision' created the impression that teachers had become permissive in their approach to spoken language and that standards would rise if, right from the start of schooling, pupils were taught to speak English properly:

> BRUSH UP YOUR ENGLISH: 'SLOPPY' TEACHERS UNDER ATTACK IN THE BATTLE AGAINST POOR GRAMMAR
> Sloppy teachers must be made to master the Queen's English before teaching it to their pupils, a senior Government advisor said yesterday. Too many were not up to the standard needed to teach a new slimmed down, back-to-basics timetable, Mr David Pascall, chairman [*sic*] of the National Curriculum Council declared. . . . The new timetable aims to banish dialect and ungrammatical phrases such as 'you ain't seen nothing yet' from schools. . . . Primary school teachers will be required to correct pupils aged five to seven who make errors such as 'we was (were) robbed', and 'we winned (won) at football'. . . . Last night Mr Patten said: 'English is at the heart of the National Curriculum. Without basic skills in this subject, pupils cannot make progress in other areas.'
> (*Daily Mail*, 16 April 1993)

There are problems with this view of Standard English. First, it contradicts what is known about children's language and literacy development. Perera, for example, a prestigious member of the Cox Committee, would advise teachers that children should move towards Standard English in *writing* before being required to use it in their speech. Her argument is that, because writing is a comparatively slow and private process, it makes it possible to monitor one's language in a way that is virtually impossible in speech. Thus she would recommend that 'statements of attainment, which set out what is to be assessed, should not include spoken Standard English until Key Stage 3 at the earliest' (Perera, 1992/1993, p. 9). Second, this view also represents a position that is linguistically unsound because it conflates important distinctions between spoken and written language as well as differences between 'planned' and 'spontaneous' speech (see Halliday, 1985). Concepts of context, register and appropriateness need real clarity for, although the new orders include a cursory reference to the differences between spoken and written forms (DFE, 1995), they are issues that are frequently muddled:

> Do you remember the Wozzies from Book 2? They were the awful family who tried to get children into trouble by making them say 'We was' instead of 'we were'. The Wozzies have some cousins, who are almost as bad. They are the Dunnits. They try to make you say 'I done it' or 'they done it' instead of 'I did it' or 'we did it'. The word 'done' is a poor feeble word, and must have 'had', 'has' or 'have' in front of it – 'I have done it' or 'we had done it'. Remember the nasty Wozzies and Dunnits when you write out these sentences correctly.
> (Moss, 1989, p. 24)

Third, there is the more important issue of cultural hegemony and social divisiveness ✓ in instilling spoken Standard English in children. For Newbolt and Sampson there was no question about the role of the teacher in this regard:

> The great difficulty of teachers in Elementary Schools in many districts is that they have to fight against the powerful influences of evil habits of speech contracted in home and street. The teachers' struggle is thus not with ignorance but with perverted power. That makes

their work the harder, but it must also make their zeal fiercer. A child with home advantages hears English used well, and grows up to use it well himself [*sic*]. He speaks grammatically, he acquires a wide vocabulary, he collects ideas. ... The latter's English may be a negative quantity, requiring great pains on his teacher's part to cancel out before any positive progress can be made. We are not surprised to be told that some children leave school almost inarticulate so far as anything like educated English is concerned.
(Newbolt, 1921, p. 59)

Even while the schools may be teaching good English, the surroundings of street and home will be teaching bad English. ... the teacher of English is continuously assailed by powerful and almost insuperable hostile forces ... The teacher's business is not simply to lay bricks on an empty foundation; he [*sic*] has first to clear the cumbered ground, and begin his edifice, as he clears, with what appears to be *a heap of rubbish*.
(Sampson, 1921, p. 43, my emphasis)

But by assuming that the teacher's role was to 'banish' or 'clear' non-standard forms from children, such a position dismisses as irrelevant the cultural background of pupils. Cultural intervention in Newbolt culminates in a combination of moral, medical and emotional invective to exhort the teacher to combat non-Standard Englishes with 'zeal'. It is, of course, a view that predates the work of Labov (1969), Wells (1986), Bryce-Heath (1983), Tizard and Hughes (1984), and their research regarding the quality of children's language in social and learning contexts *other* than school. It also predates the identification of a 'deficit theory' that has since provided an essential conceptual link between language and personal identity and that has confirmed the possibilities for linguistic imperialism within the classroom. For if in this regard the new orders demand that teachers challenge and change a child's home language – rather than add Standard English to it as an essential competence through writing initially – teachers need to be fully aware of the effect this may have on the quality of relationships between home and school. Paradoxically it could also be argued that to reject rather than build on the non-standard languages is the surest way to lower standards, for such 'bad' 'awful' 'feeble', (Moss, 1989, p. 24) children are, presumably, from communities where non-Standard spoken Englishes are considered 'Standard'. McIlvanney graphically illustrates the link between identity and non-Standard spoken English, and the pedagogical dilemma teachers may face in enforcing aspects of 'our' cultural practice:

'What's wrong with your face, Docherty?'
'Skint ma nose, sur.'
'How?'
'Ah fell an' bumped ma heid in the sheuch, sur.'
'I beg you pardon?'
'Ah fell an' bumped ma heid in the sheuch, sur.'
'I beg your pardon?'
In the pause Conn understands the nature of the choice, tremblingly, compulsively, makes it.
'Ah fell an' bumped ma heid in the sheuch, sur.'
The blow was instant. His ear seems to enlarge, is muffled in numbness. But it's only the dread of tears that hurts. Mr Pirrie distends on a lozenge of light which mustn't be allowed to break. It doesn't. Conn hasn't cried.
'That, Docherty, is impertinence. You will translate, please, into the mother-tongue.' ...
'I'm waiting, Docherty. What happened?'
'I bumped my head, sir.'

'Where? Where did you bump it, Docherty?'
'In the gutter, sir.'
'Not an inappropriate setting for you, if I may say so.'
(McIlvanney, 1991. pp. 88–9)

RAISING THE STANDARD

The dilemmas associated with teaching spoken Standard English to primary-aged children have arisen in proportion to the determination of those driven to 'revise' the Cox Orders. One reason for this is that Standard English has served as a vehicle for simultaneously promoting a quite distinct discourse concerning the nature of *standards*. Like so many terms used to discuss English teaching, the question of standards has carried with it inferences that have no logical connection with English as a subject. In this regard the distinction between Standard English, standards *in* English and the social or moral standards *of* the English, are issues that have frequently been confused in the current debate and sometimes quite intentionally. *The Parent's Charter* (DES, 1991a), for example, confirms the government's commitment to raising standards and yet the cover of the booklet intimates that the standard alluded to is none other than a pennant or banner – 'Raising *the* Standard'. The use of the singular standard to affect a sense of symbolic attachment to the cause, with the intention of arousing a nation to rally under the flag against a common enemy, that is 'falling standards', serves merely as a device for gathering support for an ambiguous agenda.

This movement between standards in English, Standard English and a cultural agenda is not new, for it has already been shown how in Newbolt these distinct discourses were overlaid and managed simultaneously. Educational polemicists more recently have also moved between these distinct concerns. Mona McNee, for example, has exhorted teachers to return to a phonics-based approach to initial reading, arguing that the rejection of traditional methods has not only resulted in 'cruel, academic child abuse' (McNee, 1993), but that there is a correlation between the influx of new methods, the lowering of standards and increased levels of criminality in the country:

> If we'd had the proper teaching of reading since 1945. ... England would be a *wonderful* place. ... We'd have one bobby at a football match and people could walk in the streets without being mugged, because the people who were mugging them would have a job because they could read. ... It all interlocks.
> (McNee, 1990, on BBC Radio 4)

This slippage from methods in English teaching to standards in English, and then interlocking this discourse to a quite distinct one regarding the moral standards of the nation, carries with it an agenda that goes beyond educational issues. Carter notes that Norman Tebbit in a 1995 BBC Radio 4 broadcast, has also made the link between the assumption of declining standards *in* English with increased criminality *of* the English, but he goes further than McNee by extending the matter to questions of personal hygiene:

> We've allowed so many standards to slip. ... teachers weren't bothering to teach kids to spell and to punctuate properly ... if you allow standards to slip to the stage where good

> English is no better than bad English, where people turn up filthy at school ... all those things cause people to have no standards at all, and once you lose standards then there's no imperative to stay out of crime.
> (Carter, 1993, p. 27)

Carter has suggested that the connection here between standards in English and standards of hygiene – with Standard English serving as the benchmark of purity and cleanliness – is no less revealing than McNee's logical equation of methods of teaching reading with street mugging. The press too has habitually stressed the need for English teachers to take responsibility for the 'future of our society'. The self-evident existence of a crisis in English teaching, the manifest need to stop standards slipping further, the indisputable worth of a literary canon containing 'the classics', the use of trigger devices like 'progressive', 'proper', 'fundamentally important', to engender unreflected allegiance, the unquestioned need for English teachers to act decisively on simple moral questions that are basic to 'our society', are all issues compacted in a telling editorial from the *Daily Telegraph*, entitled 'Queen's English':

> Because of a diminution in the rigour of English teaching, and a departure from the classics as set books, many children today leave school incapable of either writing or speaking the Queen's English properly ... . It is fundamentally important that schoolchildren, of whatever age, class or race, are taught to write and speak correct English. ... Mr MacGregor must ignore this 'progressive' thinking on the teaching of English. ... The teaching of grammar and of a distinction between right and wrong in the use of English is essential to *the future of our schools, and of our society*.
> (*Daily Telegraph*, 17 Nov. 1989, my emphasis)

Tony Crowley, in a book called *Proper English?* (1991), has suggested that during times of social, political or economic disorder, the teaching of English in England has frequently served as a focal point for political regeneration or as an instrument for national 'revision'. It has been implied in this chapter that the recent period may also serve as further evidence of Crowley's reading of history. The future of 'our nation' has provided a dominant motive in these debates. It could be argued that this is a concern that all teachers of English must share. What has been questioned, however, is whether this dominant view has eclipsed the vision that 'our' national identity may not lie with a singular view of culture, or with nationalism narrowly defined, but with plurality. Moreover, by defining literature in such a high cultural manner, by removing the defence and rejection of it not only from the sphere of scholarly endeavour but also from reference to historical and cultural contexts, some have suggested that what was proposed was a domain that was being intentionally raised above the history of 'common' culture (see Jardine, *TES*, 30 Sept. 1994). Thus whereas in the recent climate the defence of linguistic variety has proved so difficult – for to defend anything *non-standard* has been seized upon as an apology for *no-standard*, an attempt to defend something *not-yet-up-to-standard* (see Carter, 1993. p. 7) – English teachers will need to question what assumptions of 'our' nation have been implied. Moreover, because the new National Curriculum for English has been constructed in this political context, teachers will need to question whether the 'revision' now encoded by the new orders will prepare children adequately for the rapidly changing literacy demands of the twenty-first century. Does it, for example, adequately provide for languages *other* than English in primary schools? Will it create critical readers of both print *and* media texts?

Newbolt was right in this respect. The literacy needs of children in the future is an issue that relates *both* to the question of standards in English, as well as to the vision of our social futures as English.

REFERENCES

Allen, D. (1987) *English, Whose English?* Sheffield: NATE.

Anderson, B. (1994) Get modern. *The Times Educational Supplement*, 3 June.

Armstrong, M. (1993) Much too proper English. *The Times Educational Supplement*, 26 May.

Balance (1992) *Balance: A Manifesto for Balance in the Teaching of Literacy and Language Skills*. Truro: Balance.

Barrett, P. (1992a) What is your definition of a horse? (The case for not revising the order). In NATE (November 1992) *'Made Tongue-Tied by Authority': New Orders for English?* Sheffield: NATE.

Barrett, P. (1992b) Only obeying orders?. *Language and Learning*, October.

Barrs, M. *et al.* (1993) A love of nostalgia. *The Times Educational Supplement*, 7 May.

Batsleer, J. (1995), *Rewriting English: Cultural Politics of Gender and Class*. London: Methuen.

Beard, R. (1993) New Order takes the right line on early reading. *The Times Educational Supplement*, 21 May.

Board of Education (1921) *The Teaching of English in England*. London: HMSO (Newbolt Report).

Brown, R. *et al.* (1994) Author's word on required books. *The Times Educational Supplement*, 13 May.

Bryce-Heath, S. (1983) *Way with Words*. Cambridge University Press.

Cameron, D. and Bourne, J. (1988) No common ground: Kingman, grammar and the nation: a linguistic and historical perspective on the Kingman Report. *Language and Education*, 12, pp. 147–60.

Carter, R. (1991) Caught out on a point of grammar. *The Times Educational Supplement*, 21 June.

Carter, R. (1992) *Keywords: Discourses About Language and Literacy*. Oxford Polytechnic Conference Report, 9 May.

Carter, R. (1993) Proper English: language, culture and curriculum. *English in Education*, 27, no. 3.

Carter, R. (1994) Standard English in teaching and learning. In Hayhoe, M. and Parker, S. *Who Owns English?* Buckingham: Open University Press.

Cashdan, A. (1990) The great unproven failure. *Education*, 28 September.

Cashdan, A. (1991) Bearing the standard. *Child Education*, November.

Chew, J. (1991) Learning phonic rules makes soundest sense. *The Times Educational Supplement*, 4 Oct.

Clanchy, J. (1993a) Terse but not to the point. *The Times Educational Supplement*, 5 March.

Clanchy, J. (1993b) A definite difference of emphasis. *The Times Educational Supplement*, 23 April.

Conniff, C. (1992) It ain't what you say, it's the way that you say it. *The Times Educational Supplement*, 13 April.

Cox, B. (1992a) Curriculum for chaos. *Guardian*, 15 Sept.

Cox, B. (1992b) Keeping faith in the English revolution. *The Times Educational Supplement*, 25 Sept.

Cox, B. (1992c) Politicians and professionals. In NATE (September 1992) *'Made Tongue-Tied by Authority': New Orders for English?* Sheffield: NATE.

Cox, B. (1992/1993) English to be rejected. *Language Matters: Whose Orders?*, 3. London: CLPE.

CRE, see Seaton, N.

Crowley, T. (1989) *The Politics of Discourse*. London: Macmillan.

Crowley, T. (1991) *Proper English? Readings in Language, History and Cultural Identity.* London: Routledge.

Daily Express,
– School blitz on English: now Patten sends in classroom hit squads. 10 Sept. 1992.

Daily Mail,
– Blueprint for English: back to basics as Minister overrules the progressives. 10 Sept. 1992.
– Patten sets new goals for teaching Standard English. 16 April 1993.
– Prince attacks 'fashionable theorists' who undermine Britain: Charles goes back to basics. 5 May 1994.

Daily Mirror,
– 'Pupils not taught to read properly' shock. 10 Jan. 1991.
– Shake-up in English as government admit they got it wrong. 10 Sept. 1992.

Daily Star,
– Charles gives school trendies a good canning. 5 May 1994.

Daily Telegraph,
– Queen's English. 17 Nov. 1989.
– Tests reveal fall in standard of pupils' reading. 29 June 1990.
– 5 per cent of children, aged 11, 'hardly able to read'. 10 Jan. 1991.
– After 30 years English lessons go back to traditional methods: 'Progressive' teaching is abandoned. 10 Sept. 1992.
– Prince attacks 'fanaticism' of trendy experts. 5 May 1994.

Department of Education and Science (DES) (1975) *A Language for Life.* London: HMSO (Bullock Report).

DES (1978) *National Primary Survey.* London: HMSO.

DES (1988a) *Report of the Committee of Inquiry into the Teaching of English Language.* London: HMSO (Kingman Report).

DES (1988b) *English for Ages 5–11: Proposals.* London: HMSO.

DES (1990a) *English in the National Curriculum.* London: HMSO.

DES (1990b) *The Teaching and Learning of Reading in Primary Schools.* London: HMSO.

DES (1991a) *Citizen's Charter: The Parent's Charter.* London: HMSO.

DES (1991b) *The Teaching and Learning of Reading in Primary Schools 1991.* London: HMSO.

DES (1991c) *Standards in Education: 1989–90.* London: HMSO.

DES (1992, 9 March) *Background No Bar to Good Reading – Clarke* (Circular 103/92). London: HMSO.

Department for Education (DFE) (1995) *English in the National Curriculum.* London: HMSO.

Dixon, A. (1994) The baby. And. The bathwater. *The Times Educational Supplement,* 17 June.

Dombey, H. (1991) Countering conspiracy theorists. *The Times Educational Supplement,* 18 Jan.

Dombey, H. (1992/1993) Some thoughts on the proposals for reading. *Language Matters: Whose Orders?* London: CLPE.

Dombey, H. (1994) Slim pickings from softer English line. *The Times Educational Supplement,* 25 Nov.

Doyle, B. (1989) *English and Englishness.* London: Routledge.

Evens, A. (1993) Social class split infinitively. *The Times Educational Supplement: National Curriculum Update,* April.

Fairclough, N. (1992) *Critical Language Awareness.* London: Longmans.

Gorman, T. and Fernandes, C. (1992) *Reading in Recession.* Slough: NFER.

Gramsci, A. (1985) *Selections from Cultural Writings.* London: Lawrence and Wishart.

Guardian,
– Prince says schools teach English 'bloody badly'. 29 June 1989.
– Children's reading ability plummets. 29 June 1990.
– Reports fuel debate on poor reading. 10 Jan. 1991.
– A quarter of 7-year olds 'read poorly'. 10 Jan. 1991.
– New review of English teaching. 10 Sept. 1992.

– Political row as prince takes swipe at trendy theorists. 5 May 1994.

– Prince names villains who threaten heroic tradition of great British character. 5 May 1994.

Hackman, S. (1993) The age of conformity. *The Times Educational Supplement*, 5 March.

Halliday, M. (1985) *Spoken and Written Language*. Oxford: Oxford University Press.

Harding, P. (1994) Still not quite on course. *The Times Educational Supplement*, 25 February.

Hayhoe, M. and Parker, S. (eds) (1994) *Who Owns English?* Milton Keynes: Open University Press.

Hester, H. (1992/1993) Editorial. *Language Matters: Whose Orders?* London: CLPE.

HMI (1990) *The Teaching and Learning of Reading in Primary Schools*. London: HMSO.

HMI(1991) *The Teaching and Learning of Reading in Primary Schools*. London: HMSO.

Hodgkinson, K. (1991) The great primary school reading crisis – or, a year is a long time in education. *Education*, **3** (13), October.

Hollindale, P. (1993) English, whose English? *The Times Educational Supplement*, 19 February.

House of Commons (1991) *Standards of Reading in Primary Schools: Third Report of 1990/91*, Vol. 1. London: House of Commons.

Huey, E.H. (1908), *The Psychology and Pedagogy of Reading*. New York: Macmillan.

Independent,

– Authors divide on best books for children. 10 Sept. 1992.

Jardine, L. (1994) Goodbye Little England. *The Times Educational Supplement*, 30 Sept.

Johnson, G. (1994) Up the river. *Language and Learning*, June/July.

Johnson, J. (1992a) Season of discontent. *The Times Educational Supplement*, 12 June.

Johnson, J. (1992b) Introduction. In NATE, *'Made Tongue-Tied by Authority': New Orders for English*. Sheffield: NATE.

Jones, G.E. (1994) Bordering on the new Renaissance. *The Times Educational Supplement*, 30 Sept.

Jones, K.L. (1991) New 'crisis' over training is imaginary. *The Times Educational Supplement*, 18 Jan.

Knight, R. (1994a) Free the native spirit. *The Times Educational Supplement*, 18 Feb.

Knight, R. (1994b) Lost in a desert of verbiage. *The Times Educational Supplement*, 20 May.

Kress, G. (1994) Cut the link between content and resource. *The Times Educational Supplement*, 25 Feb.

Laar, B. (1993) Platefuls of forked tongue. *The Times Educational Supplement*, 30 April.

Labov, W. (1969) The logic of non-Standard English. In Williams, F. (ed.) *Language and Poverty*. Chicago: Markham.

Lake, M. (1991) Surveying all the factors: reading research. *Language and Learning*, **6**, June.

McArthur, T. (1993) Language used as a loaded gun. *Educational Guardian*, 20 April.

McCartney, K.(1984) Effects of quality of day-care environment on children's language development. *Developmental Psychology*, **20**, pp. 244–60.

McIlvanney, W. (1991) *Docherty*. London: Hodder & Stoughton.

Mackenzie, R. (1992) The Right's wrong to rewrite English. *The Times Educational Supplement*, 2 Sept.

McNee, M. (1990) *Phonics and Reading*. London: BBC Radio 4, 4 April.

McNee, M. (1991a) False logic. *The Times Educational Supplement*, 6 Sept.

McNee, M. (1991b) Parent concern. *The Times Educational Supplement*, 18 Jan.

McNee, M. (1993) *Language and Literacy News*, **12**, Autumn.

Mail on Sunday,

– Exclusive: how the left use English lessons to promote their cause. Class war returns to Britain's schools: Marxist teachers aiming to wreck education plans. 31 Jan. 1993.

Marenbon, J. (1987) English our English: the new orthodoxy examined. In Crowley, T. (ed.) (1991) *Proper English: Readings in Language, History and Cultural Identity*. London: Routledge.

Marenbon, J. (1994) English, government and the economy. In Hayhoe, M. and Parker, S. (eds) *Who Owns English?* Buckingham: Open University Press.

Meacher, M. (1994) *Today in Parliament*. London: BBC Radio 4, 24 May.

Moss, P. (1989) *Word Patterns: Book 3*. London: Collins Educational.

National Association for the Teaching of English (NATE) (1992) *'Made Tongue-Tied by Authority': New Orders for English?: A Response.* Sheffield: NATE.

NATE (1994) *Guidance on the Completion of the English Response Form.* Sheffield: NATE.

NATE/NAAE (1992) *The National Curriculum in English: Success or Failure?* Sheffield: NATE.

National Curriculum Council (NCC) (July 1992) *National Curriculum English: The Case for Revising the Order.* York: NCC.

Newbolt, see Board of Education.

Patten, J. (1993) Battle for your child's mind: Militants campaign to disrupt the tests. *Sunday Express,* 7 Feb.

Pearson, N. (1982) *The State and Visual Arts: A Discussion of State Intervention in the Visual Arts in Britain 1760–1981.* Milton Keynes: Open University Press.

Perera, K. (1992/1993) Standard English in Attainment Target 1: speaking and listening. *Language Matters: Whose Orders?* London: CLPE.

Quirk, R. (1993) More than just talking proper. *Independent on Sunday,* 18 April.

Rosen, M. (1992/1993) Conversations and literary discourse. *Language Matters.* London: CLPE.

Rosen, M. (1994) Talking and writing proper. *The Times Educational Supplement,* 17 June.

Sampson, G. (1921) English for the English: a chapter on national education. Cambridge: Cambridge University Press.

School Curriculum and Assessment Authority (SCAA) (1994) *English in the National Curriculum: Draft Proposals.* London: HMSO.

Seaton, N. (ed.) (1991) *Higher Standards and More Choice: A Manifesto for Our Schools.* York: Campaign for Real Education.

Seaton, N. (1992) *Teacher Training: Public Funding for Progressivism?* York: Campaign for Real Education.

Stierer, B. (1990/91) Simply doing their job? The politics of reading standards and 'real books'. *Language Matters 3.*

Sun,

– Queen's English fury as Prince attacks his staff: 'You Can't Write Proper'. 29 June 1989.

Tate, N. (1994) Target vision. *The Times Educational Supplement,* 2 Dec.

Times (The),

– Inspectors find low standard of reading in 20% of schools. 10 Jan. 1991a.

– Clarke 'deplores' reading standards. 10 Jan. 1991b.

– Traditionalists gain ground against progressive teachers. 10 Sept. 1992a.

– Patten orders shake-up in the teaching of English. 10 Sept. 1992b.

Times Educational Supplement (The), (TES)

– Cox committee spells out new consensus. 18 Nov. 1988.

– Psychologists alarmed by fall in reading scores. 29 June 1990a.

– A sorry story that has been told before. 29 June 1990b.

– Claims that reading standards are falling have been disputed: specialists sceptical about leaked research. 6 July 1990.

– Streams of polemic but only a dribble of facts: falling standards? The evidence. 28 Sept. 1990.

– 'Confused' reading picture emerges. 14 Dec. 1990.

– Primary reading 'not good enough'. 11 Jan. 1991.

– Poor reading standards follow classroom change. 18 Jan. 1991.

– 5–16 reading between the headlines: Chief HMI's report. 22 Feb. 1991.

– Reading link with poor homes. 21 June 1991a.

– Seeing the thrills and skills of reading. 21 June 1991b.

– Students ill-prepared for reading. 1 Nov. 1991.

– Class control vital says reading study. 21 Feb. 1992.

– Little change in reading. 13 March 1992.

– English as she is variously spoken: battle for the curriculum. 18 Sept. 1992.

– Government attacked by its old trusties. 30 Nov. 1992.

– Lack of evidence for curriculum rewrite. 11 Dec. 1992.

– Split over stress on a definitive English. 5 Feb. 1993.
– Advisers in England and Wales draw up conflicting proposals: compromise over English expected. 16 April 1993.
– Picking over bones of 'dead white males'. 23 April 1993.
– 'Softer' English condemned. 29 Oct. 1993.
– Best-sellers support traditional methods. 11 March 1994a.
– Compulsory reading list critics face defeat. 11 March 1994b.
– Dons throw the book at great works. 25 March 1994a.
– English borders on great divide. 25 March 1994b.
– Second act of English canon is 'futile' farce. 8 April 1994.
– Staff make ready for English row. 15 April 1994.
– Too much blue in the colour scheme. 22 April 1994a.
– Secrets of the quango tango. 22 April 1994b.
– New consensus suffers an early rift. 13 May 1994a.
– English advisers in revolt. 13 May 1994b.
– Vast English list upsets Welsh staff. 13 May 1994c.
– All present, but not quite so correct. 13 May 1994d.
– Curriculum anger grows. 20 May 1994a.
– Quasi autonomous?. 20 May 1994b.
– Turned off by an excess of English. 27 May 1994.
– Quangos and the sleaze factor. 28 Oct. 1994.
– Queasy about the quangocracy. 4 Nov. 1994a.
– Scanty justification for political briefs. 4 Nov. 1994b.
– A case of Dearing done. 11 Nov. 1994a.
– Controversy comes to a full stop. 11 Nov. 1994b.
Times Higher Education Supplement (THES), (The)
– Oxford dons consider running remedial English classes. 9 June 1989.
Tizard, B. and Hughes, J. (1984) *Young Children Learning*. London: Fontana.
Turner, M. (1990) *Sponsored Reading Failure*. Surrey: IPSET Educational Unit.
Wells, G. (1986) *The Meaning Makers*. London: Hodder and Stoughton.
West, A. (1994) The unacceptable face of change. *The Times Educational Supplement*, 20 May.
Williams, R. (1976) *Keywords: A Vocabulary of Culture and Society*. London: Fontana.
Wragg, E.C. (1991) The standards debate in the mass media. In D. Wray (ed.) *Standards in Reading*. Exeter: University of Exeter.
Wragg, E.C. (1994) Nasty noises under the curriculum bonnet. *The Times Educational Supplement*, 3 June.
Wray, D. (1992) Debate around fixed poles. *The Times Educational Supplement*, 14 Feb.

Chapter 3

Mathematics in the National Curriculum

Mike Spooner

INTRODUCTION

Whilst the seven years that span the time between the setting up of the initial Working Group for Mathematics in the National Curriculum and the publication of the third and latest version of the orders in November 1994 will be the main focus of this chapter, it will be useful to consider contributions to the debate about the teaching of mathematics which were made prior to this time.

It will also be important to identify the distinct groups who have traditionally held an interest in the mathematics curriculum, for it is the interplay between these competing interests which has always created and modified the curriculum and influenced teaching approaches. Ernest (1991) identifies educators, academic mathematicians and the representatives of industry and society as groups that will have distinct aims and expectations for the mathematics curriculum.

The idea that mathematics should be part of the core curriculum is largely un-challenged. A survey commissioned by the Schools Curriculum and Assessment Authority (SCAA) (June 1994) of parents' views on the National Curriculum revealed that mathematics is considered as second only to English in importance within the curriculum. Her Majesty's Inspectorate (HMI) (1979) suggest that the case for mathe-matics holding a position near the top of the curriculum hierarchy has traditionally been advanced on three main grounds: mathematics offers life skills which are essential within education, employment and everyday life; the subject is a prominent part of the culture and helps us to understand and describe the world we live in; mathematics trains the mind by offering an approach to problem-solving.

Amongst the distinct interest groups we could expect a level of agreement about these statements as descriptions of the purposes of studying mathematics but an analysis of the emphasis that each group places on each statement would reveal considerable disparity. In examining the discussion that surrounded the initial con-struction and subsequent revisions of mathematics in the primary National Curriculum we will see how the different priorities of the various groups manifested themselves.

None of the groups would be satisfied with the extent to which their aims are being met and each group would include the effect of the competing priorities of the other groups within their explanation for the consistent failure of mathematics education.

The introduction of the National Curriculum has been justified by the need to raise standards. Whenever the issue of standards in education arises, mathematics, or more accurately arithmetic, always figures strongly in the ensuing debate. Knowledge of the times tables and the ability to perform the techniques of written calculation are amongst the traditional benchmarks used by those who wish to point to how standards are falling. Research findings (see, for example, ACACE, 1981; ABLSU, 1990) suggest that there are a great many people who experience difficulty in dealing with the mathematical needs of everyday life. The ACACE study established that, even amongst people with high academic qualifications, apparently simple mathematical tasks could induce feelings of inadequacy and panic.

It is in the diagnosis of this situation that we see the different perspectives of the distinct interest groups most clearly. From outside the educational establishment the image of falling standards is seductive. It is sustained by a belief in the prior existence of a Golden Age when standards were upwardly mobile or lodged securely on a satisfactorily lofty plateau. From this perspective, falling standards are explained as the result of the introduction of progressive teaching approaches and a shift away from the traditional emphasis on basic skills in primary education.

The idea that progressive approaches to mathematics teaching are widespread and that the practice of basic skills features less prominently in the primary curriculum has been challenged by research projects and a succession of official reports. In a Department of Education and Science (DES) Primary Education Survey (1987a), a national sample of junior classes were found to be spending an average of 49 per cent of each week on English and mathematics. HMI (1992) reported that around 53 per cent of the time spent on mathematics in Year 2 classes inspected was devoted to number work. All the evidence suggests that the effects of the 'primary revolution' in teaching approaches (see Chapter 5) proved to be as hard to detect in mathematics as in other areas of the primary curriculum.

Despite the wealth of evidence to the contrary the popular image of mathematics teaching as being dominated by progressive approaches, which neglect the basic skills of arithmetic, persists. After the publication of *Science and Mathematics in Schools* (OFSTED, 1994) the majority of the tabloid newspapers offered editorial comment lamenting the state of children's arithmetical ability and suggesting that a primary cause of the perceived low standards was that schools let children use calculators. The assertion that the use of calculators has a detrimental effect on children's mathematical ability is contradicted by research evidence (Shuard *et al.*, 1991) but as a feature of mathematics teaching that is readily identifiable as a departure from tradition it is a predictable target within a 'falling standards' debate.

The explanation of the problems of mathematics teaching offered by those working within education is likely to include reference to the continued use of teaching approaches which have been found to be ineffective in establishing a meaningful understanding of the subject. Yet these discredited approaches form part of older generations' images of the Golden Age. It is common for teachers to encounter a fascinating ambivalence from parents who will readily admit to a dislike of mathematics and lack of confidence in their own mathematical ability whilst simultaneously express-ing anxiety that their children's mathematical education does not correspond more exactly to that which they experienced themselves at their own primary schools.

Those who seek to explain the consistent underachievement of mathematics educa-tion by suggesting that modern teaching approaches are to blame are challenged by both research, as recorded above, and history. The methods used to teach mathematics have been questioned consistently over a long time, McIntosh (1977) provides a useful historical survey of written comment on mathematics education. Three extracts from the survey are illustrative:

> If a child be requested to divide a number of apples between a certain number of persons, he [*sic*] will contrive a way to do it. . . . They should be allowed to pursue their own method first. . . . When pupils learn through abstract examples, it very seldom happens that he [*sic*] understands a practical example the better for it.
> (*Intellectual Arithmetic*, IV, p. 1840, quoted in Floyd, 1981, p.9).

> When children obtain answers to sums and problems by mere mechanical routine, without knowing why they use the rule ... they cannot be said to have been well versed in arithmetic.
> (*Reports*, 1895, in Floyd, 1981, p.9)

> Instruction in many primary schools continues to bewilder children because it outruns their experience. Even in infant schools, where innovation has gone furthest, time is wasted in teaching written 'sums' before children are able to understand what they are doing.
> (*Children and their Primary Schools*, 1967, p. 196, in Floyd, 1981, p.8).

These extracts certainly cast doubt on the 'Golden Age' theory but they also emphasize the distressing consistency with which efforts to enhance the general understanding of how mathematics can be learned have been dismissed or ignored. The following passage taken from the most recent official review of mathematics education suggests that there is little reason to believe that such messages will not continue to go unheeded:

> It is important to note that most pupils can perform the basic skills adequately if they know which operation (e.g. addition, subtraction, multiplication or division) is required. They can usually do the calculation. Problems arise when the question is in a context and the individual pupil has to decide which mathematical operation to use.
> (OFSTED, 1994, p.20)

When mathematics is presented as a collection of techniques and routines to be rehearsed and facts to be committed to memory the lesson of history appears to be that it seldom results in the acquisition of skills or knowledge that can be applied. The Cockroft Report *Mathematics Counts* (1982), to date the most comprehensive review of mathematics education in this country, made the issue of the application of mathemat-ical knowledge and skills one of its central themes.

The report consists of the findings of a Committee of Inquiry, commissioned in 1978 in response to popular concern about the state of mathematics education. The report provided little evidence of a decline in standards in numeracy. It also conducted surveys, the results of which contradicted the idea that there was widespread dissat-isfaction amongst employers about the mathematical ability of employees recruited straight from school. The committee did however identify major problems in the attitude that many people developed towards the subject as a direct result of their mathematics education and concluded that, whilst there was no evidence to suggest that the situation was any worse than in any previous era, there was considerable room for improvement.

The report suggested that problem solving, which was defined as 'the ability to apply mathematics to a variety of situations' (para. 249) needed to be at the heart of the subject. Teaching approaches that provided opportunities for discussion, practical work and the application of skills in meaningful contexts were recommended as the essential ingredients of a diet which could produce confident and capable mathematicians.

DEVELOPING THE NATIONAL CURRICULUM FOR MATHEMATICS

The differences between the explanations for the underachievement of mathematics education offered by the distinct interest groups meant that, when the first Mathematics Working Group was convened, different parties were working to distinct agendas. The representatives of mathematics education saw an opportunity to establish the principles of practice outlined by the *Cockroft Report* within a statutory framework, whereas the overriding political imperative was for a curriculum that could be monitored and regulated through the use of standardized assessment. A review of the nature and content of the debate, which characterized the operations of the various working groups, illustrates the difficulty that was encountered in reconciling these different aims.

The following section contains a chronological summary of the activities of the working groups from 1987 through to 1994. Commentary on some of the recurrent themes that are evident in this section will be offered later.

April 1987: The Secretary of State for Education and Science, Kenneth Baker unveiled plans for a national core curriculum which would be determined by professional educators, primarily teachers.

July 1987: The Mathematics Working Group was formed, chaired by Professor Roger Blin-Stoyle. Of the 20 people who held membership of the working group, during the time it remained in operation, two were primary headteachers but no practising class teachers were included.

November 1987: A confidential report compiled by the Centre for Educational Studies, King's College, London, which amounted to a feasibility study of a national curriculum for mathematics, was delivered to the Secretary of State. The report had been commissioned by a previous Secretary of State, Sir Keith Joseph, and it is doubtful that many of the findings would have been welcomed by his successor. The report suggested that, whilst the concept of a system of national targets was feasible, it was estimated that it would need between nine to 15 years to construct. It was felt that this time would be needed to carry out research into children's learning and provide adequate in-service training for teachers in both the delivery and assessment of the new curriculum. The report rejected the idea that targets should be related to ages and stated that children should not be assessed by the use of written tests before the age of 8.

December 1987: An *Interim Report* was published the DES (1987b). The working group complained of the inadequacy of the time that they had to respond to their brief and expressed concern about how the establishment of programmes of study would effect the chances of the continued development of the mathematics curriculum. The Secretary of State expressed great disappointment in the lack of detail on age-related targets provided by the group and picked out other areas of the report that did not correspond to his own thinking about mathematics education. He rejected the idea of equal weighting for all areas of the curriculum and suggested that arithmetic should receive greater emphasis. He cautioned that, if the use of calculators was to be extended, as recommended by the working group, teachers would need to be able to recognize the risks as well as the opportunities associated with their use. He suggested that careful thought should be given to achieving a balance between the open-ended activities promoted by the group and more traditional pencil and paper tasks. The idea that some areas of the subject could be most effectively taught through the use of contexts provided by other curriculum areas was regarded with suspicion.

December 1987: Professor Roger Blin-Stoyle resigned as Chair of the Working Group and Duncan Graham, who was later to become Chief Executive of the National Curriculum Council, was appointed as his replacement.

December 1987: Professor Sigbert Prais of the National Institute of Economic and Social Research and a member of the working group published a note of dissent from the *Interim Report*. He commented on the astonishing lack of urgency demonstrated by his fellow group members in their approach to establishing testable standards. He declared his interest as primarily vocational and alleged the existence of an appalling attainment gap between UK children and their overseas peers, which he did not feel could be remedied by the direction being followed by the group. Prais resigned from the group in January 1988.

June 1988: The final report of the working group was delivered to the Secretaries of State. In effect the group had just six months to respond to the far more exact brief that was contained within Kenneth Baker's response to the *Interim Report*. In their introduction to the report, the group stated that they felt the restricted time-scale had increased the likelihood of error in the age-related targets they had produced and had precluded a proper exploration of the potential for cross-curricular links. The group worked to the structure for the reporting of pupils' results proposed by the Task Group on Assessment and Testing (TGAT, 1987). TGAT had recommended the use of attainment profiles. The working group offered three profile components for mathematics. They saw the curriculum consisting of two broad areas; knowledge, skills and understanding and the ability to apply mathematics. The 'content' of the curriculum was to be divided between number, algebra and measures (PC1) and shape, space, data handling (PC2). The third profile component, practical applications, was to carry the heaviest weighting for assessment purposes, 40 per cent, whilst PC1 and 2 had 30 per cent each. The group had used the TGAT ten-level scale (see Chapter 1) for the 'content' components, but felt that they could not specify levels in the same way for the practical applications element. Instead they offered descriptions of the qualities they felt the average child should be capable of demonstrating at the four reporting ages.

August 1988: The full report of the working group was published together with a brief statement of proposals from the Secretaries of State. These proposals contained significant departures form the curriculum envisaged by the working group. The Secretaries of State felt that, as the practical applications component would be hard to assess unambiguously, it should be integrated into the targets for knowledge and understanding. In anticipation of the results of the consultation exercise the National Curriculum Council was directed to arrange for the integration of the third profile component and adjust the weighting of the profile components accordingly.

December 1988: The Consultation Report was published. Through the consultation process strong support emerged for retaining the practical applications component as a separate entity. The responses urged that the difficulty in specifying age-related targets for the use and application of mathematics should not be used as a reason for failing to include the area within the statutory curriculum. The general view was said to be encapsulated within one response which emphasized that the important must be made measurable and not the measurable important. The NCC offered the compromise of including an attainment target for using and applying mathematics within each of the two knowledge and understanding components. The assessment weighting was adjusted and the first profile component, which contained number, was allocated 60 per cent. The final balance of alterations which had been made as a result of consultation indicated that the proposals of the Secretaries of State had proved the most influential by far. With the diminution of the status of the practical application component and explicit reference to pencil and paper calculation the final document was widely regarded as evidence of a return to traditional approaches.

March 1989: The first Mathematics in the National Curriculum document was distributed to schools.

June 1989: The non-statutory guidance was published. The Council which had expressed some misgivings about the final form of the statutory document, which had to a large extent been prescribed by the Secretaries of State, took the opportunity to restate some of the messages that had appeared in their original proposals and, before that, in the Cockroft Report. The guidance contains many statements which appear to contradict the view of mathematics offered in the statutory orders. In offering advice about planning schemes of work for children, it is stated that it is impossible to predict the order in which a child's mathematical understanding will develop, that mathematics is more usefully conceived as a network of ideas than a hierarchy and that children should be actively involved in determining their own targets. The guidance also calls for the different areas of mathematics to be brought together in designing activities and promotes the cross-curricular integration of the subject. Given the relative status of the guidance it seemed likely that the statutory document's definition of mathematics as an autonomous subject, consisting of a collection of topics arranged in clearly defined progression, would prove more influential.

August 1989: The provisions in the orders and documents came into force for Key Stages 1 and 3.

March 1990: The National Curriculum Council (see Chapter 1) published *Curriculum Guidance 3: The Whole Curriculum*. In the Consultation Report the Council advised that discussion on cross-curricular aspects should be postponed until other core and foundation subjects were in place. This publication sets out a brief rationale for cross-curricular links which is stunning in its naïvety. The guidance contains the memorable prediction that in due course schools were likely to throw all the attainment targets in a heap on the floor and reassemble them in a way which provided for them the basis of a whole curriculum. Whilst the heap of attainment targets proved to be an attractive image, suggestions for the next move often varied from the Council's prediction.

August 1990: The provisions of the orders and documents came into force for Key Stage 2.

January 1991: The Secretary of State, Kenneth Clarke, announced a review of the statutory orders for the core subjects. The objective of the review was to simplify the structure of the attainment targets so as to make assessment more manageable without altering the content of the curriculum.

May 1991: New draft proposals were distributed and the consultation process began.

July 1991: Consultation ended.

September 1991: The Consultation Report was published. The curriculum was rearranged into five attainment targets; Using and Applying Mathematics, Number, Algebra, Shape and Space and Handling Data, each carrying equal weight for purposes of reporting. The Council took the opportunity to make some minor amendments to the wording of some statements and adjusted the level of a few items. Apart from this, the only other notable change was in the form and presentation of the programmes of study and statements of attainment. The statements of attainment were reduced in number (296 to 147) and sampled the content of the programmes of study which were far more detailed. The programmes of study and statements of attainment were shown side by side on the same page. Whilst a majority of respondents welcomed the reduction in the number of attainment targets from 14 to five, many pointed out that, without a reduction in the content of the programmes of study, there would be no real effect on the burden of assessment. Measurement no longer occupied an attainment target of its own and the items in the programmes of study which related to this area of the subject were distributed between the number and shape targets. Many respondents questioned the wisdom of this move and suggested that a sixth attainment target would be the obvious remedy. The Council's response to this suggestion, which amounted to explaining that, for the purposes of reporting on assessment, six was a far less convenient number than five, emphasized the true priorities of the exercise. Many respondents commented that the proposals made insufficient reference to issues of cultural diversity, equal opportunities and cross-curricular links. Closer inspection of the orders reveals that the term insufficient, suggesting as it does that there is some, is clearly a euphemism.

January 1992: The new order was distributed to schools.

August 1992: The new order came into force.

April 1993: Sir Ron Dearing was appointed Chair of the National Curriculum Council and the Schools Examinations and Assessment Council, prior to the two bodies being merged to form the Schools Curriculum and Assessment Authority (SCAA). The Secretary of State, John Patten, stated that Sir Ron's initial objective should be to map out a strategy for simplifying the National Curriculum and its assessment arrangements. The threat posed to the testing programme by mounting unrest amongst teachers over issues of manageability and educational merit inspired the proposed review (see Chapter 1).

July 1993: The *Interim Report* requested by the Secretary of State was published. It contained the suggestion that all ten curriculum orders should be revised simultaneously.

December 1993: Sir Ron Dearing's *Final Report* was published, setting out the procedure for a review of each subject order. The brief given to the subject teams was to reduce the volume of statutory content, enhance the clarity of the programmes of study and provide more scope for teachers to use their professional judgement.

April 1994: Draft proposals on the completely revised National Curriculum were published and distributed to signal the start of a four-month consultation period. The published proposals contained material that surprised the majority of the advisory group involved in its construction. An appendix containing a version of the curriculum in which the Using and Applying attainment target had been integrated into the remaining targets had been added. Nine members of the advisory group wrote to SCAA to express their dismay that the contents of the appendix directly contravened the group's recommendation that the Using and Applying attainment target should remain as a separate entity. Whilst the idea of cutting the amount of statutory content within the National Curriculum as a whole was widely accepted as necessary, the *Evaluation Report* (SCAA, 1993) found that the majority of teachers questioned about the mathematics orders wanted no changes to be made. The research team who complied the report advised that redrafting should only be undertaken as a result of careful analysis of the existing orders. The advisory group obviously found the process of identifying what could be removed far from straightforward. They settled for deleting material that they felt was covered by implied reference in other areas of the programmes of study, taking out items which appeared in other subject orders and removing a small number of topics for which no further development was suggested in the orders. At first sight the orders appeared considerably slimmer, with only three attainment targets remaining at Key Stage 1 (Using and Applying, Number and Shape, Space and Measures) and the attainment target for Data Handling re-emerging at Key Stage 2. Closer inspection revealed that remarkably little had actually been removed. Far more had been relocated. Other major changes included the presentation of programmes of study for key stages rather than in levels, the inclusion of descriptions of opportunities, which the pupils should be offered in their work on each attainment target, and the replacement of statements of attainment with level descriptions.

November 1994: Page-proof copies of the new orders were distributed to schools. A report on the consultation process (SCAA, 1994a) was published. The report suggested that the majority of respondents agreed that the content was about right and alleged general approval for the idea of deferring some themes so as to provide more time for basic number work at Key Stage 1. In a press release that accompanied the launch of the revised curriculum, the Secretary of State, Gillian Shephard, summarized the changes to the mathematics order as: more emphasis on arithmetic particularly in the primary years; the use of calculators by 5 to 7-year-olds had been restricted to the more complex calculations as calculators could not be a substitute for arithmetic skills. The points she chose to emphasize in this statement offer a useful illustration of the 'back to basics' nature of the political agenda. The manner in which they were offered suggests a fair degree of confidence that the principle of a return to the traditional values of mathematics education would gain wide acceptance. A closer inspection of the orders does reveal an increase in emphasis on arithmetic. Although the differential weighting of attainment targets was abandoned in the 1991 revision, number has remained dominant by virtue of the quantity of material contained within the programmes of study for this area. This dominance is even more noticeable in the new orders. It is possible, however, to identify the influence of the professionals within SCAA and the advisory group in the revised orders. Within the statements of the opportunities to be offered to children, which open the programmes of study for each attainment target, it is possible to detect how some of the recommendations contained in the non-statutory guidance have now become law.

December 1994: The London Mathematical Society, a national organization representing the interests of university mathematics departments, announced that they were to mount a campaign to urge the government to undertake a radical revision of the curriculum. The society suggested that there was a strong consensus amongst university mathematicians that, over the last few years, there had been a rapid deterioration in the mathematical skills and understanding of pupils completing their secondary education. The group felt that the nature of the National Curriculum has been unduly influenced by the emphasis that mathematics educationists have placed upon the development of process skills. They suggest that process is being emphasized at the expense of content and that, as a result, the subject is being diluted to such an extent that it is failing to motivate students and discourages them from opting for mathematics degree courses.

ACHIEVEMENTS AND MISSED OPPORTUNITIES: REVIEWING THE STORY SO FAR

Achievements

When OFSTED (1994) reviewed the inspection evidence of the preceding academic year they concluded that mathematics was the weakest subject in the curriculum at Key Stage 2. If it is fair to offer any evaluation of the National Curriculum on the basis of such evidence, it can only be that it has failed to make a great impact in overcoming the long-standing problems of the subject for this age-group.

The history of mathematics education is characterized by consistent failure. Whilst the National Curriculum can be conceived as the product of various theories of how to remedy these shortcomings, there was no explicit attempt to use the mistakes of the past as a starting point for a better future. The National Curriculum offered a new definition of the subject. The description of mathematics provided in the orders is the product of mathematics educators working within parameters set by politicians. The primary curriculum for mathematics prior to 1987 was generally defined by published mathematics schemes. Such schemes were generally the result of mathematics educators working to a brief shaped by the commercial interests of the publishing companies.

Even if this evokes images of frying pans and fires there is a lot to be said in favour of having one definition of the subject to work to. It has provided a common focus for in-service education in mathematics, making it much easier for schools and teachers to work together. It has also provided a basis for involving parents in their children's mathematics education by eliminating grounds for suspicion that pupils are being subjected to an educational experiment dreamed up by the staff of the local school. Encouraging the involvement of parents remains the key to combating the effect of negative attitudes towards the subject and a statutory curriculum provides a useful starting point for further development in this area.

OFSTED (1994) suggests that the effect of the National Curriculum at Key Stage 1 has been positive, with children being introduced to aspects of the curriculum earlier and teacher expectations being raised. Would it be reasonable to expect a similar effect at Key Stage 2 when junior teachers have amassed the same amount of experience of the new curriculum as their infant colleagues?

Missed opportunities

One feature of the development of the National Curriculum that stands out through the preceding chronological review is the unseemly haste in which the work has been carried out. By presenting the summary with dates to mark the timing of the major events in the development of the mathematics orders, it is possible to appreciate the way that the time-scale influenced the nature of the discussion. Debate about issues that would appear to provide the natural starting points for the creation of a curriculum, such as the nature of the subject, the purposes of mathematics education and views about children's learning were to a large extent sacrificed to the need to produce the substance of the curriculum in the form of written targets. If we accept the analysis that genuine progress in mathematics education has been hampered by the competing priorities of those groups who hold an interest and can exert an influence over the curriculum, the implications of the absence of wider and more open discussion are particularly profound.

Whilst the time-scale provides an obvious culprit for the paucity of discussion, it may not be the only cause. Lawton (1989) offers the view that, as a nation, the English prefer to approach curriculum planning from the perspective of common sense, treating abstract ideas and theories with distaste or suspicion.

The opportunity to engage in the type of open discussion which may have provided a rational basis for the curriculum has now been missed on three occasions. The consultation exercises constrained discussion by limiting requests for comments to the successive versions of the orders. There was no mechanism for dealing with any response that offered alternative structures.

Whilst it is possible to detect the influence of the educators in the structure of each version of the orders, there can be little doubt that the curriculum has been fashioned in response to the dominant political imperative of each phase. The paramount political objective has been the introduction of a system of standardized assessment which, by offering information that could be reported and compared, provides a means of gaining greater control over the curriculum and its delivery. As a consequence, assessment arrangements became the starting-point for curriculum design. The TGAT model provided a rigid framework for all of the original subject orders (See Chapter 1). The departure from elements of that model which can be seen in the latest version of the mathematics orders was inspired by the need to counter the threat posed to the assessment system by the risk of losing the co-operation of teachers.

The restricted nature of the debate also meant that the mathematics educators were forced to prioritize items on their own agenda. They were obliged to enter into a recurrent battle over the use and application element of the orders. The messages of history and research into adults' ability to use mathematics were clear in pointing out the need for an emphasis to be placed on the development of mathematical thinking and problem-solving strategies. In the words of Papert (1972), children needed to learn how to be mathematicians rather than be taught about mathematics.

The fact that the ability to apply mathematical ideas can only be described in terms of process skills and attitudes meant that it did not fit comfortably into the TGAT model and did not correspond with the classical mathematics curriculum. In consequence the education lobby was forced to fight a retreat from an opening position in which the practical application of mathematics was offered as the most important area of the subject to a position of staving off the threat to the separate identity of this area, contained in the appendix to the 1994 Draft Proposals. This protracted struggle sapped the energy of the professionals to such an extent that other issues were forfeited.

The next section will examine in more detail some of the issues that have largely been omitted from the discussion and briefly consider some of the implications of their absence.

THE MATHEMATICS ORDERS AND LEARNING THEORY

It could be argued that learning theory is an issue for curriculum delivery rather than curriculum design. This view underestimates the extent to which learning programmes and teaching approaches can be influenced by the content of a statutory curriculum. Thought should have been given to the amount of time that children would need to develop an understanding of any targets that were set. The recommendation made in the King's College Report (1987) that research into children's learning needed to precede the construction of the curriculum was ignored and instead the working group based their proposals on their 'collective experience and knowledge of good teaching practice' (DES, 1988). The working group recognized the inherent fallibility of the approach they had followed, stating that: 'it would be surprising … if we had got everything right first time', and recommending that their efforts should be tested empirically through use in schools.

Whilst the initial working group was justified in claiming that the time available to them, around six months, precluded the initiation of new research, Dowling (1990) notes that they appeared to make little use of existing material, preferring instead to go on a globe-trotting junket to look at mathematics teaching in Japan, the Netherlands, West Germany and France. The concerns of the working group about this 'trial and error' approach to curriculum design appears to focus upon the possibility of the misplacement of some targets. I would suggest that such errors of arrangement are insignificant when considered alongside another possible outcome.

The way in which the extent of the requirements will effect the amount of time children are allowed to assimilate and try out new ideas and skills needs to be monitored carefully. The structure of the curriculum and the immensity of the statutory content appears to suggest a model of learning which is hierarchical, linear and atomized, i.e. concerned with the acquisition of discrete items of knowledge. Whilst it is possible to identify lines of progression within the mathematical themes developed in the orders, the idea that to learn new skills and knowledge children need time to apply them in a range of situations is challenged by the imperative of comprehensive coverage. The *Evaluation Report* (SCAA, 1993) records a significant number of teachers complaining about too much to get through and comments on the impression gained in interviews with these teachers that the perception of inappropriate demands was based upon teachers' teaching rather than children's learning. Other teachers interviewed in the survey indicated that the pressure of excessive content had altered their teaching style, noting that there was less time for practical work or following up lines of investigation suggested by the children.

CROSS-CURRICULAR APPROACHES TO MATHEMATICS

Views about how the National Curriculum has effected the development of cross-curricular work within mathematics will depend upon how interdisciplinary work is conceived in general. Alexander *et al.* (1992) suggest a distinction between two positions: integration which entails bringing together subjects whilst maintaining their separate identities; and non-differentiation which contends that separate subject divisions are inappropriate for the young child.

If integration is the objective, the wide range of contexts provided by the other areas of the curriculum should draw children's attention to the relevance of mathematics and offer opportunities to use and apply mathematical skills and knowledge. It could be argued that the successful integration of subjects is dependent on a clear definition of each subject as a distinct entity. If we accept this idea the National Curriculum could be seen as providing a basis for effective cross-curricular work. In reality it seems likely that the advent of the National Curriculum has had little effect on the extent to which mathematics is integrated. Prior to the National Curriculum, HMI reported that mathematics, along with physical education and music, were the subjects most likely to be taught separately in primary schools.

For the National Curriculum to have played a more proactive role in promoting cross-curricular work the intention of NCC/SCAA to remain neutral on matters of curriculum delivery would have been compromised. The cross-curricular themes provided in the *Curriculum Guidance* series (NCC, 1990) could be considered a model for what might have been, although there is reason to believe that the non-statutory status of this material has severely limited its impact on the curriculum. It is reasonable to assume that the inclusion of cross-curricular content within the statutory orders would have provided the necessary impetus for the further development of this approach to mathematics. Areas of statutory provision have provided the focus for the bulk of in-service education and school development activity over the last seven years. Evidence from the *Evaluation Report* (SCAA, 1993) suggests that the potential of the approach is far from being realized particularly at Key Stage 2.

EQUAL OPPORTUNITIES AND MULTICULTURALISM IN MATHEMATICS

The accusation that the orders have failed to make a contribution to the development of mathematics education in areas such as the provision of equal opportunities or providing a wider multicultural perspective of the subject could be countered by reference to the clearly stated intention to leave matters of curriculum delivery to the schools. The most generous interpretation of this position is that an opportunity to raise awareness of these issues and to promote a wider participation in initiatives to establish the social context and responsibilities of the subject had been wasted. Alternatively it can be viewed as a failure to comprehend and/or take responsibility for the situations of disadvantage that can be created by curriculum design.

The final report of the initial working group (NCC, 1988) includes sections on equal opportunities and ethnic and cultural diversity. The discussion of the issues offered in these sections is heavily dependent on the type of 'folk wisdom' which is referred to earlier in the document as having informed decisions about the setting of targets. Research into the differential participation and achievement of girls in mathematics is reviewed (paras. 10.13 – 10.17) and the conclusion is reached that the identified causes make it a matter for teaching practice rather than curriculum construction.

On cultural matters the opinion is offered: 'that undue emphasis on multi-cultural mathematics ... could confuse young children' and that 'priority must be given to ensuring that they have the knowledge, understanding and skills which they will need for adult life and employment in Britain in the twenty-first century.' The working group expressed confidence that 'most ethnic minority parents would share this view' (para. 10.20).

The assumptions upon which such pronouncements are made again illustrate the weakness of the serendipity approach to curriculum design. In the light of the doubtful quality of this opening to the debate it is difficult to know whether to express regret or relief over the fact that there are no more explicit references to these issues in any of the succeeding National Curriculum documentation. The absence is perhaps most con-spicuous in the non-statutory guidance (B4–B11) which seeks to offer advice about the framing of school policy documents and describes the range of experiences that should be offered to the child through the school mathematics curriculum. In a collection of 13 statements which generally begin with the words 'Activities should', it is strange that none are concluded by ideas like: illustrate the way in which different cultures have contributed to the subject or be set in contexts which are likely to be familiar, relevant and interesting to all of the students.

THE IMPACT OF ASSESSMENT

The government sees assessment as the key to raising standards. Gipps and Stobart (1993) suggest that this belief has received little critical attention and that it is difficult to find an explanation of the nature of the causal link between testing and improved results. The belief appears to be based on the strength of the incentive to improve performance provided by the publication of results and the opportunity offered thereby to make judgements about the effectiveness of the school and its staff (see Chapter 1). The only link between assessment and improved results that can be substantiated through research is the result of teachers 'teaching to the test'. Teachers are more likely to make the emphasis of their teaching correspond with the content of the test when the results are potentially highly significant.

Items within the curriculum that are to be tested by the SATS are likely to receive a greater emphasis within teaching programmes. At Key Stage 1 in 1994 the standardized assessment was limited to number and, whilst the standardized materials currently available for Key Stage 2 (SCAA, 1994b) offer tasks to assess ATs 2 – 5, we might reasonably expect future moves to narrow the focus of testing to the 'basics' of arithmetic. These developments must cast doubt on the sustainability of the broadening effect that the orders have been reported to have had on the primary mathematics curriculum.

The influence that testing will have over the curriculum extends beyond the problems caused by stressing some areas at the expense of others. In the revised orders (DFE, 1995) non-statutory exemplification has been omitted, leaving the possibility that test items will become the accepted examples. This development would be worrying as it would subvert the purpose of the statement of attainment/level descriptions and cast them in a role for which they are inadequate. Programmes of study provide the outline for curriculum objectives, and the statements of attainment/level descriptions offer a sample from these objectives and provide the basis for assessment. If the test items become the curriculum objectives we would be offering children a narrow and im-poverished mathematical education.

The format of written tests also provides unhelpful messages about the subject. There is an obvious attempt within the test materials to set the mathematics in context. Whilst there are no baths being filled without plugs or men digging holes, the contexts remain, by necessity, artificial, and the perception that one of the main purposes of learning mathematics is to attain the skill of placing numbers in spaces on pages is reinforced.

CONCLUSION

The revised National Curriculum Orders have been presented with promises of greater stability and a decrease in the pace of curriculum change. The intention to impose a five-year moratorium on major curriculum changes (SCAA, 1995) has been welcomed by teachers, trainers and publishers, who have had to come to terms with a limited shelf-life for their plans and resources. We must hope, however, that the opportunities provided by this pause for breath are not missed. One of the major problems with statutory curricula is the way in which they can constrain experimentation, thought and debate about the curriculum. Mathematics for the new millennia should provide a focus for a debate about the purposes of the subject and the relevance of the curriculum to the mathematical needs of everyday life.

The issue of children's learning has to a large extent become sidelined in the debate about the National Curriculum. A continuation of this trend will severely limit the chances of improvement in levels of mathematical understanding and skill. If the proposed moratorium is observed, it would be nice to think that the resultant savings in resources could be used to fund research into how children learn mathematics. The perspective that could be provided by such research together with discussion about the aims that the various interested parties have for mathematics education would provide a firm basis for further development of the curriculum.

It is possible that the most enduring legacy of the last seven years will prove to be the wealth of opportunity that has been provided to learn from mistakes. The process which has featured the dominance of ideology over reason and speed over circumspection should have created enough political embarrassment to ensure against its repetition. The errors in the product will only be detected if the evaluation extends beyond the performance of children against the targets it defines. We will need to see how the presentation of the orders and their assessment affect teaching approaches and through them attitudes towards the subject. Making the right decisions about the mathematics which is appropriate for various age-groups will prove to be of little use unless children develop the ability and confidence to apply what they have learnt.

REFERENCES

Adult Literacy and Basic Skills Unit (ALBSU) (1990) *Basic Skills Accreditation Initiative: How Well Can Adults Add Up?* London: ABSLU.

Advisory Council for Adult and Continuing Education (ACACE) (1981) *Use of Mathematics by Adults in Daily Life.* London: ACACE.

Alexander, R. *et al.* (1992) *Curriculum Organisation and Classroom Practice in Primary Schools.* London: DES.

Committee of Inquiry into the Teaching of Mathematics in Schools (Cockroft Report) (1982) *Mathematics Counts.* London: HMSO.

Dearing, R. (1993a) *The National Curriculum and its Assessment: Interim Report.* York/London: NCC/SEAC.

Dearing, R. (1993b) *The National Curriculum and its Assessment: Final Report.* London: SCAA.

DES (1987a) *Primary Education: Some Aspects of Good Practice.* London: HMSO.

DES (1987b) *National Curriculum Mathematics Working Party: Interim Report.* London: HMSO.

DES (1988) *Mathematics for Ages 5 to 16.* London: HMSO.

DES (1991) *Mathematics for Ages 5 to 16.* London: HMSO.

DFE (Department for Education) (1995) *Key Stages 1 and 2 of the National Curriculum.* London: HMSO.

Dowling, P. and Noss, R. (1990) *Mathematics versus the National Curriculum.* Basingstoke: Falmer Press.

Ernest, P. (1991) *The Philosophy of Mathematics Education.* Basingstoke: Falmer Press.

Floyd, A. (ed.) (1981) *Developing Mathematical Thinking.* London: Addison-Wesley.

Gipps, C. and Stobart, G. (1993) *Assessment: A Teachers Guide to the Issues.* Sevenoaks: Hodder and Stoughton.

HMI (1979) *Mathematics 5–11: A Handbook of Suggestions.* London: HMSO.

HMI (1991) *Mathematics Key Stages 1 and 3.* London: HMSO.

HMI (1992) *Mathematics Key Stages 1, 2 and 3.* London: HMSO.

HMI (1993) *Mathematics Key Stages 1, 2, 3 and 4.* London: HMSO.

King's College, London (1987) *Targets for Mathematics in Primary Education.* Coventry: University of Warwick.

Lawton, D. (1989) *Education, Culture and the National Curriculum.* London: Hodder and Stoughton.

McIntosh, A. (1977) When will they ever learn. In Floyd, A. (ed.) (1981) *Developing Mathematical Thinking.*

National Curriculum Council (1988) *Consultation Report: Mathematics.* London: NCC.

National Curriculum Council (1990) *Curriculum Guidance 3: The Whole Curriculum.* London: NCC.

Office of Standards in Education (OFSTED) (1994) *Science and Mathematics in Schools.* London: HMSO.

Papert, S. (1972) Teaching children to be mathematicians versus teaching about mathematics. In Floyd, A. (ed.) (1981) *Developing Mathematical Thinking*.

School Curriculum and Assessment Authority (SCAA) (1993) *Evaluation of the Implementation of National Curriculum Mathematics at Key Stages 1,2 and 3*. London: SCAA.

SCAA (1994a) *The Review of the National Curriculum: A Report on the 1994 Consultation*. London: SCAA.

SCAA (1994b) *Mathematics Tasks Key Stage 2*. London: SCAA.

SCAA (1995) *An Introduction to the Revised National Curriculum*. London: SCAA.

Shuard, H. *et al.* (1991) *Calculators, Children and Mathematics*. London: Simon & Schuster.

Task Group on Assessment and Testing (TGAT) (1987) *A Report*. London: DES.

Chapter 4

Science in the National Curriculum

Ron Ritchie

INTRODUCTION

Science is one of the success stories of the National Curriculum, although the introduction of science into the curriculum of every primary school in England and Wales has not been without its problems. In 1986, when the Secretary of State announced his plans for the National Curriculum, the biggest surprise for many primary teachers was the inclusion of science as a core subject. At that time, many primary schools had only recently introduced science into the curriculum and it was usually tackled in a fairly *ad hoc* manner, was often regarded as an 'optional extra' and involved work in the natural rather than physical sciences. However, that situation was a considerable improvement on what HMI reported in their 1978 survey of primary schools:

> Few primary schools visited in the course of this survey had effective programmes for the teaching of science. There was a lack of appropriate equipment; insufficient attention was given to ensuring proper coverage of key scientific notions; the teaching of processes and skills ... was often superficial.
> (DES, 1978; p.58)

From this situation to science as a core element of the National Curriculum was a considerable change in a decade. Since its introduction into the core National Curriculum, progress, in terms of the amount and quality of science work going on in primary classrooms, has been slow but continuous. The original orders (DES, 1989a) proved problematic and their implementation challenging and demanding for teachers. They were revised within two years (DES, 1991c), but still found to be unworkable. The current revision (DFE, 1995), initiated by the Dearing Report, provide a more manageable framework for consolidating and building upon current practice.

   This chapter explores the development of science education over the last ten years, identifying significant influences and constraints teachers experienced. The evolution of the National Curriculum in science is outlined, tracing the origins of the original proposals through to the new orders that have applied from September 1995. It is a story of a profession defending its view of science education against the constant pressure from the government for a science curriculum that emphasized facts and content over process and the development of scientific skills. It is a story that has involved primary teachers dealing with at least ten versions of what the curriculum should look like and having to implement unrealistic requirements. Put simply, no primary teacher could have implemented the original, nor the 1991 version of the National Curriculum in science; at best, conscientious teachers could decide to do what they did as well as they could whilst recognizing that it was impossible to do all that was expected. In many other classrooms the attempts made to cover the unworkable and overloaded curriculum led to an increase in the amount of science being taught but not to a corresponding increase in the quality of learning. If we have learnt anything about children's learning in science over the last decade, it is that it takes time to support children in developing scientific competence and conceptual structures that help them understand the world around them; skipping from one area of content to another is not the way to achieve this goal.

BACKGROUND

This section sketches briefly the context in which the National Curriculum was introduced. There have been major curriculum development projects in primary science for many years, although their impact in classrooms has, in most cases, been limited. One of the first and most influential was the Schools Council Science 5–13 Project which began in 1967 and introduced many primary teachers to an enquiry-based approach to science (Harlen, 1975). The work of this project was developed by the Learning Through Science Project (Richards, 1983) which produced pupil and teacher materials based upon an enquiry approach. Common to these and many other initiatives was the recognition that learning in science involved young children in practical activity and that the development of skills and attitudes was as important as the development of knowledge and understanding. Indeed, in some, the focus of children's learning was almost exclusively on the process of enquiry rather than the content covered; the claim was that as long as children were behaving as scientists it was almost irrelevant what they were gaining by way of increased knowledge or understanding.

Alongside these projects, and others like them, the Assessment of Performance Unit was making a contribution to teachers' awareness of children's learning in science through the dissemination of the results of its testing programme which was carried out throughout the first half of the 1980s (APU, 1988). The reports stressed the importance of giving particular attention to developing children's specific scientific skills, such as hypothesizing, fair-testing and predicting. There was evidence that primary children were able to use more generic skills but lacked opportunities to develop and practice those skills at the heart of scientific endeavour.

A pivotal point for primary science occurred in 1985. The government made its commitment to science for all pupils explicit in one of its first subject policy documents, *Science 5–16* (DES, 1985). This stated, 'science should have a place in the education of all pupils of compulsory school age . . . ' (p.1). The message was clear: science should be taught by every primary teacher. This policy statement was generally well received by the science education community and it set an agenda which informed debate in the period prior to the implementation of the National Curriculum. It signalled a shift away from the process emphasis of early initiatives, recognizing that children 'should gain a progressively deeper understanding of some of the central concepts of science' (p. 9). Principles for planning a science curriculum were identified which remain relevant today: breadth; balance; relevance; differentiation; equal opportunities; continuity; progression; links across the curriculum; teaching methods and approaches; assessment.

In the same year, the government provided funds to support the implementation of its policy. Education Support Grants for science provided 50 Local Education Authorities (LEAs) with advisory teachers whose work involved supporting teachers in classrooms, running courses and producing curriculum and teacher support materials. For many teachers, organizing and managing the practical aspects of science teaching proved difficult and advisory teachers played a significant part in helping them re-evaluate and change their teaching approaches, sometimes with knock-on effects beyond science. This work was evaluated nationally (Initiatives in Primary Science: an Evaluation (IPSE), 1988). In 1986, the funding was increased to cover nearly all the other LEAs and an infrastructure was established to support the major professional development programme necessary for supporting the introduction of the National Curriculum in science. For a few years, primary science was a growth area, projects sprang up all over the country, publications flourished and there was a belief that science was finally on the agenda of most schools. Unfortunately, the optimism was short-lived and the influence of these teams sometimes overestimated. By 1990 the number of science advisory teachers had been cut dramatically and Education Support Grants were no longer available to cover their cost; the government failed to maintain its financial support for science education at a crucial time in its development in primary schools. The National Curriculum was introduced at the same time as an essential infrastructure for its support was removed. The rationale offered at the time was that LEAs would continue to fund advisory teachers. However, most LEAs were suffering financial cutbacks. When cuts were necessary, advisory teachers, who did not directly affect pupil–teacher ratios, were inevitably the first to go. Much of the work of these teams failed to be consolidated by teachers in their classrooms because there was no ongoing support. The short, sharp approach to encouraging curriculum development proved of limited benefit when evaluated in terms of impact in classrooms upon children's learning.

A positive influence on developments in primary science which proved longer lasting came from the Association for Science Education (ASE). As it recruited more and more primary teachers, the emphasis of its activities and publications shifted from being almost exclusively secondary towards supporting all phases. The annual conferences, which attract thousands of teachers each year, and its journal, *Primary Science Review*, have provided a focus for the ongoing debate about the implementation of science in primary schools.

During the 1980s local initiatives flourished and most LEAs produced primary science guidelines, set up centres and offered a range of support for schools and teachers. These guidelines often stressed that good practice in primary science involved science being included in topic work as part of a cross-curricular approach (County of Avon, 1981). There was agreement in many guidelines that primary science should not be a 'watered-down' version of secondary science but should build on the natural curiosity and drives a child brings to school at 5. The content of science was seen to extend beyond nature study, including more of the physical sciences. At the school level, polices were written and co-ordinators or teachers with particular responsibility for developing science were appointed for the first time. The specific content of the science curriculum at this time was a decision taken by individual teachers or in some cases a whole school, perhaps based on LEA guidelines. Schools began to build up their resources for science. Some purchased commercial science schemes, although these were generally not used systematically or found supportive of the approach to science many teachers were adopting. Local authorities and institutions of higher education increased the number of courses available to teachers in science. This was in response to the perceived need of teachers for further professional development in this area. There was an increased variety in the courses; some continued to offer the less confident teacher support in starting science, but others addressed the particular needs of post-holders and some the problem of improving primary teachers' background knowledge in science.

By 1989, HMI reports (DES, 1989b) indicated that far more teachers were including science in their teaching but many still lacked confidence in this area of the curriculum. A key reason for this was the lack of background scientific knowledge of many primary teachers. This was due to the limited, inappropriate and inadequate science education most of them received at school and during training. Research by Kruger, Palacio and Summers (1988–91) confirmed that most primary teachers they interviewed had problems with their own understanding of science concepts and felt they had received a poor science education. They found primary teachers holding alternative ideas about the world around them similar to those held by pupils they taught. How could such teachers implement and assess a balanced science curriculum? Many primary school teachers, of whom the majority are women, have no formal qualifications in science and were trained at a time when science was not regarded as an important element of the primary curriculum. The options system in secondary schools had allowed many, especially girls, to avoid science beyond the age of 14. Those who do have qualifications tend to have studied biology or the natural sciences. Fortunately, this situation should be improving as new recruits to teaching will have experienced a National Curriculum that includes science as a core element throughout their own schooling. Indeed, applicants to initial teacher education straight from school are now required to have science GCSE. For existing teachers, the government funded 20-day courses which have been offered by higher education institutions since 1989. These have focused upon improving teachers' subject knowledge and understanding in order to improve their confidence to deliver a science curriculum. Unfortunately, as with the earlier advisory teacher funding, the support for such courses was drastically reduced before the needs of teachers had been fully met. Although a small minority of teachers (mainly co-ordinators) benefited from substantial in-service support, provided by these courses, the vast majority of teachers remained in need of professional development to improve their knowledge and understanding in the area of science. For them, the only support available was in the form of material from the National Curriculum Council (NCC, 1992–94), the Curriculum Council of Wales (CCW, 1992) and the Open University (OU, 1994) which aimed at addressing this problem through the medium of distance-learning materials.

CHILDREN'S LEARNING IN SCIENCE

An exciting and valuable aspect of the development of primary science has been the increasing interest in and understanding of the nature of children's learning in science. The framework for analysing learning of skills and processes, knowledge and under-standing and attitudes, articulated by the early primary science curriculum developers, and reflected in most LEA and school policies, remains appropriate in the current climate. However, research carried out in the 1980s and 1990s has provided new insights into the relationship between these dimensions. These projects have addressed the question of how young children learn to behave scientifically and how their scientific ideas about the world around them develop. The Children's Learning in Science Project (CLIS), based at the University of Leeds, and Science Processes and Concept Exploration (SPACE), based in Liverpool are two projects providing teachers with valuable information about children's learning. CLIS researchers collected and analysed evidence of children's ideas in science from age 5 to 16 (CLIS, 1988-92). The project disseminated their findings, and through INSET packs encouraged secondary teachers to modify their teaching to ensure such ideas were taken seriously and used as the basis of further learning. The SPACE team worked with primary teachers and elicited children's existing ideas in most areas of science, analysing these ideas to identify those which were common in children. The teachers, in collaboration with the researchers, planned and implemented interventions to challenge the children's exist-ing ideas. The success of these interventions was evaluated by the researchers. The findings, which make fascinating reading, were published in a series of research reports (SPACE, 1990–93). This research underpinned the recently published and well-received Nuffield Primary Science material (Nuffield, 1992–93). This is in the form of curriculum support material for teachers and pupils.

Both research projects highlighted the importance of recognizing that learners actively construct ideas for themselves and that existing ideas that children bring to the classroom have a significant influence on the development of new ideas. Crucially, these existing ideas will often not be acceptable in a scientific sense. Considerable evidence has now been collected that shows children hold common alternative ideas about the world that are uninfluenced, or influenced in unanticipated ways, by science teaching! For example, the CLIS project has found many 16-year-olds hold the alternative idea that 'cold' is something substantive that can travel from one place to another. When asked to explain why the metal part of a bicycle's handlebar feels colder than the plastic grip, many talk in terms of 'cold moving from the metal parts into the body'. Because these alternative ideas make sense in the pupils' own terms and are supported by direct and indirect evidence they are often very strongly held. This alternative idea will no doubt have been reinforced by adult comments such as, 'Shut the door, don't let the cold in' and have been retained despite at least five years of formal science teaching in secondary schools. Alternative ideas have their origins earlier in children's education and primary teachers have a responsibility to identify and confront them. Teaching strategies which support this view of learning, sometimes labelled 'constructivist approaches', have been advocated by those involved in such projects (see Ollerenshaw and Ritchie, 1993). These approaches often include phases of orientation (arousing children's interest and curiosity), elicitation (helping children to find out and clarify what they already think), intervention (encouraging children to test their ideas: to extend, develop or replace them) and application (helping children to relate what they have learned to their everyday lives). They place emphasis upon the inextricable links between the process skills children use and the concepts they develop. Scientific activity involves exploratory work, which ideally will lead to questions that can be investigated systematically. Crucially, these approaches take children's existing ideas seriously, using them as the basis for deciding upon appropriate teacher interventions aimed at supporting learners in using their skills and the processes of science to test out their own or other people's ideas. According to Ausubel, 'the most important single factor influencing learning is what the learner already knows; ascertain this and teach him [*sic*] accordingly' (1968, p. 685). Although many would argue this approach is the basis of a learner-centred philosophy of education, its particular implications for science education in terms of the common alternative ideas children hold are considerable. The validity of a constructivist view of learning and teaching approaches based upon such a view is now widely agreed by the science education community (Harlen, 1992; Newton, 1992). However, the child does not learn science in isolation, and any view of a child's learning in science must also take account of the social context and the influence of peers and more knowledgeable adults involved. In this respect a social constructivist view is most commonly accepted and the interactions within a group, the use of language and the role of the adult scaffolding a child's learning become vital aspects (Ollerenshaw and Ritchie, 1993). Learning in science (and indeed anything else) involves the individual actively constructing a unique and provisional understanding of the world around them, but the nature of that understanding will be affected by the social context in which the learning occurs.

Prior to the introduction of the science National Curriculum good practice in primary science, as defined by HMI (1989) was evident in some classrooms and schools. These teachers had become competent at identifying opportunities for science experiences for their children within the classroom and beyond. They planned appropriate science activities within an integrated curriculum as well as focusing at times on specific science topics. The science activities were planned to suit the individual needs and interests of the children and to begin from the existing ideas that they already held. The content and contexts used were chosen to reflect our multicultural society and to motivate girls and boys. These teachers provided broad and balanced science experiences for all the children in their classes. The extent to which the National Curriculum endorsed and extended this good practice is now explored.

A NATIONAL CURRICULUM FOR SCIENCE

The evolution of the National Curriculum has been complex as illustrated in Table 4.1, with over ten versions produced (and almost as many Secretaries of State for Education attempting to influence it). In some ways, the last decade has been a constant battle between the profession and the government: the profession struggling to hold on to a view of science education which reflected the model of good practice outlined above whilst the government attempted to enforce a science curriculum which emphasized a traditional view of science as a body of knowledge. The debate concerning the relationship between process and content, skills and knowledge and understanding, had been ongoing for many years. However, government intervention in the curriculum led to the science education community becoming a much more unified voice

Table 4.1 *The changing National Curriculum for science*

Date/Publication	Attainment Targets	Profile Components	Notes
1987 *Science Working Group Interim Report(Dec.)*	5 themes: living things; materials; energy and matter; forces; Earth in space		
1988 *Proposals of Secretary of State Final report SWG* (August)	1 – 16 17 – 18 19 – 20 21 – 22	Knowledge & understanding Exploration & investigation Communication Science in action	
NCC Consultation and Recommendations (December)	1 2 – 17	Exploration of science Knowledge & understanding of science	
1989 *Draft Orders* (January) *Statutory Orders* (March)			Implemented Aug 1989 – KS1 Aug 1990 – KS2
1990 *NCC Non-statutory Guidance*			
1991 *Proposals of Secretary of State* (May)	1 2 – 5	Exploration of science Knowledge & understanding of science	Summer 1st SATS (KS1)
NCC Consultation & Recommendations (September)	1 2 – 4	No longer profile components for reporting purposes	
Draft Orders (October)			
Statutory Orders (December)	1 – Scientific investigation 2 – Life and living processes 3 – Materials and their properties 4 – Physical processes		Included examples to support teachers; implemented Aug 1992
1992 Spring/Summer			Slimmed down SATs (KS1) – AT 1 not covered; first reported results
1993 *Dearing Report* (Dec.) **1994** *Draft Proposals* (May)	1 - Experimental and investigative science 2 – Life processes and living things 3 – Materials and their properties 4 – Physical processes		Level descriptors replace SoA; summer – no KS1 SATs
1995 *Statutory Orders* (Jan.)			Pilot KS2 SATs; implemented Aug 1995

seeking to defend the importance of process and skills in the curriculum. It was to be a battle, that despite some set-backs, the profession were to win.

Science, mathematics and English were the first subjects to be introduced as National Curriculum subjects. In July 1987 the then Secretary of State for Education set up a working group of those involved in science education to recommend attainment targets and programmes of study for science. Wynne Harlen, who was highly respected in the primary sector, chaired the primary group . The construction of a National Curriculum for science was a daunting task for the group, tackled on a part-time basis over a relatively short period. On reflection, some saw it as similar to trying to do part of a jigsaw without a picture (West, 1988). One of the dilemmas of approaching a National Curriculum in the way required by the then Secretary of State was that essential thinking about the structure of the whole curriculum did not occur. Each subject team had to produce its own view of the overall curriculum. This made co-ordination and integration of different curriculum elements/subjects extremely difficult. It also led to overambitious proposals, especially for primary schools, which did not take into account the demands upon a teacher of delivering the whole curriculum.

The philosophy articulated in the working group's *Interim Report* (Science Working Group, 1987) was widely commended by the science education community and is worth revisiting. Statements about the need for science experiences to be 'based on real experience' and developed as 'part of the whole curriculum' (p. 6) were close to the heart of those who had been advocating such an approach for many years. The group's final report *Science for Ages 5–16* was published in August 1988 (DES, 1988). This document was accepted by many in the profession as an excellent overview of the nature of school science. In the report's own words (p. 4):

> We show how we see the acquisition of knowledge and understanding as inextricably linked with the development of investigative skills and practical work, and with learning to communicate effectively . . . We also stress the importance we attach to the development of appropriate attitudes.

The report said little about methodology and how the curriculum should be implemented but it clearly endorsed a constructivist approach.

> In their early experiences of the world, children develop ideas which enable them to make sense of things that happen around them. A child brings these ideas to the classroom or laboratory, and the aim of science education is to adapt or modify these original ideas to give them more explanatory power. Viewed from this perspective, it is important that we should take the child's initial ideas seriously so as to ensure that any change or development of these ideas, and the supporting evidence for them makes sense and, in this way, become 'owned' by the child.
> (p. 7).

The programmes of study, for each attainment target at all key stages, were listed together in the report and provided what was for many its most important section. The programmes of study, which indicated in broad terms the learning experiences the pupils should have, were advocated as the aspect of the National Curriculum with which teachers should be most concerned when planning their teaching programmes (Ovens, 1989; Harlen, 1989). This was seen as a way of avoiding an assessment-led curriculum based on attainment targets and statements of attainment whilst ensuring continuity and progression. The statements of attainment were defined at ten levels for knowledge and understanding but those for exploration and investigation were grouped for each key stage. This (according to the report) was to reflect the holistic nature of these processes. The 50 per cent weighting of the 16 knowledge and understanding attainment targets in relation to the two for exploration and communication (science in action did not cover Key Stages 1 and 2) reinforced the group's desire to ensure that science was not seen simply as a body of knowledge. The report had separated knowledge in order to specify different components for assessment purposes. Behaving scientifically was seen as being as important as developing scientific knowledge and understanding. The then Secretary of State, Baker, in the same document, made his views, which were at odds with his panel of experts, explicit: emphasize knowledge and understanding, reduce other areas of learning.

There was a brief consultation period before the National Curriculum Council produced its report (NCC, 1988) and draft orders which reflected the then Secretary of State for Education's views of the curriculum rather than those of the profession elicited through consultation (80 per cent of respondents had opposed his proposed changes). By this time the working group had been disbanded. The Secretary of State had, as noted above, demanded an emphasis on knowledge and understanding at the expense of other attainment targets and statements of attainment at each level for AT1. Even more controversially, he insisted on a two tier approach to science in Key Stage 4, with an option which covered a narrower range of attainment targets and would allow certain pupils to spend less time on science. This contradicted the working group's aim of offering a balanced science curriculum to all children up to the age of 16. This desire for balance was particularly related to ensuring girls continued with a balanced science curriculum beyond the age of 14. The first round of the battle saw the initiative shifting towards the Secretary of State.

The orders which eventually arrived in schools in April 1989 were significantly different from those recommended by the Secretary of State's working party of 'experts in their fields'. The following knowledge and understanding attainment targets were included for the first two key stages: the Variety of Life, Processes of Life, Genetics and Evolution, Human Influences on the Earth, Types and Uses of Materials, Earth and Atmosphere, Forces, Electricity and Magnetism, Information Technology, Energy, Sound and Music, Using Light, The Earth in Space. One attainment target remained in the process domain: Exploration of Science. The programmes of study were similar to those recommended by the working group but their location in the document was subtly altered, to reduce their accessibility and, to some extent, their importance. The Secretary of State was keen to emphasize the assessment aspects of the curriculum at the expense of pedagogy and balance. The programmes of study were 'hidden' at the back of the document and all merged into one programme for each key stage. The aspirations of those who hoped the programmes of study would be the key element of the National Curriculum were thwarted by government intervention. The first round of consultation led to a developing cynicism amongst the profession about whether the process was any more than tokenistic.

The orders provided a framework for science teaching, indicating what should be taught, not how. The job of unpacking what had been produced and finding a creative way of implementing it, that did not cause them to lose sight of good practice, was the enormous task in front of primary teachers. This task was helped by the publication of the useful and well-received non-statutory guidance and support materials (CCW, 1989; NCC, 1989; 1991; 1993). These offered practical guidance and stressed the teacher's role in interpreting the programmes of study and attainment targets. However, in reality, the first National Curriculum for science was unworkable. The programmes of study were too ambitious; the statements of attainment and the model of progression involved were, at best, an educated guess, rather than one firmly grounded in research evidence concerning children's learning. To suggest children learn science in a strictly linear fashion that could be measured on a scale of one to ten was to most primary teachers a suspect model. Despite this, there was grounds for some optimism: at last science was established in the primary curriculum and the importance of behaving scientifically was still explicit in the curriculum requirements.

IMPLEMENTING THE NATIONAL CURRICULUM

A massive in-service training programme was implemented by LEAs to support the introduction of the National Curriculum and its assessment requirements, with advisory teachers and advisers running courses and school-based sessions to help teachers attempt to turn the theory of the National Curriculum into practice in their classrooms. It was a period of considerable professional development for many teachers, especially in the area of assessment which had not been prioritized in previous curriculum development projects. Nationally, and locally, teachers were receiving mixed messages about assessment. The government focus upon accountability was often at odds with models of good practice advocated by those running courses. The confusion became evident in classrooms. In some schools teachers placed too much attention on teaching to the statements of attainment and the assessment requirements dominated their planning and teaching. Others took a more measured approach, recognizing formative assessment as an essential part of good teaching. It soon became obvious, as teachers attempted to assess learners, that the assessment model of the National Curriculum was indeed problematic; teachers found some children at level 6 in one area and level 3 in another, perhaps during the same activity (Ollerenshaw *et al.*, 1991). The simplistic view of progression as strictly linear within attainment targets was based upon the original view of assessment provided by the Task Group on Assessment and Testing (TGAT). It provided one of the most unworkable aspects of the curriculum for those teachers who took children's learning seriously and based their assessments on genuine evidence of significance. The situation was made worse by the large number of attainment targets (17) and even greater number of statements of attainment (409). Assessing over 30 children in a class against all these 'objectives' and recording their achievements could not be implemented by a teacher, even if he/she only had science to teach, which was not the case. Implementing the standard assessment tasks (SATs) was also demanding and time-consuming. The emphasis of the first SATs (summer 1991) was on practical and group work and they were generally tolerated by Key Stage 1 teachers, particularly those who discovered new insights into individual children's achievements. However, on reflection one wonders whether the National Curriculum assessment requirements would have failed at the outset if the government had asked more vocal Key Stage 3 teachers, with their more effective union organization, to introduce the first SATs.

Teachers conscientiously attempted to cope with the overextensive programmes of study. This meant concept areas were sometimes covered superficially. In some cases, quality learning was being sacrificed for quantity. Many of the less confident teachers also found AT1, with its emphasis upon child-centred and child-devised investigations, difficult to implement. The treatment of science as a separate subject did not help in schools where the approach was more integrated and holistic; in most cases the teachers' preferred approach was retained and the requirements accommodated within topics and projects. In other schools, especially at Key Stage 2, some specialist teaching was used to compensate for teachers who lacked confidence to teach science. This usually involved timetabled slots and made integration with other classroom work difficult.

One of the most reassuring messages received by primary teachers from in-service providers at this stage was, 'Don't worry, you can't do it all, so do what you can do as well as you can!' Those who suffered during this period were the most conscientious teachers who naïvely believed the government rhetoric about realistic requirements and felt professionally inadequate because they could not 'make them work'.

On a positive note, one of the major benefits of this period concerned the increased collaboration that took place amongst teachers, especially when it came to planning for continuity at a whole school level. Another benefit was the obvious increase in the amount, and sometimes the quality, of science going on in primary schools. An unexpected benefit was the new respect teachers gained for the scientific achievements of young children; many were surprised by the children's existing ideas and their skills at testing them out.

HMI reported on the first year of the National Curriculum (DES, 1991a) in Key Stage 1 and found standards satisfactory or better in 75 per cent of classes with, on average 8 to 10 per cent of time being allocated to science. Planning of science had improved and they found increased confidence amongst teachers, although not where the physical sciences were concerned. HMI also found assessment was proving problematic and teachers were investing a disproportionate amount of time and energy in it. Crucially, in 20 per cent of classes the quality of work was adversely affected by the lack of suitably qualified staff. A research project surveyed over 900 primary teachers in 1989 and found only a third felt confident of their ability to teach science, and widespread anxiety was reported amongst the others in terms of their perception of their own scientific knowledge and understanding (Wragg *et al.*, 1989). A follow-up survey in 1991 showed remarkable increases in perceived confidence; science was now ranked third in the order of competence with over 40 per cent now claiming to feel competent regarding their background knowledge (Wragg *et al.*, 1991). However, some have suggested the latter findings need treating with caution; teachers with an inadequate knowledge base are not always aware of gaps or, perhaps more worryingly, of alternative ideas they hold. What the increase does show is a greater self-confidence on ᵗʰᵉ part of teachers when it came to science two years after the National Curriculum ᵇᵉᵉⁿ introduced. HMI's report on the second year of implementation (DES, 1992) ᶠᵒᵘⁿᵈ standards in the quality of teaching and learning in Key Stage 1 similar to the ᵖʳᵉᵛⁱᵒᵘˢ year. Work at Key Stage 2 was less satisfactory and restricted by teachers' lack ᵒᶠ ˢᶜⁱᵉⁿtific knowledge. Assessment continued to cause excessive workloads and ᵃⁿˣⁱᵉᵗʸ amongst teachers. The third year of National Curriculum science (OFSTED, 1993) saw progress in Key Stages 1 and 2 (the latter still lagging behind in terms of ᵈⁱˢᵖˡᵃʸ). At Key Stage 1, just over 75 per cent of lessons rated as satisfactory or better. ᴬ ˢᵘbstantial improvement was seen in Key Stage 2 classes, although whole school planning was weak and 'limited the systematic development of scientific knowledge and skills' (p.2). Little teaching by subject specialists was observed. As in the previous year, good leadership by science co-ordinators was identified as a crucial factor in the successful implementation of the National Curriculum in science.

The National Curriculum for science had made many demands upon teachers including: the need to spend more time on science; planning for science at a whole school and class level to ensure coverage of the programmes of study and continuity between classes and schools; giving greater attention to the development of children's knowledge and understanding and ensuring this is developed through their use of the processes of science; assessment and recording of progression through attainment targets and statements of attainment; reporting scientific achievements through profile components; acquiring and using appropriate resources and equipment (including IT); providing equality of opportunity and access to the science curriculum for all children. Teaching the science National Curriculum was proving an onerous task.

THE FIRST MODIFICATIONS

It became clear within the first two years that the National Curriculum, as a whole, was unworkable, and a ministerial decision was announced in January 1991 that the curriculum needed simplifying, particularly to make assessment more manageable. Sir Ron Dearing's proposals for reducing the requirements for science were published in May (DES, 1991b). The revision was carried out by HMI in consultation with the NCC (NCC, 1991). The proposals for revisions in science went further than originally suggested by the Secretary of State since the new group took the opportunity to improve aspects of progression in and between the attainment targets as well as taking into account the growing body of research into children's learning. Ironically, some teachers were resistant to the changes, having put considerable time and effort into dealing with the original orders. However, the new orders were approved in 1991 and teachers were required to teach to revised programmes of study and assess children against a drastically reduced set of attainment targets (from 17 to 4) and statements of attainment (from 409 to 176) from August 1992. The new attainment targets (scientific investigation; life and living processes; materials and their properties; physical processes) were divided into strands, most of which could be mapped to the original attainment targets. In some respects the orders returned to the content themes identified in the first Science Working Group report. Again, despite the then Secretary of State's view, the profession managed to defend the place of scientific investigation (AT1) in the curriculum and ensure the balance between it and the knowledge and understanding attainment targets remained about 50-50 at Key Stages 1 and 2.

The revised orders did not prove as manageable as was hoped, by politicians and teachers alike. The content described by the programmes of study was not reduced very much and remained problematic for many teachers; formative assessment against the new generalized statements of attainment was difficult and many teachers found themselves referring to the original detailed orders for guidance; the new orders no longer included elements which some teachers particularly valued, such as the social implications of science, multicultural aspects and health education. The assessment of the 1991 orders also provoked controversy when paper and pencil tests replaced the tasks originally set and standardized assessment of AT1 (Scientific Investigation) was removed from the SATs. This, and the demands of programmes of study for other attainment targets and the difficulties some teachers were having implementing investigative approaches, led to AT1 being less valued and less time was given to such work by busy teachers, coping with excessive content demands across the curriculum (OFSTED, 1993b, p.5).

HMI's report on the fourth year (OFSTED, 1993b) indicated further consolidation of teaching and learning standards, claiming 'the National Curriculum has secured a broad and balanced provision of science education for all pupils' (p.2). Progress in Key Stage 2, although continuous, was still restricted by lack of teacher knowledge in a significant number of schools. By 1993 a majority of primary schools, according to HMI, had matched schemes of work to the revised orders and, encouragingly, pupils were enjoying science. However, 'insufficient use was made of assessment to ensure subsequent work matched the ability and attainment of the pupils' (p.3). Another area of concern was the lack of liaison, and therefore continuity, between Key Stages 2 and 3.

Despite the positive findings from HMI, evidence from my own, and my colleagues', visits to schools, feedback from students on school placements and teachers on courses indicated that in some schools and classrooms science remained a somewhat peripheral, undervalued aspect of the primary curriculum. It was still not being accepted as a core subject alongside English and mathematics in the early 1990s. The number of these schools was diminishing, but making the teaching of science a statutory requirement did not guarantee a quality science education for all children from 5 to 11 in England and Wales.

The period from 1991–94 was one of less curriculum development in science than the previous few years. As the rest of the National Curriculum came on stream less attention was given to science. An interesting development of this period concerned the nature of whole school planning. In the first couple of years of the National Curriculum it was common for whole school planning of topics to focus upon the needs of the science curriculum and other subject areas were accommodated within these topics, such as 'water', 'weather' or 'on the move'. As other subject orders became statutory this approach proved less viable. For example, teachers found they needed to plan more history topics or projects to cover the study units. This led to a reduction in the number of science-focused topics and in some schools to an increase in separate subject teaching. The planning of science then needed to be more sophisticated, with perhaps a balance of science topics, themes within other topics, and ongoing science work (such as observing seasonal changes or plant growth). What should have been a period of consolidation for science failed to happen; the continuing demands of trying to make an unworkable National Curriculum viable meant little time was available for consolidation – almost every week teachers were faced with new documentation or requirements resulting from the 1988 Education Reform Act.

THE NEW ORDERS

The origins of the Dearing proposals for a further simplification of the whole National Curriculum were outlined in Chapter 1. The concerns from teachers about the requirements imposed on them was certainly not restricted to concerns about science: by now vocal opposition to overcrowding in most subjects and inappropriate assessment models were common. Interestingly, the battle for the retention of a process dimension to the curriculum in science was paralleled by similar concerns expressed by other professionals in areas such as mathematics, history, design and technology. The Dearing version of the science curriculum appeared in May 1994 (DFE, 1994), offering an even more slimmed-down curriculum: reductions in the programme of study content; replacement of statements of attainment with level descriptors; a revision of

AT1 (renamed as Experimental and Investigative Science). Consultations (SCAA, 1994) on these proposals were more 'genuine' than previous exercises and teachers' views were listened to and accommodated in ways not previously experienced. For example, widespread concern about the removal of electricity at Key Stage 1 in the draft led to it reappearing in the final proposals and orders and concern over 'energy sources and transfer' at Key Stage 2 led to its removal. The 'electricity' issue is particularly interesting since its original inclusion in Key Stage 1 had caused some concern: teachers claiming that young children could not deal with ideas about simple circuits and that it was an inappropriate topic for infant classrooms. Experience since the National Curriculum's introduction however, had convinced most of them that young children could cope with electricity – they even enjoyed it, and so did some of their teachers! The problem, initially, was not related to children's learning but to teachers' confidence and their knowledge. Things had indeed moved forward since 1989. Returning to the Dearing consultation, nearly 6000 response forms were submitted concerning the science proposals (only English had a higher level). By now, in science at least, it appeared the Secretary of State's opinion was no longer overriding the voice of the profession.

The new orders (DFEE) place emphasis on the programmes of study (now the level descriptions are tucked away at the back). Indeed, the programmes of study are now commonly referred to as Sc1, 2, 3 and 4, rather than AT1–4. There is a general section of the programmes of study for each key stage which applies to all four areas of the science curriculum, and is also statutory. It covers systematic enquiry; science in everyday life; the nature of scientific ideas; communication; health and safety. The first main section of the programme of study is named Experimental and Investigative Science (Sc1) and it outlines what pupils should be taught about: planning experimental work; obtaining evidence and considering evidence. Sc2, Life Processes and Living Things, covers: life processes; humans as organisms; green plants as organisms (Key Stage 2 only); variation and classification; living things and their environment. Decay and the effect of human activity on the local environment has been removed from Key Stage 1. Fossils, waste disposal procedures and seasonal changes have gone from Key Stage 2. Sc3, Materials and their Properties, is divided into: grouping materials; changing materials; separating mixtures of materials (Key Stage 2 only). Weathering has gone from Key Stage 1 and weather, and seasons have been removed from Key Stage 2. The final area, Physical Processes (Sc4) has a programme of study divided into: electricity; forces and motion; light and sound, the Earth and beyond (Key Stage 2 only). Hot and cold has gone from Key Stage 1 and heating and magnetic effects of an electric current, logic gates, structures and study of the night sky have been removed from Key Stage 2. Some content – effects of heating, fuels and Earth and beyond – have moved from Key Stage 1 to 2. Other such as acids and alkalis, chromatography, competition, colour, renewable and non-renewable energy sources, sounds as waves and the solar system have been transferred to Key Stage 3. To improve clarity, the sections include more examples than the earlier versions; each statement is given a letter for reference, and the content has been reordered. It is intended that progression in key ideas, where possible (or where known), is clearer in the new orders. For example, ideas about light can be tracked more easily across key stages using the subtitles. However, the use of brief bullet points does not help clarify what depth of understanding children might be expected to reach or what previous understanding may be needed. In making these decisions teachers will continue to need guidance and support beyond the orders. The content of the National Curriculum has not changed significantly through the revisions, although it has been reduced, and is not dissimilar to that advocated by enthusiasts for primary science in the 1970s (Harlen, 1978), the DES in the original policy document (DES, 1985) or the Science Working Group in its original proposals (SWG, 1987). Cynics might suggest the National Curriculum is simply biology, chemistry and physics, couched in different terms.

Common requirements set out at the beginning of each key stage emphasize that the programmes should, wherever possible, be taught to the great majority of pupils, making appropriate provision for those with special educational needs. In this version of the orders access for all children is given a higher profile.

The new version of Sc1, Experimental and Investigative Science, offers a broader view of practical activities than previous versions which emphasized the importance of pupil-designed investigations. The new programme of study moves away from a sequential model, of hypothesizing, observing, drawing conclusions, to encourage a variety of ways of obtaining scientific evidence and to justify observation work, exploratory work, illustrative activities, demonstrations and research based upon secondary sources as well as investigations (ASE, 1993; NCC, 1993). However, the rubric for Sc1 states 'On some occasions, the whole process of investigating an idea should be carried out by the pupils themselves.' There is less explicit reference to children hypothesizing and the language of the orders has been considerably simplified. Another modification of Sc1 concerns the use of the term 'variables'. The original orders placed considerable emphasis upon pupils controlling these in their investigative work and it proved problematic for teachers. The new proposals refer to 'factors' which is intended to include variables which can be quantified and controlled but also other things which might affect the outcome but are not easily measured or controlled. It is an attempt to broaden the definition of 'variable' to what it was before assessment requirements narrowed it. The integration between Sc1 and the other areas is explicit in each key stage. The battle for Sc1 has been won and in its current form it looks more like the original proposal than ever before.

Level descriptions (for assessment purposes) are provided for each level in each attainment target (a term retained in the orders to label assessment requirements) and are worded very generally. For example level 1 in AT1 (Experimental and Investigative Science) is:

> Pupils describe simple features of objects, living things and events they observe, communicating their findings in simple ways, such as by talking about their work or through drawings or simple charts.

In some ways these might best be called 'child descriptions'. It is intended that they are used in a 'best fit' manner; children do not need to attain each statement within the description to be awarded the level. They are a general description of what a pupil can do if they are at a particular level. This avoids the 'hurdle' approach taken to the previous statements of attainment by some teachers. Level descriptions are to inform summative assessments at the end of a key stage rather than to enable assessment of individual activities or pieces of work. However, this does not mean teachers should not refer to them earlier in a key stage to inform their teacher assessments and decisions about significant evidence to collect. The implications for simplified record-keeping based upon the revisions are considerable since many schools had devised overcomplex record sheets which covered individual statements of attainment; these will become redundant, unless teachers find them useful as a tool for more refined formative assessment. The purpose of the programmes of study as the basis for teachers' planning and assessment are more explicit in the new orders than in the previous ones, pleasing those who struggled to encourage such an approach in order to avoid an assessment-led curriculum. There is no longer any overlap between key stage programmes of study which makes it essential for teachers to know what has gone before. Unhelpful duplication across subjects has been removed but teachers need to make links between subjects in their teaching. The requirements are now set out as a series of teaching points, but decisions about how to teach are still left to teachers. This represents another success for professional consistency throughout the evolution of the science National Curriculum. From the first version the professional opinion has been firmly grounded in the belief that programmes of study are the key to successful delivery of the curriculum; they are the means by which teachers plan and implement a broad and balanced curriculum. Whether the revised programmes still contain too much content is a question for teachers to answer through experience.

Crucially, teachers are being reminded through support materials and dissemination conferences that the new slimmed down curriculum is a statutory *minimum* requirement which provides a framework for teachers' work; it is methodologically neutral and does dictate how the curriculum should be taught (although the requirement for practical work linked to Sc1 could be argued to lead to particular teaching approaches). Implementation has not put new pressures on schools since the new order is largely a subset of the previous ones and many things remain the same or are simplified.

In many ways the new orders have taken us full circle and some of the issues and proposals of the original working group of professionals, that were rejected as a result of political not educational pressure, have been reinstated. The new orders reflect a model of science education which more closely mirrors the good practice discussed in the earlier part of this chapter than the two previous sets of orders. The initial reaction of the profession to the new orders has been positive, although doubts about the relative weighting to be given to AT1 and the other attainment targets at Key Stage 2 remain a concern (Burton, 1995). It remains 51% AT1, 50% AT2–4 at Key Stage 1 but AT2–4 are given a heavier weighting at Key Stage 2 (60–40). Whether the proposals are genuinely workable, whether the level descriptions facilitate assessment will only become clear as they are implemented. There are grounds for cautious optimism. The opportunity now exists for the consolidation of science in primary schools. For a period of five years we are assured, by the Secretary of State, Shephard, that there will be no further revisions. Curriculum development in science during this period should be driven by professional concerns, interests and enthusiasms as opposed to political directive.

To return to the beginning, in the words of one of Her Majesty's Inspectors:

> the implementation of the National Curriculum leads me to the unequivocal view that primary science is a success story. It has been an eye-opener in several aspects; the competence of even very young pupils; the increasing confidence of teachers; the acceptance of science as an activity for all, retaining mystery but, thankfully, being denuded of false mysticism.
> (Evans, 1994, p.18)

In the same article Evans goes on to remind teachers of the importance of fostering creativity in children through science. This is a priority that teachers in primary schools should continue to recognize. Whatever the demands of the National Curriculum it should never deflect us from encouraging imaginative thinking because, in the words of Duckworth (1987):

> Wonderful ideas do not spring out of nothing. They build on a foundation of other ideas . . . The more we help children to have their wonderful ideas and to feel good about themselves for having them, the more likely it is that they will some day happen upon wonderful ideas that no one else has happened upon before.
> (p. 14)

REFERENCES

Assessment of Performance Unit (APU) (1988) *Science at Age 11: A Review of the Findings 1980–84*. London: HMSO.

Association of Science Education (ASE) (1993) *Primary Science Teacher's Handbook*. Hatfield: ASE.

Ausubel, D. (1968) *Educational Psychology: A Cognitive View*. NY: Holt, Rinehart & Winston.

Burton, N. (1995) Primary science focus. *Education in Science*, No.161, January.

Children's Learning in Science (CLIS) Project (1988–92) *Various Project Reports*. Leeds: Centre for Studies in Science and Mathematics Education (CSSME).

County of Avon (1981) *Primary Science Guidelines*. Bristol: County of Avon.

CCW (1989) *Non-Statutory Guidance*. Cardiff: Curriculum Council for Wales.

CCW (1992) *Energy / Light and Sound /Earth in Space: Aspects of Science for Primary Teachers*. Cardiff: Curriculum Council for Wales.

DES (1978) *Primary Education in England: A Survey by HM Inspectors of Schools*. London: HMSO.

DES (1985) *Science 5–16: A Statement of Policy*. London: HMSO.

DES (1988) *Science for Ages 5 to 16 (Proposals of the Secretary of State/Science Working Group's Final Report)*. London: HMSO.

DES (1989a) *Science in the National Curriculum*. London: HMSO.

DES (1989b) *Standards in Education 1987–88: The Annual Report of HM Chief Inspector of Schools Based on Work of HMI in England*. London: HMSO.

DES (1991a) *Science Key Stages 1 and 3: A Report by HM Inspectorate on the First Year 1989–90*. London: HMSO.

DES (1991b) *Science for Ages 5 to 16 (1991) Proposals of the Secretary of State*. London: HMSO.

DES (1991c) *Science in the National Curriculum* (Revised Orders). London: HMSO.

DES (1992) *Science Key Stages 1, 2 and 3: A Report by HM Inspectorate on the Second Year 1990–91*. London: HMSO.

DFEE (1994) *Science in the National Curriculum: Draft Proposals*. London: HMSO.

DFEE (1995) *Science in the National Curriculum (1995)*. London: HMSO.

Duckworth, E. (1987) *The Having of Wonderful Ideas*. NY: Teachers' College Press.

Evans, N. (1994) Educare: the only policy. *Primary Science Review*, **35**, pp. 18–19.

Harlen, W. (1975) *Science 5–13: A Formative Evaluation*. London: Oliver and Boyd.

Harlen, W. (1978) Does content matter in primary science? *School Science Review*, **59**, pp. 614–25.

Harlen, W. (1989) *The National Curriculum in Science: Key Stages 1 and 2*. Primary Science Review, National Curriculum Special, summer, pp. 10–11.

Harlen, W. (1992) *The Teaching of Science*. London: David Fulton Publishers.

HMI (1989) *Aspects of Primary Education: The Teaching and Learning of Science*. London: HMSO.

Initiatives in Primary Science: an Evaluation (IPSE) (1988) *School in Focus*. Hatfield: ASE.

Kruger, C., Palacio, D. and Summers, M. (1988–91) *Primary School Teachers and Science (PSTS) Project Working Papers 1– 12*. Oxford: Oxford University Department of Education Studies.

NCC (1988) *NCC Consultation Report: Science*. York: National Curriculum Council.

NCC (1989) *Science: Non-Statutory Guidance*. York, National Curriculum Council.

NCC (1991) *NCC Consultation Report: Science*. York: National Curriculum Council.

NCC (1993) *Teaching Science at Key Stages 1 and 2*. York: National Curriculum Council.

NCC (1992–94) *Forces/ Energy / Electricity and Magnetism / Chemical Change / Genetics: Guides for Teachers*. York: National Curriculum Council.

Newton, L. (ed.) (1992) *Primary Science: The Challenge of the 1990s*. Clevedon: Multilingual Matters Ltd.

Nuffield Primary Science (1992–93) *Teachers' Guides and Pupil Booklets*. London: Collins.

OFSTED (1993a) *Science Key Stages 1, 2 and 3: A Report by HM Inspectorate on the Third Year 1991–92*. London: HMSO.

OFSTED (1993b) *Science Key Stages 1, 2 and 3: A Report by HM Inspectorate on the Fourth Year 1992–93*. London: HMSO.

Ollerenshaw, C. and Ritchie, R. (1993) *Primary Science: Making it Work*. London: David Fulton Publishers.

Ollerenshaw, C. *et al.* (1991) *Constructive Teacher Assessment*. Bristol: National Primary Centre (South West).

Open University (OU) (1994) *Primary Teachers Learning Science: Life – Diversity and Evolution*. (S624) Milton Keynes: Open University.

Ovens, P. (1989) National Curriculum – pot filling or fire lighting? *Primary Science Review*, pp. 2–3.

Richards, R. (1983) Learning Through Science Project: a report. In Richards, C. and Holford, R. (eds) *The Teaching of Primary Science: Policy and Practice*, pp. 159–66. Lewes: The Falmer Press.

SCAA (1994) *The Review of the National Curriculum: A Report on the 1994 Consultation*. London SCAA.

Science Process and Concept Exploration (SPACE) Project (1990– 93) *Project Research Reports (various)*. Liverpool: Liverpool University Press.

Science Working Group (SWG) (1987) *National Curriculum Science Working Group: Interim Report*. London, DES.

West, D. (1988) Half measures for science. *The Times Educational Supplement*, 30 Dec.

Wragg, E.C., Bennett, S. N. and Carre, C.G. (1989) Primary teachers and the National Curriculum. *Research Papers in Education*, **4** (3), pp.17–31.

Wragg, E.C., Bennett, S. N. and Carre, C.G. (1991) Primary teachers and the National Curriculum revealed. *Junior Education*, **15** (11).

Chapter 5

Thematic Approaches to the Core National Curriculum

Stephen Ward

INTRODUCTION

It was in July 1987 when the first consultation document on the National Curriculum (DES, 1987) appeared. It contained two disturbing proposals for primary school teachers: first that there should be national standardized testing of the curriculum at ages 7 and 11; second that the curriculum was to be defined as nine separate traditional subjects, plus religious education. Both these were contrary to the long-held principles and practice of many primary schools. Standardized testing, especially in the 5 to 7 age-range, with the consequent stratification of children and the imposition of stressful test situations, was seen as anathema to the learner-centred ethos. Separate subjects had long been seen as a feature of secondary schools with their teaching of discrete subjects in a daily timetable. Many teachers in primary schools had, during the 1960s and 1970s, worked to develop an integrated or thematic approach to the curriculum which avoided what was seen as the overstructured logic of the subject curriculum with its arbitrary confinement of knowledge in separate compartments.

In 1989 the National Curriculum forced upon teachers a subject-centred framework which they have been left to formulate into an appropriate *primary curriculum*. The struggle between the teachers and the government over assessment is discussed in Chapter 1. This chapter relates the progress of the primary curriculum in coming to terms with the separate subject framework and explores the ways the National Curriculum can be made to be consistent with the tenets of good primary practice: children as autonomous learners within a thematic and negotiated curriculum which makes sense to children. It will be argued that the subject formulation of the National Curriculum and the accompanying guidance is a part of a two-pronged attack on teaching methods and curriculum integration, perceived as liberal progressivism.

It is now up to schools and teachers to make the decision as to whether to adopt a differentiated curriculum with separate subject teaching, or an integrated and thematic approach. This chapter is intended to help to make that decision and tries to show the importance of curriculum integration. An example is included of the way one school has managed to maintain the integrity of a topic-based approach to the primary curriculum while teaching the subjects of the National Curriculum.

THE EVOLUTION OF THE INTEGRATED CURRICULUM IN PRIMARY SCHOOLS

There is a long tradition of integration in the primary curriculum and its rationale has been made by, for example, Tann (1988), Kerry and Egglestone (1988) and Gunning *et al.* (1981). A variety of terminology has been used to describe integrated approaches: 'thematic work', 'topic work', 'centre of interest' and 'project work'. These all share common underlying assumptions about the curriculum, children's learning, and teaching.

The first of these relates to a view of children's knowledge and learning as learner-centred: the subject, such as science or mathematics, is viewed as an abstract adult construction, the logic of which does not necessarily make sense within the psychology of the child. For example, the *a priori* logic of mathematics is not evident to the child and is indistinguishable from an empirical understanding of the world. For the young child the mathematical concepts of number need to be confirmed with actual objects in reality. Whether the child is handling the abstract concepts of mathematics or the empirical concepts of science is irrelevant.

Another motive for teachers' use of a thematic approach to the curriculum is the attempt to provide learning experiences which are coherent and relevant to children. The content of the curriculum should not be entirely imposed from without. The curriculum theme is intended to provide an area of interest for children within which learning can take place. This is difficult to achieve by teaching fragmented subjects in a timetable. The theme, then, should be one which children can identify with and own. Fullan and Hargreaves (1992) argue the importance of *ownership* of the curriculum by teachers and children, and warn against the prescription of a curriculum which gives teachers no control over its content: that teachers should feel some sense of originality and individuality about the curriculum which they share with children. A thematic curriculum is the ideal vehicle for such an approach, where teachers can construct a curriculum which is relevant to their expertise and enthusiasm and share it with children.

Further, a thematic curriculum provides opportunities for children to be involved in the selection of the context for learning: the curriculum can be negotiated so that children, as well as teachers, feel a sense of ownership, a sense of distinctiveness about what they are learning. Their involvement in the decision-making about the curriculum will enhance their learning and their commitment to the content. Learning is an activity to be engaged in; it is not something which can be *done* to pupils. The more sense of ownership which children feel for the curriculum, the greater the likelihood of their being actively involved in learning through it. In this way teachers could involve children in the planning and employ their own creativity in the process. The result can be a feeling of commitment and ownership. The National Curriculum should not prevent the development of integrated topic work derived from children's initiatives. Primary school teachers have shown how this can be achieved to engage fully children's interests and enthusiasms. One criticism of the thematic approach is that the method cannot cover the whole curriculum comprehensively, especially in mathematics. However, if the unified topic which is of interest and importance to the children is at the centre of the curriculum, any additional 'routine' and discrete subject work which is necessary to complete the comprehensive curriculum will be more readily accepted by them when they know that the teacher shares their overall excitement about learning.

Children's interests are best engaged by their learning about real things. As far as possible, children should have their hands on real objects and be involved in real activities. Learning should not be a *dry run* for real life, it should be about doing real things. Education is not just a preparation for the future: it is the fulfilment of the present. This is difficult to achieve in a single subject timetabled curriculum. The Plowden Report (ACE, 1967) emphasized the importance of children's learning through direct *hands-on* activity, rather than through abstract propositions by teachers. It is often argued that the thematic approach allows more readily for this in giving children the opportunity to engage in real-life tasks such as measuring fossils in a project on dinosaurs. Activities in this context are likely to have more intrinsic worth to children.

The strongest arguments for a thematic curriculum depend on notions of coherence, relevance to children, autonomous learning, intrinsic motivation and ownership of the curriculum. It is sometimes proposed, as the DES (1989) suggested in an early document for schools, that curriculum integration allows for economy of time: that more subject learning can be fitted into a thematic project, rather than allocating specific time to each subject. However, the key feature of the integrated curriculum is not the pragmatism of time, but its link with learner-centred forms of pedagogy. Those teachers who see the child as 'the centre of learning' are inclined to provide an integrated curriculum. Those teachers who see the curriculum as the main focus of education will tend to organize on a separate-subject basis.

Thematic or topic work in schools is, of course, not above criticism. There have been examples of teachers making spurious links between subjects which are not relevant to children and sometimes it has led to a neglect of areas of the curriculum. Also, the integrated curriculum is far from universal in primary schools. Although detailed quantitative data is hard to come by, OFSTED (1995) reports that many schools use a topic-based approach to the curriculum and it is evident that there has been a wide range of pedagogy in primary schools. This derives from teachers' various ideas about the nature of teaching and learning, but also from their view of the curriculum. The following forms of curriculum planning can be determined in schools:

- fully integrated work with all subjects in the curriculum included in themes;
- partially integrated work with some subjects under a theme and some subjects, such as mathematics or PE, always taught separately. Of course, the number of subjects which are taught separately can vary and these may be determined by extrinsic factors such as specialist teaching in music;
- partially integrated work where a given theme, such as 'health', might be used to cover certain subjects – science, mathematics, information technology, design and technology, history, physical education and English – but not geography, art and music;

- separate subjects with occasional curriculum linkage, where there are direct links between programmes of study, such as sound in science and music;
- separate subjects, but taught through an *integrated day* in which children work on different tasks and subjects at the same time. There can be variation here in the extent to which the work is teacher-directed or allows some degree of pupil autonomy;
- separate subjects in which the class all work at the same subject or tasks, possibly differentiated by children's attainment, on a timetabled basis;
- separate subject teaching which includes different specialist teachers working with the whole class (the secondary school model);
- team teaching in which a team of two or three teachers work together on an integrated theme, using their own curriculum specialisms to give specialist teaching;
- team teaching in which the team of teachers teach separate subjects on a separate subject basis.

Of course, there are many variations and combinations of these various forms.

THE POLITICS OF CURRICULUM INTEGRATION AND DISCRETE SUBJECTS

The chequered post-war history of primary education, together with underlying assumptions about teaching and learning, is now well documented in, for example, Alexander (1984) and Galton (1994). The public image of progressive primary education which emerged in the 1960s and 1970s was one of universal activity-based, discovery learning, children's autonomy and an integrated curriculum. The public image and the private realities of classrooms are, it is now known, often different. Observational research into primary classrooms has systematically exposed the myth of widespread idealized progressivism. Instead, the picture is of wide variety in practice but with a great deal of individualized learning from commercially produced materials, teacher direction, relatively little child initiation and much single subject teaching. Some of the sources which present this information are: the HMI primary survey (DES, 1978); Galton, Simon and Croll (1980), Mortimore *et al.* (1988); Tizard *et al.* (1988); and, in mathematics, HMI (1989). The 'myth of the primary revolution' is discussed in detail by both Simon (1981) and Delamont (1988). It is not, then, a simple matter of professionals attempting to preserve a common framework to which everyone has worked. Instead, it is for all teachers in all schools making decisions about the best approach to the curriculum and picking their way among the combination of legislation and recommendation and guidance which is now in existence. In order to do this they need to understand it.

Chapter 1 shows that the introduction of the National Curriculum was a complex process engaging politicians and professionals in a power struggle. Two of the items of conflict became overt and subject to media attention: the debate about assessment and, as described in Chapter 2, the debate about the English curriculum. A matter which attracted much less publicity, but which caused a great deal of anxiety within schools, was the integration of the primary curriculum.

Controversy about the curriculum in primary schools originated long before the advent of the National Curriculum. A dual, and inherently conflicting, view of knowledge underlies this debate: the *political* and the *professional*. Blenkin and Kelly (1981) demonstrate the contrasting views of the curriculum which emanated from the DES, exemplified by two curriculum documents which appeared in 1980. The one, *A View of the Curriculum* (DES, 1980b) written by HMI, represents the *professional* view of the curriculum. HMI urged that the model of the curriculum as learning *processes*, rather than *product* or *content*, should be sustained and strengthened and saw the ideal curriculum for primary children as essentially integrated or 'unified':

> ways should be found to develop the existing curriculum by helping teachers both to frame essential processes more carefully and deepen their understanding of the skills and concepts that children should be developing in schools. Although confused in parts, the substance of their views focuses on the processes of education and their views of how learning should take place is that it should be essentially *unified*.
> (Blenkin and Kelly, 1981, p. 147, my italics)

The *political* model of the curriculum is expressed in *A Framework for the Curriculum* (DES, 1980a) apparently written by DES officials. In this the curriculum is seen as discrete elements of 'protected content' with an emphasis on education as product:

> They urge the inclusion of 'common elements' – notably English, mathematics and science – which should form a substantial part of the school's work. The emphasis is on the product of education and on clearer means of measuring achievement, particularly in certain skills and knowledge areas.
> (Blenkin and Kelly, 1981, p.148)

The contrasting views, then, are the *professional* one of the curriculum as an integrated whole, to be developed through increasing teachers' understanding of the educational processes, and the *political* one of the curriculum as discrete blocks of knowledge or skills to be imparted through transmissionist teaching, regardless of the learning context. The preceding chapters of this book analyse the National Curriculum documents and trace the detail of the conflicts which took place between the professionals in the working groups and the politicians, mediated by the National Curriculum Council and the School Curriculum and Assessment Authority, over the details of each core curriculum subject.

The right wing has always attacked primary progressive education. This opposition can be identified formally with the publication of the so-called Black Papers (Cox and Dyson, 1969 and 1971) and continued throughout the 1970s, often through the pursuit of scandal through popular media coverage of, for example, the William Tyndale School affair of 1975 (Gretton and Jackson, 1976). The integrated primary curriculum has always been one of the targets of this criticism, the idea being that *real knowledge* lies in grammar school subjects which should be taught as such in timetabled slots. Teachers who reject this model are portrayed as left-wing ideologues who are more concerned with self-indulgent theories drawn from Rousseau and Dewey than they are with children's learning and knowledge. Linked with right-wing notions about the discrete subject curriculum are ideas about teaching and learning. The idea of knowledge as a set of subjects which can be timetabled throughout the week is associated with the simple notion of teaching the subject to a class: knowledge exists in subjects, so it can be, and should be, imparted directly and didactically to the class, and then tested.

The relationship to other areas of knowledge and understanding and, indeed, to the child's existing knowledge, are simply a distraction.

Teachers' struggle to keep control of the curriculum has been partially lost. If control of the content is lost to the politicians, the next step may be seen as the resignation of a professional approach to methods and delivery: the collapse into the transmissionist teaching of separate subjects through didactic materials and exercises. In order to resist this the revised National Curriculum documents need to be read with care and with an understanding of the thinking which underlies them. It is necessary to see how the National Curriculum can be used to further the steady development of good primary practice.

AN ALTERNATIVE MODEL FOR THE PRIMARY NATIONAL CURRICULUM

The DES consultation document (DES and Welsh Office, 1987) determined the format of the National Curriculum as a series of separate subjects. Could the National Curriculum have been devised and presented in a different way which would have been more appropriate for primary schools? Of course it could and, if the professionals had been genuinely consulted at this early stage, this may well have been the case. Instead what we have is a collection of subject-based programmes of study and attainment targets, each of which specifies the progress of the curriculum from 5 to 16, exploring the links between one stage and the next. There is subject progression, or sequential integration over time within each subject, as shown in Table 5.1.

Table 5.1 *The Primary Curriculum presented by subject progression*

English	Key Stage 1	Key Stage 2	Key Stage 3	Key Stage 4
Mathematics	Key Stage 1	Key Stage 2	Key Stage 3	Key Stage 4
Science	Key Stage 1	Key Stage 2	Key Stage 3	Key Stage 4

An alternative would have been to present the curriculum across all subjects for each age phase (see Table 5.2).

It is now obvious that Key Stages 1 and 2 require different approaches to the planning and organization of the curriculum. Children at the upper end of Key Stage 2 can cope with, and need, a more discrete subject approach with more specialized teaching. Had the National Curriculum been devised *by Key Stage*, rather than *by subject*, these different needs could have been met. The subject structure of the curriculum means that teachers planning for 5 and 6-year-olds are forced to work with the same framework as that for 10 and 11-year-olds.

A key stage structure would have provided a set of documents dedicated to each age phase: a document for infant teachers and one for junior teachers. Of course the phasing could be shorter with, for example, separate documents for the two phases in the junior years (Year 3, Year 4 and Year 5, Year 6). This would have allowed primary working groups to devise a coherent National Curriculum for the age phase concerned, with appropriate teaching and learning methods suggested and integrated examples

Table 5.2 *The Primary Curriculum presented by Key Stage*

Key Stage 1	Key Stage 2	Key Stage 3	Key Stage 4
English	English	English	English
Mathematics	Mathetmatics	Mathematics	Mathetmatics
Science	Science	Science	Science
(Other subjects)	(Other subjects)	(Other subjects)	(Other subjects)

given across the curriculum. In this way, subject content and learning process would have been appropriately linked. What is more, a primary team would have been able much more easily to include programmes of study for other foundation subjects at the primary stage. The presentation of the National Curriculum at its introduction in 1989–90 was through definition of the core curriculum subjects in English, mathematics and science. Teachers wishing to adopt an integrated approach at this point were left with no knowledge of what the content of the other foundation subjects were to comprise. This made a serious attempt to continue the development of the integrated curriculum in the primary school difficult, to say the least, and would certainly have increased the temptation for a school to treat the core National Curriculum separately from its other work. Given rather more time than was available, a primary working party could have devised a full and integrated National Curriculum with a recommended pedagogy appropriate to the primary school.

SKILLS MODEL

It can also be argued that the traditional *subjects* of the National Curriculum are by no means the only way of conceptualizing children's learning. There are skills, common to all subjects, which children are asked to learn, and these might be considered in formulating the curriculum. The following list is only an example:

Personal and social skills
- Collaborating
- Sharing
- Discussing

Planning and evaluating
- Making choices and deciding
- Drafting
- Reflecting
- Selecting equipment and materials
- Planning
- Checking and monitoring

Communicating
- Explaining
- Recording
- Presenting
- Using information
- Reporting
- Describing
- Discussing

- Debating

Cognitive skills
- Looking for and recognising pattern
- Observing
- Exploring
- Investigating
- Raising questions
- Forming and testing hypotheses
- Interpreting
- Sorting and classifying
  (Spooner, 1993)

CURRICULUM INTEGRATION IN THE FORMATION OF THE NATIONAL CURRICULUM

Coulby (1989) has shown that the very existence of the National Curriculum is a function of the political attempt to limit the professional autonomy of teachers, with a concerted assault on the 'secret garden' of the curriculum. The first National Curriculum consultation document (DES and Welsh Office, 1987) proposed a structure comprising a bald list of subjects, with percentage time allocations, which would be tested at four stages. This was the political model in outline, as Blenkin and Kelly (1981) foresaw: a set of grammar school subjects, with heavy emphasis on the basic skills subjects of English, mathematics and science, each to be tested at four stages. The document was extraordinary in its simplicity, apparently ignoring the complex work which had been carried out on the curriculum during the previous 30 years. No alternative models were proposed; the legitimacy of traditional subjects was taken for granted. Although responses were invited, these were apparently ignored and the proposals in the document indeed became the framework for the National Curriculum. The overall structure of the National Curriculum – the political one – remained intact.

In order to create the National Curriculum in detail, the then Secretary of State, Kenneth Baker, saw fit to hand over the task to professionals in the subject working parties. It is suggested in Chapter 1 that the working parties, filled with enthusiasts for their subject, were chiefly responsible for the disastrous overloading of the curriculum. However, an analysis of the documents shows that they produced a curriculum which was far more complex and interesting than the model originally suggested and which, in essence, entails learner-centred and integrated topic work. A separate subject framework was transformed, from within, into a potentially integrated model. The professional architects of the National Curriculum can be shown to be sympathetic towards an integrated primary curriculum.

The 1989 orders, and their predecessors the working group reports (DES and Welsh Office, 1988a,b,c), reflect the original thinking of the architects of the National Curriculum which were professionally sound, thorough and generally sympathetic to *good primary practice*. Subsequent publications by authors of the original documents show how their attempts to adhere to professional principles were frustrated by the need for political compromise (Cox, 1991; Graham and Tyler, 1993). These original documents – the working party reports and the 1989 orders and non-statutory guidance

– will be stuffed into obscurity very rapidly. It is important then to record the principles upon which they were designed and which should still inform teachers' thinking about the curriculum, for, as will be shown, the post-Dearing documents offer little guidance.

Although the 1989 National Curriculum was set out in separate subject documents, at all stages the authors explained that it was perfectly possible for primary teachers to take a 'cross-curricular' approach. The most important of these documents were the non-statutory guidance which were published alongside the curriculum orders (National Curriculum Council, 1989b,c,d). These were substantial and high quality publications which gave strong hints and suggestions about ways in which there might be cross-curricular approaches. Other general documents concerning the National Curriculum, *From Policy to Practice* (DES, 1989) and *A Framework for the Primary Curriculum* (NCC, 1989e), also suggested that the possibility of curriculum integration was available to schools. However, nowhere among the documents which came to schools during 1988 and 1989 from the DES and the National Curriculum Council was there any firm statement about the direction which schools and teachers should take in addressing this issue, nor was there a consistent rationale for an integrated approach. Instead schools were offered separate subject packages with only hints and suggestions about planning an actual primary curriculum.

It is interesting that the original National Curriculum documents from the National Curriculum Council assured teachers that there would be no attempts to determine the ways in which they teach. In the widely circulated Policy and Practice Document teaching *methods* and curriculum *delivery* were depicted as technical matters for professional practitioners:

> the way in which teaching is timetabled and how lessons are planned and organized cannot be prescribed.
> (DES, 1989, para. 4.3)

This left the way open for an integrated approach to the curriculum. Analysis of the curriculum documents written by the subject working groups show an even stronger commitment to integration. In the introduction to each of the working group proposals there was the recommendation that the core subjects should not necessarily be taught as separate subjects, but could be taught within an integrated framework. In the Mathematics Working Group proposals:

> Opportunities for using mathematics across the curriculum should be exploited because, as we have argued throughout this report, it is through applying mathematics in contexts which have relevance and interest that pupils' understanding and appreciation of the subject develop.
> (DES and Welsh Office, 1988a, para. 10.34)

The need for learning in an integrated context at the primary phase was acknowledged in the Science Working Party Proposals:

> In the early phase of primary education ... children do not see the boundaries between one form of knowledge and another since they are intertwined with each other at this stage ...
>
> The context in which Science ... [*is*] developed is therefore very important. If this is chosen carefully children come to appreciate the relevance of both subject areas to everyday life, and to use their Science to solve problems. Scientific and technological experiences set in these contexts can, and should, be introduced at an early age.
> (DES and Welsh Office, 1988b, para. 2.18–2.20)

Here is the notion of children's initiatives and ownership in the curriculum planning process: what children bring to science is crucial to how it is learned.

And the possibilities for integration were summarized by the English Working Group:

> The Reports of the various Working Groups, taken together, should ... reveal possibilities for collaboration across disciplines that have not yet been widely recognised, with each making its distinctive contribution.
> (DES and Welsh Office, 1988c, para. 1.14)

In these early documents, then, the vision of an integrated National Curriculum for primary schools was embraced. It was argued that mathematics is learned effectively in the context of other topics: scientific concepts are only meaningful if they are *owned* by the child and language/English is central to children's learning in other subjects.

The final orders and non-statutory guidance also included a number of examples of integration. For example, the programmes of study for science were prefaced by well-developed suggestions about scientific activities taking place within the context of real life activities which imply links with other curriculum areas:

> **Communication:** throughout their study of science, children should develop and use a variety of skills and techniques involved in obtaining, presenting and responding to information. They should also have the opportunity to express their findings and ideas to children and their teacher, orally and also through drawings, simple charts, models, actions and the written word.
> (DES and Welsh Office, 1989c, Key Stage 1, p. 65).

> **Communication:** children should have the opportunities to continue to develop and use communication skills in representing their ideas and in reporting their work to a range of audiences, including children, teachers, parents and other adults. ... Children should be given the opportunity to participate in small group discussions and they should be introduced to a limited range of books, charts and other sources from which they gain information.
> (DES and Welsh Office, 1989c, Key Stage 2, p. 68)

Both these paragraphs might well have been included in the English orders and demonstrated a clear case for integration between English and science.

In the science non-statutory guidance there was an even more explicit approach to three-subject integration. In fact, unlike the other two curriculum documents, the science non-statutory guidance offered a special section on 'Science in the Primary School', the central feature of which is an example of a topic on making a windmill. This was given in some detail (C8–13) and included a chart showing lists of attainment targets for each of mathematics and English in the proposed topic (C9–10). There can be no doubt here that the authors of the document saw scientific activities within an integrated curriculum. The attention given to science in the primary school is particularly interesting and is as far as the non-statutory guidance could go in specifying an integrated primary curriculum from within the boundaries of the science discipline.

In the statutory orders for English in the programme of study for Speaking and Listening there occurs the following:

All activities should ... draw on examples from across the curriculum, and in particular those existing requirements for mathematics and science which refer to use of spoken language and vocabulary, asking questions, working in groups, explaining and presenting ideas, giving and understanding instructions.
(DES and Welsh Office, 1989c, p.13)

And in the non-statutory guidance for English (at Key Stage 1) there is a clear statement, derived from Bullock's (1975) insight, that language is embedded in the activities of the other curriculum subjects: 'Language provides the main instrument of learning throughout the school curriculum learning' (p.A1, 1.1).

While the working party reports, the statutory orders and the non-statutory guidance of 1989 all pointed towards an integrated approach, the document which might have articulated this was the NCC booklet, *A Framework for the Primary Curriculum*, which appeared in the last days of the Summer Term in 1989. Disappointingly it did not. It allowed for the possibility of integrated work, but emphasized the primacy of subjects: 'The National Curriculum is described in terms of subjects which will form the starting point for curriculum planning' (p.7, para. 2.12.ii) and gave no clear lead on an integrated curriculum.

The authors of the subject documents in the original working groups had to work at great speed and had no opportunities to consult with each other (see Chapter 1). They went as far as was reasonably possibly in providing hints and recommendations from within the single subject boundaries for an integrated curriculum for primary schools. However, teachers were given no central lead in developing an integrated curriculum by the National Curriculum Council which, of course, was subject to much stronger political control than had been the working groups. This is not surprising, given that the government was inclined towards the *political* curriculum for schools: a product model delivered through discrete subject teaching.

THE REVISED NATIONAL CURRICULUM DOCUMENTS, 1995

If the 1989 curriculum documents were the source of recommendation for an integrated curriculum, does the same hold for the new documents? The original core documents contained extensive non-statutory guidance. As has been shown above, much of this was directed to primary teachers and urged an integrated approach to the curriculum. The revised Dearing version comes in a most welcome compact compendium of Key Stage 1 and 2 orders (DFE, 1995). It contains no such guidance. The only non-statutory material are brief examples in italics. This, of course, was part of the attempt to keep the documents as slim as possible. So, the very slimming down of the National Curriculum has the effect of limiting guidance. Only the bare bones of the subject are given, with no suggestions about curriculum integration. For example, the English orders now contain no references to language across the curriculum and the only reference to integration is, in a yellow box at the top of page 11, the suggestion that the various English activities – reading, writing, speaking and listening – should interrelate. There is no mention of other subjects. In the programmes of study and the level descriptions there is no reference to other subjects.

The programmes of study for each of the three subjects have an initial page headed *Common Requirements*; each has a one-sentence reference to information technology and the mathematics and science ones each refer to pupils' use of language. However, in the rest of the mathematics and science orders there is no other reference to another subject. Of course, it would be perverse to complain of the lack of further guidance and suggestion in a document, the aim of which has been to present things in as brief a space as possible. It would be reasonable, though, to look to other publications for suggestions about planning.

The most recent primary guidance supplied at the time of writing is the SCAA (1995) publication, *Planning the Curriculum at Key Stages 1 and 2*. This would appear to be a most significant document for primary schools, designed to make everything come to life and to reflect the enthusiasm for integration embraced by the original 1989 documents. In fact it is deadening, concerned principally with statutory matters: assessment, curriculum balance, units of work and 'curriculum blocks'. It fulfils very much the same role as the *Primary Framework* document of 1989 (NCC, 1989e). There is a concession to curriculum integration with a section entitled *Making Links* (pp. 21–6). It is interesting that the terms *curriculum integration, thematic, project* or *topic work* are never used. It is as though these dangerous and corrupting old notions should not be entertained. Instead, the authors give only the most tentative grounds for *linking units of work*:

1. they contain common or complementary knowledge, understanding and skills, *e.g. developing reading and writing skills through work in history, or work on the water cycle in science linked with work on weather and rivers in geography;*
2. the skills acquired in one subject or aspect of the curriculum can be applied or consolidated in the context of another, *e.g. work on co-ordinates in mathematics applied to work in geography on four-figure grid references;*
3. the work in one subject or aspect of the curriculum provides a useful stimulus for work in another, *e.g. creating music from a poem or a picture.*
    (SCAA, 1995, p. 20)

A few other examples are offered in slightly more detail.

It is remarkable that in a document about planning the primary curriculum there should be no reference to the framework for planning which many teachers have used for years: the theme or topic. What teachers are offered are simply some suggestions for links between disparate subjects. There is no reference to children's and teachers' interests, no mention of any unifying principle in the curriculum, no reference to children's experience. The assumption appears to be that the starting-point for the curriculum is the discrete subject framework. Again, the teacher is left to find links.

Readers are asked to carry out a task to *establish links between aspects of the curriculum*. Here there is the acknowledgement that 'the benefits of linking subjects ... are often more to do with providing relevance and curriculum coherence than with saving time' (p.44). There is some good, but brief and unexplained, advice: 'keep work focused by restricting the number of subjects of other aspects of the curriculum to be linked; avoid contrived or artificial links between subjects or other aspects of the curriculum' (p.44). However, the third point makes clear that curriculum links are secondary and that the starting-point for planning is the curriculum subject: 'review the allocation of blocks of work to year groups to facilitate links being made, ensuring that this does not disturb progression' (p.44). This document appears, unfortunately, to embody the doubts about the integrated primary curriculum of the political right wing.

THE NEW POLITICS OF DISCRETE SUBJECTS: CURRICULUM REFORM AND THE POLITICS OF PRIMARY TEACHING

The long-standing tensions between professionals and politicians over primary education are now recreated through the National Curriculum. Hargreaves and Goodson (1995) have argued that recent curriculum reform has damaged the professional role of teachers:

> First, reform has intensified teachers' work – adding on huge additional burdens to a job that is already excessively demanding. Second, it has been anti-intellectual. It has failed to call upon the professional wisdom of teachers.
> (Hargreaves and Goodson, 1995, p.16)

One aspect of 'intellectual wisdom' which primary school teachers bring to the profession is the construction of a thematic curriculum. This has been a unique curriculum for individual teachers and their classes and has given the inspiration and excitement which the top-down prescription of content can never achieve. Examples have sometimes been, in the past, flawed and incomplete. However, curriculum development should not be about trapping teachers into the narrow corridors of a highly specific separate subject curriculum which is common to all. Instead, it should be about helping teachers to create a superior integrated curriculum which handles progression without the omission of essential content.

The National Curriculum with its statutory standardized national assessment and its separate subject framework has been used as a weapon against the primary progressive movement. As already noted, the original National Curriculum documents from the government assured teachers that there would be no attempts to legislate for teaching methods (DES, 1989). The ways in which the curriculum was to be delivered was in the hands of the professionals. However, in the politically volatile times of the early 1990s, the government found itself unable to resist the temptation to intervene in teaching methods and made primary education a target in its back-to-basics campaign, depicting primary teachers as driven by left-wing, doctrinaire theory. In 1991 the then Secretary of State for Education, Kenneth Clarke (1991), launched an attack on primary practice in a speech in which he criticized group work and individualized teaching. He announced the setting up of a short, sharp enquiry, during the Christmas period, into primary teaching methods (Alexander, Rose and Woodhead, 1992, sometimes known as the 'Three Wise Men' Report). Clarke called for a return to didactic class teaching. Alexander, Rose and Woodhead's report was designed to provide the research evidence to support this. Sure enough, the report drew on the classroom research data of the late 1970s and early 1980s to demonstrate the overuse of individualized instruction and the benefits of class teaching. Of course, the type of class teaching which the report recommends is not the didactic, transmissionist type which Clarke had in mind. It is the type of teaching where teachers pose high level intellectual demands on children in well-formed, open questions and which is balanced with appropriate group and individual instruction: 'The conclusion we draw ... is that teachers need the skills and judgement to be able to select and apply whichever organizational strategy – class, group and individual – is appropriate to the task in hand.' No one could, surely, disagree with this. But they go on to end the paragraph with the remarkable statement: 'The judgement, it must be stressed, should be educational and organisational, rather than, as it so often is, *doctrinal'* (Alexander, Rose and Woodhead, 1992, p.30, para. 99, my italics).

Robin Alexander was the academic member of the three. The notion that primary teachers are driven in their judgements by commitment to doctrinaire assumptions is a theme in his work (Alexander, 1991; Alexander and Wilcocks, 1992) and is derived largely from his research in evaluating the Primary Needs Project in Leeds. Galton (1994) shows how this project, and the situation of the Leeds teachers, is a peculiar one and not typical of primary teachers in the whole of England and Wales. By using this terminology the report played into the government's hands by depicting teachers as incompetent professionals, driven by left-wing ideological doctrine, with no rational commitment to their enterprise. It also seems perfectly designed to meet the governments back-to-basics policy by prescribing simplicity: 'Over-complex patterns of class-room organization frustrate assessment, diagnosis and task-matching, and preoccupy teachers with management matters rather than learning tasks' (Alexander, Rose and Woodhead, 1992, p. 35, para. 126). As to the curriculum, the report acknowledges the role of thematic work: 'When topic work focuses on a clearly defined and limited number of attainment targets it, too, can make an important contribution to the development of pupil learning' (ibid., p. 35, para. 123). However, the main thrust of the recommendations is towards a curriculum of discrete subjects. This is made most strongly in the suggestion that there should be specialist teaching at both primary key stages.

> The subject knowledge required by the National Curriculum makes it unlikely that the generalist primary teacher will be able to teach all subjects in the depth required. This is particularly the case in Key Stage 2, but is true also in Key Stage 1.
>
> (p. 35, para. 121)

Specialist teaching, with different teachers taking different subjects in a timetable, not only threatens the possibility of providing an integrated curriculum but also endangers the role of the generalist class teacher who is aware of each child's learning needs. Later, Alexander (1993) modified his own position on this, arguing that the specialist teaching should be provided through additional staffing to supplement the generalist class teacher. Of course, this would be admirable, but appears a forlorn hope in the current economic climate. At the time of writing, not surprisingly, little more has been heard of the specialist teaching initiative.

In appointing Alexander, Rose and Woodhead in this high profile way, the government deliberately engaged the popular media in the debate. Galton (1994) argues that Alexander used a form of rhetoric in the report which was then able to be used by politicians. This meant that national newspapers joined politicians in the call for a return to class teaching and the surrendering of progressive methods. The problem for education about the role of the popular press is that teachers themselves are readers of it and subject to the discouragements which it initiates. The integrated curriculum, depicted as a part of the criticized progressive *doctrine* is likely to be threatened by this.

The public condemnation of primary practice was continued under the next Secretary of State, John Patten. Subsequently, since the governmental losses in the assessment wars and the demise of Patten (see Chapter 1), direct political intervention in primary teaching approaches has lessened. Gillian Shephard was appointed Secretary of State in 1994 to bring peace and stability with a slimmed-down National Curriculum,

·intended to last for five years. However, the attack on progressive primary education has been sustained through the government's arm, OFSTED.

It is through OFSTED that the government can continue its attempts to exert its influence over primary teachers to modify their practice and to emulate a secondary subject model. The inspection of schools is a powerful instrument in this. Inspections are carried out on a subject basis, with each member of an inspection team allocated certain subjects. In order to do this each teacher is obliged to submit a timetable indicating when subjects are being taught. It would be possible for a teacher to submit a timetable which indicated periods of time for integrated learning activities among different groups. However, there is inevitably pressure for subjects to be driven into separate timetabled slots. That this should simply occur during the week of an OFSTED inspection is unlikely. It is far more probable that the whole curriculum would be timetabled in this way. An enormous amount depends upon the outcome of an OFSTED inspection collectively for the school and for all the individuals within it, especially the headteacher. The desire to respond by creating a curriculum framework which conforms to the separate subject model must be strong. Of course, it would be possible for schools to be inspected to ensure children's learning in each of the subjects without arranging for separate subject lessons. However, this would require an extremely sophisticated level of perceptual skill among the inspectorate. This has certainly not been provided in teams which are given a minimal five days' training per member and which are required to inspect a whole school in a few days. The model which the government has created is a simple and crude one in which the school must ensure that the subject teaching and learning is put before the inspectorial eyes. An inspecting team will only be able to report on what it sees. If it is not seen, it will be judged not to be happening.

So, while it may appear that the curriculum can easily be interpreted to be taught either in separate subjects or through integrated themes, it would be naïve to assume that everyone on the political side of the educational fence is equally happy about this. In fact, there are strong political pressures on teachers to engage in didactic class teaching of separate subjects in a timetable.

One of the three members of the 'Three Wise Men' Report, Chris Woodhead, went on to become Her Majesty's Chief Inspector (HMCI), and its themes are echoed in the OFSTED (1995) Annual Report on schools. In his commentary at the beginning he refers to teachers simply *supervising* children's activities. Further, Woodhead goes on to make the same mistake as the national press and actually to equate class teaching with *telling*: 'Why is it that in too many primary schools "learning by doing" is preferred to "teaching by telling" to the point where sitting pupils down and telling them things becomes almost a "marginal" strategy?' (OFSTED, 1995, p.7). In fact, HMI (DES, 1978) had criticized primary schools for being overdidactic in their teaching and for not providing learning situations in which children were challenged to explore and solve problems. The government appeared to have appointed an HMCI who shared its political agenda. Woodhead's own report cites one of the weaknesses in primary schools being the 'underrepresentation of investigation in science' (OFSTED, 1995, p. 26, para. 92). The reader is left wondering whether there is too little investigation or too little telling?

OFSTED found that primary schools are still using a topic work approach:

Many primary schools were continuing to review the relative contributions of topic work and separate subject teaching in meeting NC requirements. In the majority of schools the curriculum was planned as a mixture of topic work and separate subject teaching. Improvements found now in most schools included agreed long-term topic frameworks for each Key Stage and a move from broad-based topics in KS1 to a sharper subject focus in KS2. Nevertheless, inspectors judged curriculum planning unfavourably in about half of the schools in KS1 and in rather more than half in KS2. Many schools had policy statements for most or all subjects, but these policies had not always been translated into schemes of work specifying the detailed coverage required to ensure progression and continuity from year group to year group.
(OFSTED, 1995, para. 4, p.26).

Here there is no direct statement of criticism of thematic work, although it is implied in the phrase 'continuing to review the relative contributions of topic work and separate subject teaching.' So, again, primary schools are not given any inspiration or guidance in providing an integrated curriculum. They are left now with an even more stark set of separate subject statements which required formulating into a curriculum for children.

A FRESH APPROACH TO CURRICULUM INTEGRATION

While some outstandingly good work has been achieved by teachers and children in the integrated curriculum, it must be acknowledged that there have been problems with the thematic approach which teachers have taken to the primary curriculum. There is now a need for a new approach to thematic work: one which is informed by awareness of the subjects of the National Curriculum.

It was the HMI (1978) survey of primary education which first cited worries about topic work in schools. HMI found that so-called topic work tended to cover only the subjects of geography and history and involved children in limited learning activities, often copying out chunks of text books with little understanding or analysis. A good thematic curriculum should include a full range of learning activities with appropriate subjects, not simply be a means of keeping children occupied.

Another concern with topic work is with the notion of *incidental learning*: the idea that children should not be aware in any way that they are learning, but that learning will occur invisibly and silently, like osmosis. This extreme view is to relinquish the use of curriculum subjects completely. Instead, the subject can be an important way of teachers and children coming to a better understanding of the nature of their learning. To have an explicit understanding of what is being learned is now seen as important. Teachers are developing this in *plan–do– review* models in which children are asked to take some control of the planning of their own learning activities and to reflect on what they have learned. It is also consistent with developments in profiling as a form of assessment record which includes pupils self-assessment (see Ritchie, 1991).

Another criticism of the thematic approach can be the attempt to force all learning under the umbrella of a single topic. Links can be made through the simple association of words: for example a topic on 'Growth' in plants can lead to the idea of growth in a piece of music. Now the growth of a piece of music in the sense of its development and construction is an important idea in music; but its relationship to the growth of plants exists only in the use of the word, not in any reality which can be meaningful to children. The forging of spurious links between subjects can lead to damagingly irrelevant curriculum choices. This might occur when stories or poems are selected which have limited literary merit, but which are about the topic: poems and stories about dinosaurs, for example, when there might be poems or stories unrelated to the theme, but which would be much more beneficial to the children's stage of learning. Similarly, in physical education, dinosaur movements might be appropriate for children, but might be completely inappropriate in the sequence of work which the teacher has been developing. The important point to be recognized now is that the links between subjects should be real ones and ones which are identifiable within the subject content of the National Curriculum. For example, it is relevant for children to learn about sound as a physical process in science when doing a topic on musical instruments: 'that sounds are made when objects, e.g., strings on musical instruments, vibrate but that vibrations are not always directly visible' (DFE, 1995, p.49). Here there is a real connection between learning in these two subjects. It is not an artificial connection, and children should be able to understand the application in the different subjects: that the empirical observations about vibration of the string is a scientific concept and judgements about the quality of the sound is a musical one. In this way, teachers and children can become aware of the differences between subjects, but also of the links which are between them.

A good integrated curriculum is more difficult to organize and it can be difficult to ensure progression through a subject if all the content of the curriculum is to be addressed through a theme. Now that the National Curriculum specifies a clear progression in each subject it is possible for teachers to identify the curriculum content which can be taught through integrated subjects and that which will need separate treatment. This might lead towards more discrete subject teaching for certain content and to a mixture of thematic and separate subject teaching. The point is that teachers should be able to decide which curriculum content is best explored in an integrated theme, and which requires separate treatment.

Earlier thinking about topic work was critical of the use of subjects in developing the curriculum for children. Subjects were seen as an irrelevant abstraction for young children and a distraction from the reality of their learning. Much of this abhorrence could be seen to come from the notion of *timetabled* subject teaching in the secondary school model. It can, of course, be shown, that teachers and children can engage in an understanding of the role of the subject in the curriculum without it being timetabled. The National Curriculum, for all the difficulties which it has brought to primary school teachers in its cumbersome documentary format, has offered a strengthening of the understanding of subjects for teachers. It can be argued, then, that primary teachers now have the opportunity to adopt a topic-based approach which is much more informed by knowledge and understanding of subjects. The identification of subject learning can strengthen the rationale for the topic approach.

Further, thematic work is enhanced where the teacher is aware of the methodology of the subject: what it means to *know* in science, as distinct from knowing in mathematics or in language. This would be the distinction between the empirical knowledge of science – what is observable and recordable about the natural world – and the logical *a priori* knowledge of mathematics which does not need to be tested in the natural world. The mathematical statement that $7+5 = 12$ is a logical one which is true in all possible worlds, given that the meaning of the numbers is agreed. The statement that water boils at 100 degrees centigrade is knowable by testing, or by learning from someone who has previously carried out the test. Knowing in language might mean understanding that grammatical utterances are socially learned and agreed and might vary in different dialects. Children in London listening to and analysing Yorkshire dialect will learn of the linguistic varieties of English and that these different uses of English are social. This *social* knowledge is distinct from either the logic of mathematics or the empirical knowledge of science. For teachers to be aware of such matters will increase the quality of children's learning in an integrated curriculum. When writing up a science observation, it is important to distinguish helping children with the grammatical aspects of their writing from the matter of recording the scientific aspects of empirical observation.

These epistemological distinctions are themselves problematic. The statement that water boils at 100 degrees centigrade is questionable. It depends on the purity of the water, the atmospheric pressure and the accuracy of the measuring instrument. Children can discover the temporary and relative nature of scientific knowledge when they come to make observations in the real world and they can challenge the nature of the knowledge which they are dealing with. This gives them the potential to query all assertions and purported 'facts'. For this reason, at Key Stage 2 in particular, it is desirable that children should understand the nature of subjects and the problematic nature of knowledge.

The National Curriculum, with its separate subjects, can then lead towards a new formation of thematic work which has the following features:

- subject coverage
- an appropriate mixture of thematic and discrete subject teaching
- real subject links, not spurious connections
- teachers' awareness of subject methods (knowing what is *knowing* in English, mathematics and science)
- children's awareness of subject methods
- progression within subjects
- whole school planning which preserves the teacher's ownership of the curriculum

The following description of a school's approach demonstrates how this is possible.

A SCHOOL CASE-STUDY

Chapters 6, 7, 8 and 9 in this book give examples of the ways in which individual subjects can be linked through integrated thematic work. This case-study is intended to show how a school manages the integrated curriculum within the context of the statutory National Curriculum with its separate subject orders.

Walwayne Court Primary School, Trowbridge, Wiltshire, was opened in 1991 and has developed its approach to the curriculum alongside the emerging National Curriculum. From the outset, staff were keen to establish key principles for the school and a learning policy. The key principles include the following:

> Walwayne Court should provide a happy, caring, secure environment in which children feel valued, respected and enjoy learning.
> Through experiencing success and appropriate praise, children should be helped to develop a positive attitude to themselves and others.

Children's individuality should be respected and their achievement in all areas, including non-educational achievements, should be given due recognition.

Children are best helped to cultivate their natural impulse to learn when provided with relevant first-hand experiences and good quality second-hand experiences which build on what they already know.

New experiences require an appropriate period of exploration/play.

Children need to develop independence, confidence and responsibility.

Expectations of children's work and behaviour should be high, clearly explained and consistent.

The physical environment provided should be challenging, stimulating and supportive.

Learning is helped by a continuity of approach and organization through the school.

Good communication is required to ensure that Walwayne Court is understood, respected and valued by parents and the local community.

(Walwayne Court Primary School, 1991a)

From these principles the learning policy is derived. This includes the following elements:

In reviewing work covered and planning new work, the needs of individual children are taken into account. Teachers plan in detail to provide an appropriate balance of new experiences over time. They take due account of the requirements of the National Curriculum, the school's policies and schemes of work and children's previous experiences.

We believe that a curriculum presented through a combination of cross-curricular topic work and discrete subject teaching is the approach which provides the best opportunity for achievement and enjoyment of learning. The choice of method will depend on the age of the children and the identified learning aim.

We recognise that grouping children in a variety of ways offers the best opportunity for learning. Children work individually, in small groups and as a class, taking account of the nature of the activity and the age of the children. When forming groups we take account of learning aims, the nature of the subject matter being covered and the social and intellectual needs of the children.

'Circle Time' is used throughout the school as an opportunity for discussion of social and personal issues. During this time issues can be raised by the teacher or the children. Ground rules are established to provide security for contributors.

Children learn by building on and extending their existing knowledge. The difficult task of matching child and task is best facilitated by providing good quality first-hand experiences which provide the child with a knowledge and understanding which can then be explored and developed. Without such experiences there is a risk of a gap in understanding which makes real learning much less likely. Second hand experiences can also be effective if good quality resources are used, such as

- out-of-school visits
- visitors to the school
- artefacts from the museum and library service
- the local environment
- dramatisations, such as 'drama days'
- a good quality reference library
- good quality resources within the school
- involving children in relevant practical activities in the classroom

- video and audio tapes
- children bringing objects from home
- LEA advisory service personnel
  (Walwayne Court Primary School, 1991b)

The school's approach to the curriculum derives from these principles and policy for children's learning. Central to this policy is the issue of the integrated curriculum and discrete subject teaching. The staff in the school believe that the thematic approach is the better one in addressing their principles. However, it is recognized that, in addressing the statutory requirements of the *coverage* of the National Curriculum subjects the ideal of delivering the whole curriculum through integrated themes cannot be realized. There is a tension between *themes* and *coverage*. As the headteacher, Richard Brown, says,

> We are really committed to topic work, but we know we must cover the National Curriculum. It is difficult to ensure that a topic will cover sufficient elements of the statutory curriculum, so we include some discrete subject teaching in order to ensure sufficient coverage.

There is, then, a combination of thematic and discrete subject teaching as appropriate. Topics are designed to cover some aspects of the National Curriculum. For example, a half-term topic on 'Changes in Plants' for Years 2 and 3 will cover subjects as shown by Table 5.3. This topic covers some work in most subjects, but nothing is included in geography and history which, during this time, may be covered by some discrete subject teaching as appropriate. Alternatively, geography and history may be addressed later in the year through another topic.

Decisions about whether to cover an aspect of a subject through discrete subject teaching or through a theme may depend on the type of resources available. For example, study of the Romans in history may well be studied in a thematic topic because there are good resources available in the nearby city of Bath. This enables the topic to be used to generate a wide interest among children and to extend the learning across other curriculum subjects. Study of the Egyptians, on the other hand, may be judged to offer less immediate tangible resources and so may be treated differently, perhaps through a short and intense cross-curricular topic of about a week's length.

It is the policy in some schools to devise a series of topics in a 'cycle' which cover all the required programmes of study in each subject year by year, and some such packs are available commercially. However, such a predetermined approach is rejected at Walwayne Court:

> We just don't believe in having a series of pre-formed topics which cover everything. First of all, to try to force all the subjects into a topic leads to false links between subjects. Secondly, it robs the teacher of the creativity of devising and making the topic with the children. The topic should be generated, and owned, by the teacher and the children.

How, then, is the school working towards progression and coverage through its thematic approach? The answer to this is in the systematic recording of programmes of study in each topic on a half-termly basis. The teacher then uses the record in selecting the next topic which will be appropriate in terms of curriculum coverage and relating to the children's interest.

The school uses two main strategies to address the issue of curriculum coverage, progression and teachers' and children's creativity and ownership of the curriculum:

Table 5.3 *Curriculum work through a topic on* Changes in Plants *(Year 2 theme)*

English	Science	History	Art	PE
'Magic bean' stories, concentrating on narrative structure. Descriptive writing about plants. Research on plants: use of contents and index in books. Keywords (e.g. stigma).	Concept mapping before and after work on plants. Sorting seeds. Observation of inside of seeds. Seed dispersal. Fair-testing: growing cress under different conditions. Observing growth of beans. Recording growth over time. Recording daily weather.		Colour mixing and matching to plant and flower colours. Emphasis on pastel colours. Paint imaginary plant from story writing. Drawing and painting Spring flowers.	Dance: movements of plants growing, using World of Plants video.

Maths	Technology	Geography	Music	RE
Time: growth in days, weeks and months. Measurement of length. Interpreting graphs of growth records.	Design and make imaginary plant from the story writing. IT Artisan		Making music for the plants movement. Jack and the Beanstalk pack from Silver Burdett Music Scheme.	Spiritual response to the wonder of growth in plants seen in the World of Plants video.

- combined curriculum integration and discrete subject teaching;
- themes selected by the teacher, taking account of children's interests and available resources.

An example of the record of that part of the curriculum covered through topic work for one class of children is given in Table 5.4. This is in note form and not a detailed account of the whole curriculum. It gives each teacher an at-a-glance view of the main areas which have been covered in the series of topics over two years. It should be emphasized, thought, that this is a record *only* of the curriculum taught through the topic, and not a complete record of the curriculum.

CONCLUSION

It has been shown that two views of the curriculum, and of teaching, underlie the National Curriculum orders: the first from the professionals, in which knowledge is seen as process and derived from the learner's activity; the second political, in which knowledge is divided into compartments and is seen as a set of prescribed skills to be acquired. While an integrated curriculum, negotiated with children as autonomous learners, is *implicit* in the National Curriculum orders, it is the discrete subject model which is presented to schools through the *structure* of the documents. Although the 1995 revised curriculum presents the whole National Curriculum in a single volume, rather than an array of subject folders, it is a very bald statement of requirements, still in separate subject compartments. There is no more support to schools in developing a

Table 5.4 *Record of the curriculum through topic work – Key Stage 2*

TOPIC DATE	English	Maths	Science	Technology	History
OUR SCHOOL Autumn 1991	Questionnaire – interviewing adults; story writing; playground games; handwriting	Data handling; measurements; model making; number work		Designing, making and evaluating models of equipment for school grounds. IT – Picture Builder	Schools in the past; interviewing adults about their school; visit to Trowbridge Museum
THE ROMANS Spring 1992	Research skills; dictionary work; factual writing; Roman stories, myths and legends; distinguishing fact/fiction	Roman numerals; tessellation in mosaics; rotational symmetry and measurement		Designing and making a temple and statue of Apollo	Finding out about Romans using different sources of evidence. Using artefacts. Visit to Roman Baths
WATER Summer 1992	Reporting results of experiments; sea poems; descriptive words	Grid references; capacity: estimating/ measuring quantities of water; water clock; sunken water clock	Floating/ sinking: high/ low floaters, shape, material, prediction and testing; drawing conclusions; evaporation, condensation		
MEXICO Autumn 1992	Research skills: envoying. Class story. Drama – Pitt Rivers. Listening to and questioning visitors; newspaper articles	Multiplication tables; number skills	Prediction and observation of Mexican fruits	Model of Tenochtitlan. Designing posters; designing and making Mexican toys that move	Timeline of Aztec/Mayan way of life; legacy; Cortes invasion of Mexico
WEATHER Spring 1993	Research James and the Giant Peach; Met Office: videoing presenting weather forecast; story writing	Compass directions; right angles; measuring weather graphs; area; fractions	Recording the weather with own instruments; how clouds are formed; causes of weather conditions	Designing and making equipment to record the weather; using computer database	
MY BODY Summer 1993	Floor book: how body works; research into major organs; share key words; hot-seating; Piggy book; questionnaire; poems based on fact; nouns, verbs, adjectives; creative writing after visit to waterfall at Penderyn Danywennalt	Database: our personal measurements; graphs using various scales; averages; ordering information; fractions	Labelling parts of the body; lung capacity; effect of exercise; digestion; strength of ones; personal hygiene; bodily changes; birth, reproduction; electricity: conductors, circuits, parallel and in series; safety; mammal traps; habitat	Designing, making body boxes; how joints work	Personal history; stories of personal achievements; big pit mining

Table 5.4a *Record of the curriculum through topic work – Key Stage 2* continued

Geography	Art	Music	PE	RE
	Introductory activities to clay; pen and ink handwriting; sketching and painting part of the school; view finders	Playground rhymes; steady beat; repeating patterns	Jumping and landing; balancing; forward rolls; ball skills; swimming	Care and respect for the school and people in it; Harvest story
Map of European countries the Romans conquered; place names; key places in Britain	Sketches of artefacts; designing mosaics; making clay tiles and glazing them for class mosaic; pinch pots	Expressive qualities. Pitch high and low. Melody; sounds of the Roman world	Balancing; stretching and curling; games: skittles, ball games; swimming	Roman gods; temples; Christianity; Easter Story
Water cycle; some map work; beach features; erosion; visit Wookey Hole Caves and the Beach of Southbourne	Beach sketches; observation drawing of shells; pastels; water colours; clay shells; miniature paintings; marbling, brusho	Using water words; water cycle as a stimulus for composition; recording composition. Following notations. Tone colour	Skills for summer sports: catching, throwing, teach games, travelling; swimming	Significance of water; John the Baptist
Naming places on world map; map of Mexico; Mexican way of life; food: maize	Pastel sketches of artefacts; paintings of gods; clay masks; poster advertising Mexico	Form: binary/ternary. Class composition based on four pictures of Mexico and the patterns on a sombrero	Jumping/landing; hockey skills; use of space; team games	Aztec/Mayan religious practices
Predicting temperatures in different parts of the world; movement of earth around the sun; seasons; general weather observations; Beaufort scale	Sketches of models from different angles. James and the Giant Peach display	Music for the story of Noah's Ark	Compass directions; joining movements; changing directions; parts together and apart; lifting and lowering	Noah's Ark; Mothering Sunday; Easter Story; Easter Garden' Easter cards
Formation of valleys, gorges; erosion; rock formation; source of rivers	Portraits by various artists; facial features; portraits; Acrimboldo		Importance of exercise; summer sport skills; stretching, curling	Valuing self, others; personal shields; feelings, fears etc.

thematic approach to children which they will find exciting and relevant to their lives. Indeed, there is even less than was contained in the original orders and the non-statutory guidance of 1989.

The OFSTED framework for the inspection of schools and the 1995 report by Her Majesty's Chief Inspector of Schools also militates against a cross-curricular model. The notion that the curriculum is a neutral body of content to be delivered in any way which is 'convenient' is uninspiring and unfortunate. It was first embodied in the advisory documents, *The National Curriculum: From Policy to Practice* (DES, 1989) and *A Framework for the Primary Curriculum* (NCC, 1989e) and has since been reiterated in the planning guidance issued by the School Curriculum and Assessment Authority (SCAA, 1995). Again, teachers are being left to makes sense of a clutter of curriculum documents for which a pedagogy has not been devised and systematically thought through; again, there has been minimal provision for in-service training. Those teachers not already committed to developing an integrated approach could well be led further towards adopting an approach which involves 'exercises' in discrete subjects. If account is to be taken of children's priorities and interests then it is necessary to consider integrated themes which are relevant to their lives and experiences.

REFERENCES

Alexander, R.J. (1984) *Primary Teaching*. London: Holt Rinehart and Winston.

Alexander, R. (1991) *Policy and Practice in Primary Education*. London: Routledge.

Alexander, R. (1993) Whose consensus? *The Times Educational Supplement*, 5 February.

Alexander, R. and Wilcocks, J. (1992) *Sixty Primary Classrooms*. Leeds: University of Leeds.

Alexander, R., Rose, J. and Woodhead, C. (1992) *Curriculum Organisation and Classroom Practice in Primary Schools*. London: DES.

Blenkin, G.M. and Kelly, A.V. (1981, 1st edn.) *The Primary Curriculum*. London: Harper and Rowe.

Central Advisory Council for Education in England (CACE) (1967) *Children and their Primary Schools* (Plowden Report). London: HMSO.

Clarke, K. (1991) *Primary Education – A Statement by the Secretary of State for Education*. London: DES.

Cox, B. (1991) *Cox on Cox: An English Curriculum for the 1990s*. London: Hodder and Stoughton.

Cox, C.B. and Dyson, A.E. (1969) *Fight for Education: A Black Paper*. London: Critical Quarterly Society.

Cox, C.B. and Dyson, A.E. (1971) *Black Paper Two*. London: Critical Quarterly Society.

Coulby, D. (1989) From educational partnership to central control. In Bash, L. and Coulby, D. (1989) *The Education Reform Act: Competition and Control*. London: Cassell.

Delamont, S. (1988) The primary teacher 1945–90: myths and realities. In Delamont, S. (1987) *The Primary School Teacher*. Lewes: Falmer Press.

DES (1975) *A Language for Life* (Bullock Report). London: HMSO.

DES (1978) *Primary Education in England*. London: HMSO.

DES (1980a) *A Framework for the Curriculum*. London HMSO.

DES (1980b) *A View of the Curriculum*. London: HMSO.

DES (1989) *National Curriculum: From Policy to Practice*. London: HMSO.

DES and Welsh Office (1987) *A Framework for the School Curriculum*. London: DES and Welsh Office.

DES and Welsh Office (1988a) *Mathematics for Ages 5 to 16*. London: DES and Welsh Office.

DES and Welsh Office (1988b) *Science for Ages 5 to 16*. London: DES and Welsh Office.

DES and Welsh Office (1988c) *English for Ages 5 to 11*. London: DES and Welsh Office.

DES and Welsh Office (1989a) *Mathematics in the National Curriculum*. London: HMSO.

DES and Welsh Office (1989b) *Science in the National Curriculum*. London: HMSO.

DES and Welsh Office (1989c) *English in the National Curriculum*. London: HMSO.

DFE (1995) *Key Stages 1 and 2 of the National Curriculum*. London: HMSO.

Fullan, M. and Hargreaves, A. (1993) *What's Worth Fighting for in Your School*. Milton Keynes: Open University Press.

Galton, M. (1994) *Crisis in the Primary Classroom*. London: David Fulton.

Galton, M., Simon, B. and Croll, P. (1980) *Inside the Primary Classroom*. London: Routledge and Kegan Paul.

Graham, D. and Tyler, D. (1993) *A Lesson for Us All*. London: Routledge.

Gretton, J. and Jackson, M. (1976) *William Tyndale: Collapse of a School or a System*. Harmondworth: Penguin.

Gunning, S., Gunning, D. and Wilson, J. (1981) *Topic Teaching in the Primary School*. London: Croom Helm.

Hargreaves, A. (1993) *What's Worth Fighting for in Your School?* Milton Keynes: Open University Press.

Hargreaves, A. and Goodson, I. (1995) Let us take the lead. *The Times Educational Supplement*, 24 Feb. 1995.

HMI (1989) *Aspects of Primary Education in Mathematics Teaching in Schools*. London: HMSO.

Kerry, T. and Eggleston, J. (1988) *Topic Work in the Primary School*. London: Routledge.

Mortimore, J., Sammons, P., Stoll, L., Lewis, D. and Ecob, R. (1988) *School Matters: The Junior Years*. Wells: Open Books.

National Curriculum Council (NCC) (1989a) *English 5–11 in the National Curriculum: A Report to the Secretary of State for Education and Science on the Statutory Consultation for Attainment Targets and Programmes of Study in English at the First Two Key Stages*. York: NCC.

NCC (1989b) *Mathematics: Non-Statutory Guidance*. York, NCC.

NCC (1989c) *Science: Non-Statutory Guidance*. York, NCC.

NCC (1989d) *English Key Stage 1: Non-Statutory Guidance*. York: NCC.

NCC (1989e) *Curriculum Guidance 1: A Framework for the Primary Curriculum*. York: NCC.

OFSTED (1995) *The Annual Report of Her Majesty's Chief Inspector of Schools*. London: HMSO.

Ritchie, R. (1991) *Profiling in Primary Schools: A Handbook for Teachers*. London: Cassell.

School Curriculum and Assessment Authority (SCAA) (1995) *Planning the Curriculum at Key Stages 1 and 2*. London: SCAA.

Simon, B. (1981) The primary school revolution: myth or reality. In Simon, B. and Wilcocks J. (eds) (1981) *Research and Practice in Primary Classroom*. London: Routledge and Kegan Paul.

Spooner, M. (1993) Commonalities in curriculum planning. Unpublished.

Tann, C.S. (1988) *Developing Topic Work in the Primary School*. Lewes: Falmer Press.

Tizard, B., Blatchford, P., Burke, J., Farquhar, C. and Plewis, I. (1988) *Young Children at School in the Inner City*. London: Lawrence Erlbaum Associates.

Walwayne Court Primary School (1991a) Key principles for the school. Unpublished.

Walwayne Court Primary School (1991b) Policy for teaching and learning. Unpublished.

Chapter 6

Implementing English in the National Curriculum

Sally Yates

INTRODUCTION

The arrival in 1995 of the final revised version of English in the National Curriculum had been long awaited by teachers who had felt ready to review their existing provision for English for some time. The new orders would therefore inevitably act as catalysts for change and, as it was six years since the first English orders were implemented, this review of practice was timely. The reflection on existing practice and planning for development which was initiated by the original orders was soon slowed down, and in some cases halted altogether, by the immense demands of the orders for the other curriculum subjects which followed. English had been left to 'tick over', as the content was on the whole more familiar and perceived as perhaps less problematic than aspects of the other core and foundation subjects. The criticisms in reports on the implementation of English (DES, 1992) would seem to demonstrate that this complacency was misplaced, although it was an understandable approach for schools to take as a survival strategy. The main area where development continued, through INSET supported by DES funding, was the focus on knowledge about language through the Language in the National Curriculum (LINC) project (Carter, 1990) which ran from 1989 to 1992. When in 1991 the DES made funds available for teachers to be released from classrooms for 20 days to attend designated courses in the other core subjects, mathematics and science, there was no provision for English. When funding *was* later made available for DFE courses in English in 1994, it was only when courses in several other foundation subjects had already been established and, because of funding cuts, the courses had been reduced to ten days. This is particularly ironic as the lack of support for English came at a time when great controversy raged in government, educational circles and the media about standards of literacy and teaching approaches (Turner, 1992; DES, 1992; see Chapter 2).

Now that English is back on school development plans and there is funded INSET available, schools are keen to review their English policies and develop schemes of work which will function to support the teaching and learning of English within the broader framework of curriculum planning which most schools have now constructed. Also, OFSTED, in their inspection of schools, expect to see schemes of work and policies 'currently used', and which 'must be presented in a form appropriate to a wider audience than the staff' (Wiltshire LEA, 1993). This review is opportune because English as a *subject* has also suffered through language and literacy being the medium through which learning in other curriculum areas takes place. An integrated approach to teaching English through other subjects ensures that language and literacy develop in real contexts and not in decontextualized exercises. However, this can lead to a utilitarian attitude in which English can lose its worth as a subject in its own right. Consequently there can be a lack of clear planning for development in some areas such as 'responding imaginatively' to aspects of literature (DFE, 1995, p. 13).

POLICY AND PLANNING

Curriculum planning in many schools is now approached through topics, either age/ stage specific or whole school, within which subject needs are then addressed. The problem with this for all subjects, and particularly for English, is that not everything can be neatly slotted into topics, and some aspects of children's learning need regular, ongoing planning to foster effective development. Although topic based work is an effective and economical approach to delivering the primary curriculum (see Chapter 5), there has always been the danger of creating spurious links between subjects to include them neatly in a topic plan, when some elements may be far better approached separately, or via the many 'mini-topics' related to seasons, festivals or current events, which are an important supplement to main topic planning. For example, the selection of books to read aloud to a class cannot be linked exclusively to the themes and content of the topic in hand, or the children will lose opportunities to explore a wide range of literature.

The planning document developed by SCAA (SCAA; 1995) to support the implementation of the revised orders addresses this. It suggests that teachers should note which aspects of each subject should be taught as 'discrete and cohesive' blocked units of work, and which should be planned as continuing units requiring 'regular and frequent teaching' and running alongside any blocked units. Elements of both blocked and continuing units may be included in topic work, linking different subjects, but there must also be provision for the elements which sit outside the topic. So a programme for the initial teaching of reading will clearly be a continuous unit, some elements of which may be drawn into the current topic, but continuing none the less as discrete teaching alongside the topic.

SCHEMES OF WORK

This approach to planning for a subject is useful as a framework for developing schemes of work for English and will encourage schools to plan again, as they did in the post-Bullock period before the National Curriculum's innovation overload, for coherent programmes for language and literacy learning.

Example from a primary school in South London

Prior to the introduction of the National Curriculum, the English co-ordinator had developed a policy for language as an aid to planning across the curriculum. This advice included a policy for handwriting, indications of which reading skills and strategies might be introduced at each stage of development and when particular aspects of punctuation should be covered. When planning topics teachers checked through to ensure that language development was being included too.

With the introduction of the full range of National Curriculum subjects, however, English had been allocated little time within the school's staff development programme, although the English co-ordinator had run occasional workshops to disseminate good practice and ideas from conferences and courses she had attended. School-based INSET was focused on each new subject's requirements or was governed by the need to respond to 'external forces' such as the necessity for producing behaviour policies and special needs policies, leaving little time for maintaining development in English. The English co-ordinator felt that, although writing, for example, was firmly embedded within the topic work, teachers' responses tended to focus on the subject content and lacked clear aims for writing development. It was only when the London reading test scores for the school dropped to below the local average that the need to focus on English again was realized. This coincided with plans to overhaul the school library and, in reviewing bookstock, it was realized that books for English were old, battered and uninspiring and had been neglected in resourcing areas of need in other subjects. This came as a shock to a school which had always prided itself on high standards of reading and which had achieved success in implementing other areas of the curriculum and other new initiatives, such as a 'green club', an environmental group within the school. The old policy is to form the basis of a new policy and scheme of work which will make planning 'as quick and painless as possible', containing specific requirements and suggestions, linked to resources which have proved effective.

Where schemes of work have been developed, they have helped to draw a staff together again on English and to ensure a common approach. This is vital to effective teaching and learning in English (HMI, 1992).

Besides helping the teacher to plan for a class, the scheme of work can be used to aid differentiation both in initial planning and through continual assessment. Progress mapping, for example, where one child's development is tracked through and reviewed to evaluate progress and to set appropriate teaching and learning goals for the future, ensures that all children are working within the scheme of work at appropriate levels, not only at a supposed 'norm' for their age. If children are to be empowered through their language and literacy, particularly those with learning difficulties, they must have appropriate individual programmes drawn from the overall guidelines. High-achieving children also benefit from progress mapping, as there is always a danger that both they and the teacher will be content with the fact that they are achieving more than other children, instead of reviewing particular progress and setting personal goals.

Whilst the scheme of work must indicate how a school plans to implement the National Curriculum for English, it should not be just a reorganization of the programme of study, and should leave scope for including detail in areas such as information technology (IT), media education and drama which are fundamental to developing language and literacy and which play so small a part in the revised orders. It should also include some reference to the introduction and valuing of languages other than English, not only to enable bilingual children to 'make use of' all the languages they speak (DFE, 1995, p. 2), but also to develop 'intercultural and international understanding' (Andrews, 1994, p. 34) and metalinguistic awareness for *all* children through acquisition and exploration of other language systems.

Example from Widcombe Infants School, Bath

The head of this school has introduced a programme to enable all children to understand and speak French through 'immersion' in the language. Her own experience of coming from a bilingual Welsh family helped to convince her of young children's ability to operate comfortably in more than one language, and French was chosen as the most familiar language to the adults in school. One member of staff is a fluent French speaker who takes the children from each class for sessions which are conducted solely in French, so that the children tune in to the sound of the language. As the sessions may be RE lessons, art or RE, the vocabulary particular to the subject and organization is soon acquired and through songs and rhymes more French is introduced and enjoyed.

The role of the co-ordinator is critical in identifying needs and, in collaboration with the Head and the rest of the staff, drawing up a viable programme for creating policies and schemes of work. One of the 'factors influencing good practice' identified by HMI (1990) was the school having

> a teacher with overall responsibility for language and literacy, and appropriate status for the exercising of that responsibility.
> (HMI, 1990, p.28)

The mere existence of a co-ordinator with subject expertise does not on its own guarantee effective practice, and the same HMI report found that in schools with designated teachers responsible for language,

> only a minority of these effectively influenced the work of the school, mainly because they lacked the time to act as consultants and to work alongside other teachers.
> (HMI, 1990, p.6)

The provision by the DFE of in-service courses for co-ordinators also reflects the increased awareness of the particular skills required by subject specialists beyond their subject knowledge if they are to effect change and foster good practice.

The next section illustrates aspects of practice in implementing the National Curriculum. It is organized under the headings of the attainment targets. However, the interrelationships between the language modes means that these distictions are not discrete. The revised orders require that language should be developed 'within an integrated programme of speaking and listening, reading and writing' (DFE, 1995, p. 4) and the following reflects that blurring of boundaries.

ATTAINMENT TARGET 1: SPEAKING AND LISTENING

While the importance of valuing and developing children's spoken language has been realized since the Bullock Report (DES, 1975) this aspect of English has required much support for teachers. The detailed outline of requirements for speaking and listening focused on the *range* of opportunities children should have for developing their spoken language and the National Oracy Project (NOP) has been significant in disseminating useful practice (Norman, 1990; 1992). This, and other key studies of classroom talk, have also encouraged teachers to reflect on their own interactions with children and the facilitating strategies they can use to foster effective spoken communication (Edwards and Mercer, 1987; Brown and Wragg, 1993; Wells, 1986).

Language and culture

The culture of the school is still alien to many children, with language serving different purposes to those at home (Tizard and Hughes, 1984, Bryce-Heath, 1983; Wells, 1986), and it is the teacher's job to create an environment where children feel confident to use language for learning. The power of language to alienate can be exemplified in the continuing insistence in many schools that children should address teachers formally by their titles and second names, Mr Smith, and Mrs Jones, rather than by their first names, despite the changes in society that mean most children now address neighbours and adult friends by their first names. The formal titles are often abbreviated by children to 'Sir' and 'Miss' which have a further alienating effect. Where schools have addressed this, there has not been a perceived lack of respect and growth in indiscipline, but relationships improve, with school seeming a less remote culture.

> culture shapes our behaviour patterns, and a great deal of our behaviour is mediated through language.
> (Halliday, 1978, p.23)

Speaking and listening across the curriculum

The requirements within other subject orders for children to have opportunities to discuss, explore and present their work to others have prompted teachers to focus on talking to learn across the curriculum. For example, in mathematics pupils are required to:

- explain their thinking to support the development of their reasoning
- describe and discuss shapes
- ask questions and follow alternative suggestions.

(DFE, 1995, pp. 22, 25, 26)

Most of the subject orders also expect that children will develop vocabularies which allow them to discuss their learning using the terminology of the subjects: for example, in art (DFE, 1995, p.101), in geography (p.88), in history (p.77), in design and technology (p.59). Children are also learning the language relating to English AT1 such as *discuss, debate, argue, question, listen, respond, decide,* and being explicit about how and why they are using language aids children to reflect on their own developing competence.

There is an expectation that children should ask *questions* to support their learning in the orders for mathematics, science, history and geography, but the provision of a learning environment where children feel confident to ask questions is not to be underestimated, as the work of Wells (1986) and Tizard and Hughes(1984) have made plain. It is unfortunate that the continuing controversy about the status of Standard English within the orders has deflected attention from some other issues, such as questioning, relating to expectations for children's speaking and listening within the orders. Not only are teachers creating opportunities within the classroom to develop a spirit of enquiry within the learning environment so that the children are asking questions as they would at home, but they are also examining their own strategies for facilitating talk. These include asking open rather than closed question and following lead questions with 'tag' questions to elicit further responses. They are also using strategies other than questioning to encourage speaking and listening; these include active listening strategies: nodding and other body language, making encouraging noises, acknowledging what has been said. Talking for different purposes is highlighted in English AT1, and there is a major focus on the use of speaking and listening in discussion with others.

Teachers need to be aware of gender issues in class discussion. Some of the early videotapes made by the NCC (1992) and the Cumbrian Oracy Project to illustrate speaking and listening include sequences where in mixed groups working on practical maths and science tasks, the boy in each group takes over, ending any discussion. The fact that the commentaries on these filmed tasks do not acknowledge the lack of debate and the gender dominance illustrates how easy it is to forget that effective discussion for working and learning co-operatively is not instinctive behaviour but has to be fostered:

> Several studies have suggested that boys' dominance is the outcome of strategies employed by boys *and* girls *and* teachers. If gender-typed talk is regarded as normal it is likely it will be supported by all participants in an interaction.
> (Swann, 1992, p.69)

There has been some innovative and effective development within classrooms. Teachers are realizing that changing a task very slightly can allow greater opportunities for discussion and reporting, and there has been an increased confidence in focusing on the *process* of learning rather than always having a written end product. However, time spent in speaking and listening can often put the teacher under pressure, with children claiming they 'did no work today'. There has been a realization that feedback on attainment in speaking and listening is as vital as feedback in other areas of the curriculum, and peer reflection has now become more commonplace. It is not enough simply to set up situations where talk is required and assume that children will learn to discuss effectively; there needs to be careful planning to enable children to practise the skills needed to work in collaboration.

These skills are developed in the Avon LEA materials on 'Collaborative Reading', the scope of which extends beyond reading to encourage effective collaborative work across the curriculum. The collaborative approach in these materials involves the children considering what makes an effective group and setting clear targets for learning and deciding how effectiveness will be evaluated before they commence the actual task. The children work on a given task within a structured framework involving four parts (Avon LEA, 1994):

Preparation   setting specific learning goals and outcomes for the task
Planning   structuring the work to be done and allotting roles within an action plan
Action   carrying out the action plan
Review   evaluating against the outcomes, reflecting on both the task and the group's effectiveness in working together

Besides the evident benefits for the children's immediate learning, this structured framework, which encourages autonomous learning, has organizational benefits for the management of the class. This in turn facilitates higher attainment; it is documented that well-organized classrooms lead to more effective learning (Mortimore *et al.*, 1988; HMI 1990; Alexander *et al.*, 1992).

So the range of *curriculum* contexts for talk is not difficult to provide because there are expectations of opportunities for speaking and listening across the National Curriculum subjects. Teachers can use any subject areas in which they feel confident to develop effective strategies for fostering discussion in which some children are not dominated by others. These skills are transferable to other subjects, promoting improved communication and facilitation of discussion. Because the focus is on the *nature* of the investigation, the context becomes a 'context of joint enterprise', which Wells (1986) found to be such an effective strategy for the development of talking and learning in the home. In focusing on talk across the curriculum, though, talk for developing other aspects of English should not be overlooked.

The task of having older children produce story-books for younger children has been used by one teacher to develop the older children's writing and support reading with the younger children. The teacher described these speaking and listening opportunities within the task:

Reading a range of popular books for young children to each other and discussing common features

- talking with and listening to younger children to discover their own particular attitudes and preferences to books;
- discussing as a group the outlines for their own particular story, and writing collaboratively with continued discussion;
- functional talk during the design and creation process;
- reading aloud to the young children from the finished books, having discussed together who would be best to do this in terms of clarity of voice;
- discussion during evaluation, both with the young children and within their own group.

This one writing task, then, had provided opportunities to cover all the main elements of AT1 at Key Stage 2:

Pupils should be given opportunities to talk for a range of purposes, including:

- exploring, developing, and explaining ideas;
- planning, predicting, and investigating;
- sharing ideas, insights and opinions;
- reading aloud, telling and enacting stories and poems;
- reporting and describing events and observations;
- presenting to audiences, live or on tape.
  (DFE, 1995, p.11)

The task also enabled them to consider how they should adjust their language for the particular audience of younger children, the nature of the oral evaluation with the younger children taking a different form from the group's own evaluation. Another teacher developed this idea with the older children acting as scribes for the younger children to create their own books. This added another dimension to the opportunities for talk, with the older children reflecting their awareness of the younger children's language needs.

> Types of linguistic situation differ from one another, broadly speaking, in three respects: firstly, what is actually taking place; secondly, who's taking part; and thirdly, what part the language is playing.
> (Halliday, 1978, p.31)

Another example of speaking and listening within English activities comes from a school in Bath. The teacher of a class of Years 5 and 6 wanted to provide children with opportunities to gain in confidence in speaking and listening in different contexts whilst working on story structures. Over a period of two or three weeks, the children were read and told a wide range of traditional stories, collections of tales being made available for the children to read in their own time too. The stories were read by the class teacher and told by a visiting lecturer. The children discussed the stories which had been told, volunteering their own versions of the tales they recognized. 'My version's different to that' was a common response which would invite an alternative account. The children then worked in pairs telling a story of their choice to each other. They were asked to provide feedback: two things about their partner's story-telling they thought were good, one thing which the partner might work on to make the retelling better. The pair retold the stories again, taking on the constructive criticism; then the pairs went into fours, a slightly bigger audience, and told their tale again.

The teacher provided opportunities for the children to tell their stories onto tape so that they could be self-critical, and to record on paper the story outlines to help them remember. Eventually the children were comfortable with telling to larger groups, and they set up a database on the computer of which tales children in the class told and whether they preferred a small or larger audience group. This list was circulated to other classes, who could 'book' a story-teller to come and entertain a small group or the class. The children's writing also improved dramatically during the story-telling project, as they focused on story structures, characterization and choices of language.

Social contexts for talk

The provision of a range of social contexts in which children may work has also challenged some approaches to classroom organization. In moving away from whole class teaching, a common pattern of organization has been for the class to be grouped in either attainment groups or mixed groups which rotate through a range of activities (Mortimore *et al.*, 1988). Whilst organizationally convenient, this does not allow for variety of teaching and learning strategies and means children cannot experience working with different social groupings. The National Oracy Project helped teachers to explore different groupings such as 'envoying', where one child from each group moves to another group, either in a reporting or information-seeking capacity, reporting back to the original group on his/her findings (Howe, 1992). In 'jigsaw' groupings, a base group allocates expert roles to each member. For example, if a class had been collecting minibeasts from the school grounds, one person from each base group might be allocated to look at woodlice, one to ants; or in a project on Vikings, one person might look at weapons, one at food. The experts gather to work in their expert groups, returning later to the base group where they report back. This has been found to have an enabling effect for many children, and is particularly useful with quiet children, or those not fluent in English who may not contribute readily to either base or expert groups initially, but will be enabled to contribute when acting as representatives or 'experts' in reporting back to their base group.

The issue of the use of Standard English has been a difficult one for teachers, particularly when assessing talk during informal discussions where talk is more likely to reflect social and regional variation. Teachers are developing children's implicit aware-ness of register through the preparation and feedback for different uses of talk. These include presenting work to others in more formal situations, such as 'sharing assem-blies', reporting to the class, as well as opportunities in drama and literature. Books such as Robert Westall's *The Kingdom by the Sea*, set in Tyneside, include use of dialect and reflection on code-switching according to social context:

> 'Do sit here. I expect you're ready for your supper. I see you've been camping! You haven't had very good weather for the first week of your holiday!'
> 'No, it's been a bit wet.' He realized how posh her voice was, against his own. Even though he was talking to her the proper way he talked to the teachers at school.
> (Westall, 1990, p.114)

Just debating the use of the word 'proper' in that passage raises major questions for discussion with children.

Formal debates have also been introduced by teachers to allow children to prepare what they might say on an issue and reflect on the persuasive power of language. In taking on opposing roles in historical debates, for example, children may be playing devil's advocate and having to convince others on issues they do not actually agree with. Such activities provide a link with media education, which suffers from 'vagueness and confusion' about its place within the National Curriculum (Bazalgette, 1991) and needs embedding in classroom practice.

Drama too has wide potential for exploring and extending oracy, and the links between media and drama have been exploited well by teachers who capitalize on children's broad knowledge of television genres.

Assessing and recording children's speaking and listening

The most difficult element of this attainment target to implement has been assessing and recording talk, and yet the observations made of children by observing them in a range of both curriculum and social contexts have challenged teachers' preconceptions about children's linguistic competence. Formal assessment of talk through the SATs was dropped, although teachers' own continuous assessment continued. Many teachers are still trying to find a form of record which allows for the recording of speaking and listening without duplicating information. Observation of a small group engaged on an investigation of the speeds of toy cars running down a ramp, for example, may be relevant to English, science and mathematics AT1, as well as to personal and social development. So, even in schools with well-established records in each curriculum area, this can pose problems. If it is recorded under mathematics, the note is lost when reviewing speaking and listening, for example. There are solutions however: one teacher records all observations for one individual across the curriculum on the same sheet, but then goes through her observation colour coding entries according to the National Curriculum. A one or two-line entry on the above task could then easily be seen to relate to AT1 as it would be marked in yellow for English. The matrix of social and curriculum contexts used in the Primary Language Record (Barrs *et al.*, 1988, p.38) is another effective tool for planning and recording opportunities for talk.

ATTAINMENT TARGET 2: READING

The revised orders for AT2 interpret reading in a broad sense to include reading both in print and on screen, reflecting the complex range of 'new literacies' which children need to acquire (Meek, 1991). Schools recognizing this have reviewed traditional practices to include use of environmental print, information technology and other media in developing children's literacy.

An inner city school ran a parents evening focusing on the ways print is used in everyday life, encouraging parents to be more explicit when engaged in reading and writing activities to deal with such text as:

- sifting through junk mail
- reading letters from school
- noting events on a calendar/diary
- leaving and reading written messages
- reading recipes and menus
- reading food labels and instructions for reheating
- looking up TV programmes in the newspaper or TV guide
- reading horoscopes in magazines
- looking up telephone numbers
- writing and reading from lists

This focus was developed by encouraging parents to add comments on children's own involvement in 'reading for living' in the reading record which went home and had previously been used just for notes on the child's reading from the school 'reading book'. Another consequence of this was that the teachers' own awareness of opportunities for reading and writing outside planned curriculum contexts were raised and there was greater exploitation of such opportunities in class.

This development of reading beyond books reflects an awareness of the culturally related literacies in which children engage before schooling and outside school (Harste *et al.*, 1984, Goodman, 1990; Ferreiro and Teberosky, 1982). Children exist in a print-rich environment outside school and the school should be providing at least as rich an environment (Smith, 1988). The listing of literature for children in drafts of the revised orders has been controversial, and is now reduced at Key Stages 1 and 2 to categories of texts. Although this includes reference to 'stories and poems from a range of cultures', it makes no explicit reference to popular culture. Yet if the barriers between home and school are to be breached, then having materials for reading which are already familiar to children in school is important, whether it is print on packaging and signs or books.

A school in Yate, near Bristol, is in an area with no bookshop, but the children are provided with books at home through shopping at Tesco, which has now sponsored the printing of a booklet on supporting children's reading produced by the school. The quality of books sold in supermarkets is often impressive, with Walker Books working with Sainsbury's supermarkets to produce a creditworthy list. However, even where some may feel that providing books familiar to the children involves compromising on 'quality' of language and style, the importance of reflecting popular culture is enough of an incentive to encourage many teachers to ensure that *some* texts related to television and other influences are available in classrooms.

The revised English order lists some of the 'knowledge, understanding and skills' children should use when reading:

- phonic knowledge
- graphic knowledge – word recognition
- grammatical knowledge
- contextual understanding
  (DFE, 1995, p.7)

Although there has been an insistence by the School Curriculum and Assessment Authority (SCAA) that the order of skills in this list is neither indicative of their importance nor of their order of teaching, the level descriptor for AT2 level 1 belies this, demanding that pupils should

> use their knowledge of letters and sound-symbol relationships to read words and to establish meaning when reading aloud.
> (DFE, 1995, p.28)

Only at level 2 are pupils required to 'use more than one strategy' (ibid, p.28). In fact while attention to print is implicit in the first two categories listed above, two of the three most important prerequisites to reading cited by Clay (1979) do not appear here. They are attention to print, talking like a book and left to right directionality.

Although absent from AT2, Reading, the language of books *is* listed as a key skill in Attainment Target 1 at Key Stage 1:

> Pupils' vocabulary should be extended through activities that encourage their interest in words, including exploration and discussion of:

- characteristic language in story-telling, *e.g. 'Once upon a time'.*
  (DFE, 1995 p.5)

Fortunately, teachers have long realized the importance of introducing the language of books to children, informed both by their own experience and the work of others (Meek, 1988; Barrs, 1991; Clark, 1976). The provision of opportunities for children to develop their knowledge, understanding and skills through sharing good literature, rather than through decontextualized exercises, is also a major concern for teachers of reading. The language of books is introduced through frequent readings and discussions and the use of 'big books', enlarged versions of picture books selected for the patterning of the text, has enabled teachers to extend to whole classes the sort of experience children have when sharing a book one-to-one with an adult (Holdaway, 1979). Texts which have repetition, rhyme, alliteration, clear sequencing and good symbiosis of text with the pictures are particularly useful. Just the title of 'Noisy Nora', (Wells, 1978), which is so pleasing to say aloud, immediately encourages association of sounds and words (grapho-phonic association); it provides clues about the central character and allows the child to predict the possible content of the book.

Using the patterns of language in books with clear repeated sequences of language allowed one teacher to create big books with the children, scribing for them as they created their own versions of a favourite book based on their own experience. So, for example, *Goodnight Owl* by Pat Hutchins inspired 'Goodnight Children', and instead of

> The Robin peeped
> pip pip
> and Owl tried to sleep
> (Hutchins, 1972)

The children's version read:

> The baby cried,
> Waah, waah,
> and Adrian tried to sleep.

The creation of the book enabled the teacher to model writing, reinforcing left-right directionality, one-to-one correspondence of words, discussion about what each word would begin with, how to write the letters and grammatical structures. The book then became another reading resource for use with individuals or groups.

The concept keyboard has also been used effectively to enable children to create their own texts based on familiar language patterns. One teacher, for example used *The Monster Sandwich* from the Storychest series to enable children, at the touch of a picture on the concept keyboard, to add their own foods to the format of the original book. This created individual mini-books which the children could illustrate and keep as their own, or put into the book corner for others to read.

The sequencing of pictures from books to retell the story is also invaluable for aiding prediction, as is the 'reading' of stories from books without pictures, such as Jan Ormerod's *Sunshine* (1981) and *Moonlight* (1982), Briggs's *The Snowman* (1978), or Collington's *The Angel and the Soldier Boy* (1987). Wordless comic strips such as 'Biffo the Bear' in *The Beano* can be highly motivating and effective for 'reading' and sequencing for older non-fluent readers, especially those dependent on word-recognition or phonics who need encouragement to predict and use context cues.

The introduction of the CD Rom to classroom computers is providing teachers and children with yet another resource for reading. The text and pictures from whole books can be reproduced on the computer with high quality graphics and animated with high quality sound, both speech and music. The current applications are excellent in the field of non-fiction, with encyclopedias such as Encarta and interactive packages like 'Dinosaurs' facilitating information retrieval. However, the potential of fiction in the early years has still to be fully explored. There has been some criticism of the packages which transfer books to the screen with some interaction, e.g. *Just Grandma and Me*, for not fully exploiting the potential of interactive media, nor substantially adding to the experience of reading and understanding fiction (Moore, 1994). As more primary schools acquire CD Rom, the applications will no doubt evolve into more dynamic forms, just as the picture book has continued thie century to develop with increasing sophistication.

The HMI (1992) report on the teaching and learning of reading, whilst reassuring in the recognition of much good practice, was extremely critical of the lack of planning for effective reading development:

> In KS2 the children's reading skills and the range of their reading experience were insufficiently extended in the majority of classes. . . . teachers of KS1 pupils generally gave sufficient time to the teaching of reading but the time spent on reading was not always well used and tended to fall away too steeply in KS2.
> (HMI, 1992, p.1)

Teachers have been working to redress this, exploring ways of meeting the requirement that pupils should:

> be taught to consider in detail the quality and depth of what they read . . . They should be taught to use inference and deduction . . . to evaluate the texts they read.
> (DFE, 1995 p.13)

In Wiltshire, a Key Stage 1 teacher realized that the quiet reading time in her classroom every afternoon was not as productive as it should have been. When she observed the children closely she found that, whilst some children were fully absorbed, many were off-task, flicking through books without engaging in them, drifting off the task, or spending large parts of the session 'choosing', only to return the partly read book to the shelf at the end. She tried some different reading practices and evaluated how effective each was in engaging the children and providing constructive reading experience. She was then able to draw up a plan for using the afternoon reading time for activities which were varied each day and had a marked effect on progress, such as:

- reading with older children
- groups reading multiple copies of books individually and having time to discuss the text together
- groups reading plays aloud
- individuals or groups listening to tapes with headphones
- sharing books in pairs

She also ensured that the children chose their books before lunch to minimize time spent in avoidance strategies, and discussed ways of choosing books, without losing the enjoyment of browsing through books.

Structured reading schemes where the next book to be read is the one listed in the scheme, or is always given by the teacher, may not provide adequate strategies to support children's ability to choose books. One of the positive aspects of teaching reading without schemes is the way less readily quantifiable aspects of successful reading can be fostered: children's motivation, knowledge of authors and genres, their ability to choose books and the perception of their own reading capacity. Where teachers are using schemes, many are refusing to be seduced by the hard sell of the publishers, especially those who have produced glossy new materials which have the same drawbacks as older traditional schemes. Instead, they are selecting materials such as *Literacy Links*, (Shortland, 1993) *Storychest* (Shortland, 1983) *Collins Bookbus*

(Collins, 1987) and *The Flying Boot* (Ginn, 1994) which are less structured. No one scheme can fulfil the requirement that pupils should have 'extensive experience of children's literature' (DFE, 1995 p.6).

The term 'higher order skills' is now no longer used, with the realization that from the earliest stages children are engaging in texts at 'deep structure' level, not simply decoding the 'surface structure' (Smith, 1985). Even the earliest picture books may expect children to read beyond the lines to 'fill in the gaps' in the text (Meek, 1991). 'The best picture books are open to interpretation because they leave so much unsaid' (Baddeley and Eddershaw, 1994, p.1). This early experience of visual literacy encourages children to read between and beyond the lines, to go beyond the literal in reading and is extended through their other great visual experience of watching the television. The 'reading' of the expressions on the faces of characters in the closing shots of 'Neighbours', for example, encourages interpretation of the characters' feelings, prediction about what will happen in the next episode, motivation to continue watching and a desire to talk about it with others. Any adult eavesdropping on children discussing characterization and plot in their favourite television serials will realize that children are already sophisticated 'readers' of media texts, and this can be exploited in the classroom.

A student teacher gave each group of children in the class a picture book with some of the pages clipped together, leaving a picture from the centre of the book for them to 'read' in as much detail as they could. They discussed the setting, the characters, who they were, what they felt and what the text might be about. They discussed what might have happened before this page and what might happen next. The children were then able to look at the preceding page and following page, and talk about how what they saw affected their 'reading'. The group then wrote a story based on the three images, before reading the whole book. The quality of the children's dialogue during this activity was impressive in revealing how they brought to it their previous experience of literature and life.

Although the class in this example were Year 5 children, similar techniques can be used at any level. Many picture books work well with older children, and increasing numbers of picture books without text are being published which have a high interest level to excite and interest older children.

Another technique is to use speech or thought bubbles to record what particular characters might be thinking or saying. For example, what might Goldilocks have said when she returned home? What did the wolf think when he couldn't blow down the house of bricks? These can be used to 'read' a picture, or in response to events within the text, particularly where this has been left to the inference of the reader. It can be done individually or in groups and fosters debate about different interpretations of the text.

Examination of character by tracing someone through the text can demonstrate how the reader is manipulated by the text, with first impressions often changing as the reader understands more about a character's motivation and experience, such as Edmund in *The Lion, the Witch and the Wardrobe* (Lewis, 1950), Jason in *Dinner Ladies Don't Count* (Ashley, 1981) or Andrea in *The Suitcase Kid* (Wilson, 1992).

At a school in Chippenham, a teacher taking over a Year 5 class assessed the children's story-writing skills and planned her programme of books to read aloud to support children's needs in creating their own stories. So she read Susan Cooper's *The*

Dark is Rising (1973) to focus on settings and books by Betsy Byars for characterization. Besides enjoying the stories, the discussion and writing resulting from these readings had an effect on the children's own use of language and story structure in their writing.

Consideration of the range of books for reading aloud in any programme of reading development has often been neglected at Key Stage 2, through a lack of coherent planning, and time for reading aloud has suffered in the overcrowded curriculum. The revised orders allow more time for reading and expect teachers to provide a wider experience for pupils.

At Key Stage 1 teachers are accustomed to planning which books to read aloud, including some new texts and some old favourites in a reading session. Criteria teachers at Key Stage 2 have used in selecting a range of books for reading aloud include:

- a range of authors, with supporting displays of further titles;
- books from series;
- a range of genres to widen all children's reading and reflect the interests of each class member;
- a range of levels of difficulty, so that the non-fluent readers are also having books at their reading level read aloud. All the children enjoy reading books at varying levels;
- stories from anthologies and single authored collections of short stories which can be 'dipped into';
- poetry;
- books written in different styles, e.g. first- and third-person narrative, use of flashbacks;
- books written by the children themselves.

Chambers stresses the importance of the 'enabling adult' in introducing literature to children:

> everything begins with selection – selection of a book to read is essential before 'reading' can begin; equally, selection of something to talk about is essential before any talk can begin.
> (Chambers, 1993, p.12)

Adults have a tendency to select books to read within the genres they enjoy themselves, but teachers need to meet the needs of all the children in their classes. They need, therefore, to identify genres where they may not be able to recommend suitable books for children and fill in their own gaps of knowledge. Another useful strategy for teachers to use in introducing books to older children is to take the idea introduced by Webb (1986), in *I like this Story*, of introducing a book and presenting the first chapter or two. Audiotapes which introduce the story and the author with a reading of the opening chapters can help the child decide whether s/he likes the book; these introduce characters and vocabulary and style, and facilitate the child's continued reading. Although time-consuming to make, some schools have found that half an in-service day spent with each teacher producing a tape provides a useful bank which can be copied for each class.

The increased use of reading logs or journals, particularly at Key Stage 2, is conducive to critical reflection and consideration of personal patterns of reading. It enables the teacher to monitor the range and frequency of individual children's reading, and to suggest other possible texts. This careful reading of text is in contrast to the different sorts of reading that the use of non-fiction texts often require.

Attainment Target 2 is explicit in requiring children to:

> find information in books and computer-based sources by using organisational devices to help them decide which parts of the material to read closely. They should be given opportunities to read for different purposes, adopting strategies appropriate for the task.
> (DFE, 1995, p.14)

And in their report on the teaching and learning of reading, HMI (1992) found that

> many Key Stage 2 teachers had insufficient knowledge of the books which their children were reading to be able to discuss them critically.
> (HMI, 1992, p.6)

The improved approach to topic planning in one Avon school was perceived by a teacher to have reduced the opportunities for children to use information-retrieval skills as the books and other resources necessary for the topic had been gathered by the teacher in advance and displayed conveniently for the children' use. She decided to introduce each term's topic to the class at the end of the previous term, so that they could gather resources themselves and use the library systems to find appropriate books and consider other useful resources. They recorded the sections of the Dewey system which contained books relevant to the topic. The teacher made further opportunities for research skills by encouraging more focused enquiry by individuals or small groups on aspects of the topic which had not been covered as a class, and by encouraging personal topics as ongoing projects to foster individual interests.

Certainly the use of non-fiction texts is now much more refined, with children less likely to copy out sections of books (HMI, 1990). Children are taught to record what they already know, then extend their knowledge by drawing on a range of texts and include a bibliography of books they found useful. The work of Bobbie Neate (1993) and Margaret Mallett (1992) have supported teachers' practice in working with non-fiction.

Assessing and recording reading

Techniques such as miscue analysis and running records have been used to enable teachers to plan appropriate programmes for reading development for individuals, ensuring that each child develops the ability to draw on a wide range of strategies and background knowledge about text in any reading. This focused support prevents the overreliance on one strategy which leads so many children to struggle with reading. In particular, phonics is often stressed at the expense of other strategies and leads to what Margaret Phinney (1988) calls 'overphonication' where every word is attempted phonically. The use of the running record in the Standard Assessment Tasks (SATs) has been a sad underexploitation of an opportunity to raise reading standards. The running record is a useful formative assessment technique, used by Clay (1993) in the Reading Recovery programme for initial assessment, but is used summatively in the SATs, to determine levels of reading attainment. There are thousands of completed running records around the country which could have been used to determine *how* each child read the given texts, what strengths the child had and what further learning experiences may benefit the child.

In the original working party report (DES and Welsh Office, 1988), the chair, Brian Cox, called for a national system of record keeping to be introduced. Seven years later this still has not been addressed, although concern about reading standards has continued to be voiced. In one of SCAA's early publications (1994) the use was suggested of elements of the Primary Language Record (Barrs *et al.*, 1988) for recording and assessing reading, exactly what Cox had recommended in 1988. With the reiteration of the importance of teachers' own assessment in the 1995 SATs booklet (SCAA, 1994), the need for effective records to maintain continuity and progression is vital and these should include the involvement of children and parents in recording reading. It is the interpretation of the evidence gained from reading with children that is particularly difficult, and skilled work, with in-service training in reading for all teachers, is needed. The Reading Recovery Programme (Clay, 1993) which has attracted so much publicity involves tightly structured training for the teachers involved, and this must be part of the success of the technique.

ATTAINMENT TARGET 3: WRITING

The work of the National Writing Project (1989) informed the original orders for English and continues to influence literacy practices in schools. Dissemination of good practice through publications following the National Writing Project (Czerniewska, 1992; NWP, 1989) has encouraged teachers to review their classroom organization and to create environments which provide opportunities for literacy to be embedded in both directed and non-directed activity. The writing produced through free-choice time in writing areas, and through 'play', both structured (small world area homes, shops, offices, cafés) and unstructured, has revealed to teachers the extent of children's literacy experience outside school and their ability to write for a range of purposes and in a variety of forms. Through the examination of lists produced by children, Gibson (1994) has questioned the simplistic divisions of writing into chronological and non-chronological in the original orders and demonstrated the complexity of such an apparently simple form frequently used in play or family-oriented activities.

Harste *et al.* (1984) demonstrated how the varied experience of writing at home often narrows when children enter school, and HMI (1992) found that the most effective teachers at Key Stage 1 linked reading and writing and drew from children's literary experiences at home.

> Children do not learn to write through some form of spontaneous creative force; they learn what their culture and their school have constructed for them to learn.
> (Czerniewska, 1992, p.128)

If the early months in school teach children that writing is only about copying correctly what the teacher has scribed for them, and not about taking risks in attempting to communicate in writing with others, they soon learn to discount their wealth of previous experience.

Teachers capitalize on their increased awareness of children's motivation and potential as writers and attempt to meet the requirements of the National Curriculum in the provision they make for writing within topic work. However, the concept of the 'author' is more often applied to children's story-writing than to their other writing and this can affect the attention paid by adults in fostering development. The language co-ordinator quoted earlier found that most writing outside story occured within topics and that it was not sufficiently supported. However, the scope for writing has increased and there has been some exciting development within many classrooms.

For children in the early years, shared writing has already been mentioned as a way of modelling writing and drawing on their own experiences to create texts, but this technique has other uses. In a reception class, a 'big book' was created to function as a class diary. Each day the date was written, with discussion about the order of days of the week, the months and ordinal numbers. The day was reviewed and items selected for inclusion in the diary, the teacher modelling writing for the children. The events recorded were not only those experienced within the classroom, but extended beyond to the local community:

John's mum had her baby yesterday and he is going to see his new sister tonight;
Carlie's Dad crashed his car but he is not hurt;
Kamran's family are celebrating the end of Ramadan;
Lots of children went with their parents to vote in the junior school yesterday.

Besides becoming a reading and writing resource the diary helped to create an atmosphere of community within the class, with respect for the similarities and differences in the children's lives inside and outside school. This relates to the 'dimensions' of the National Curriculum, 'treating pupils as individuals with their own abilities, attitudes, backgrounds and experiences' (National Curriculum Council, 1992, p.15), and the theme of education for citizenship, which is still of importance in the revised curriculum.

Writing within different genres

The class diary provides the experience of writing within a particular genre.

'Genre' is a term used in literacy pedagogy to connect the different forms text take with variations in social purpose. Texts are different because they do different things.
(Cope and Kalantzis, 1993, p.7)

This provision of experience within a range of writing styles and purposes is funda-mental to AT3, the revised orders reflecting the need to explore form and function even at Key Stage 1 where pupils 'should be taught to write in a range of forms, incorporating some of the different characteristics of those forms' (DFE, 1995, p.9). Teachers are reviewing how they are supporting children to cope effectively with this breadth of writing. This will help to clarify issues raised in the current debate about how explicitly different genres should be 'taught'. The work of Halliday (1978) and Kress (1992) has suggested a need to deal much more systematically with children's writing within different genres:

> The child has to gain mastery [*sic*] over the forms and the possibilities of the different generic types, as part of the process of learning to write. The different genres each make their own demands in terms of their formal structures, their ordering of thematic material, their conception of knowledge.
> (Kress, 1992, p.100)

But there is a fear that approaches to diverse genres will become formularized and stifle children's creative exploration of genres (Barrs, 1991), and publishers have already produced many resources for dealing with forms of writing through textbook tasks. Completing exercises on decontextualized text is a very different experience from writing for audiences other than the teacher, for real communication. Meanwhile, many teachers *have* found ways of exploring genre in context.

With older children, the creation of a class newspaper has been used for collaborative writing and for exploring style and audience. Children read and discussed some national and local newspapers, gathering information on what might be included in their own paper. They examined the ways language was used in headlines, advertisements, sports reports and horoscopes, concentrating on choices of words, grammatical structures and differing styles between papers, before allocating roles and creating their own paper. This involved reflecting in their own writing the stylistic devices they had studied. Desk-top publishing packages allowed for authentic presentation, although handwriting on paper divided into columns was also effective.

In writing stories there has often been an expectation that children should write from imagination, and recounting known stories in 'creative writing' was often thought to reflect a 'lack of imagination' or 'ability' in the children. But interviews with published adult authors invariably lead them to discuss the *influences* on their writing. It becomes apparent that, far from plucking ideas from the air, they are influenced by other stories they have read or heard, their own family, friends and experiences, all mingle with the imagination to create something new. Robert Westall, for instance, drew on his own experience of living in Tyneside as a child in the war, his interest in 'the way children can wriggle through the chinks in adult pretence', plus a newspaper article he read about some Dutch children who found a machine gun in 1969 and the 'fact that one night in 1941 some people on Tyneside really thought the German invasion had begun' to create his story *The Machine Gunners* (Westall, 1975).

Graves (1983), Calkins (1983) and Rosen (1989) have stressed the importance of children writing from their own experience, and Fox (1993) has demonstrated the impact of children's experience of literature on story. The storying in television and film, plus the broader general knowledge acquired from watching television, also appear in children's stories, reflecting their enjoyment in recalling storylines of favourite programmes (Buckingham, 1993, p. 31). Fox, however, found that television-influenced stories lacked the structural strength of book-influenced stories which, she felt reflected the 'repeatable' nature of book experience.

Teachers capitalize on children's own experiences and retellings of known stories to create foundations for expanding writing experience, moving into other genres. These draw also on the broader knowledge children have of literacy. For instance, in a history-based topic, to help children to empathize with the Roman soldiers invading Britain, a teacher drew on the children's own experiences of going somewhere new, such as changing classes, moving to the juniors, joining Brownies or Woodcraft or moving house. They read literature which covered similar themes: *Grace and Family* by Mary

Hoffman (1995), *Gaffer Samson's Luck* by Jill Paton Walsh (1984), *The Little Princess* by Frances Hodgson Burnett (1907) and discussed characters' responses. These provided further material for writing and reflection.

The old orthodoxy of writing in an exercise book for the approval of the teacher has gone, but in some cases has been replaced by a 'new orthodoxy' of writing within the extended developmental model of:

- plan
- draft
- revise
- proof-read
- present
  (DFE, 1995, p.15)

However, the rewriting of drafts with no real development and reflection on content ignores the potential for growth that discussion, review and revision can play, both in writing and language study generally, and which is required in AT3. In classrooms where teachers are encouraging children to match approach to purpose and audience, children select the most appropriate strategy for writing. Some tasks will be in note form or lists and will be developed no further; some, such as reading logs and journals, will be written once and not revised unless extracts are required to be used for wider audiences. This may occur, for example, when a book review is published for others to read, or simply for personal gratification. More complex tasks or texts produced for a wider audience than the writer and teacher, (e.g. letters to be sent to others or stories for publication in class books) will necessitate going through the full process described above.

A teacher in South London whose class was involved in a project at the British Film Institute decided to focus not only on the films watched, but on the whole experience of being in a cinema as part of an audience. The children wrote about the anticipation of what they were to see, buying popcorn, the tiered seats and the moment when the lights went down. They contrasted the cinema with live theatre, writing about the eye contact made in the theatre and the desire to applaud. The sharing of experience was important, but it was essentially personal writing, although carefully crafted to satisfy each child's desire to encapsulate the experience.

Children can be supported in setting appropriate goals for their writing when the criteria for any writing task are made explicit. In Wiltshire, one school introduced 'reflections on learning' books for children to use, a development of earlier 'think books' for planning writing. Before the children started writing, the particular learning aims for the task were considered with the children, making explicit the criteria for success. After the task was completed, the children reviewed their writing, both process and product, reflecting on what they had achieved and where they needed support. These books encouraged self-awareness and ownership of the learning process and informed the teachers' own assessments.

Although redrafting text on the word-processor is relatively simple, the common current provision of one or two computers for a class means that individual use is restricted, so teachers are introducing similar techniques for developing writing on paper, including

- using the insertion symbol (^) to add words and phrases;

- using asterisks to insert short pieces of text;
- cutting and pasting the first draft onto fresh sheets of paper to make space for longer revisions without having to rewrite the whole text.

In developing stories with children one teacher in Southwark stops when they have completed the openings of the stories. These openings are shared as a class and then each child talks about the action which will take place, the main thrust of the story. Children are encouraged to challenge each other's thinking and comment critically, always picking up on positive aspects to praise before adding constructive criticism or asking questions. It is at this stage that substantial development of language takes place, with children themselves spotting long streams of writing (. . . and then . . .) which could benefit from revision. Repetition of basic verbs to describe action, such as 'went' and 'said' is spotted and alternatives discussed. Exploring alternative language to use serves to highlight the subtleties of meaning which can be obtained by substituting one word for another. For example, 'strolled', 'dawdled' or 'tiptoed' instead of 'went' or 'ran'. Inevitably, someone suggests an adverb instead of a verb, and the way adverbs qualify the action of verbs is explored and introduced into writing within a real context, rather than a decontextualized exercise.

> Pupils should be given opportunities to reflect on their use of language . . . to develop their understanding of the grammar of complex sentences . . . to distinguish between words of similar meaning, to explain the meanings of words and to experiment with choices of vocabulary. Their interest in words should be extended by the discussion of language use and choices.
> (DFE, 1995, p.16)

Of course, none of this is quite as *ad hoc* as the example above suggests; the teacher will take up issues raised by the children, but will also operate within a cohesive plan of what is appropriate to cover in a particular year or term. So, in working on the content and quality of the children's writing through revision, and peer group review or conferences with the teacher, aspects of language study are also introduced. The editing stage provides further opportunities for language study, perhaps with some taught sessions on particular aspects, such as when to start a new paragraph. Thus, in editing their own work, alone or with support, children are practising what has been taught.

Spelling and handwriting, besides being addressed through the editing and presentation of curriculum work, are also developed as 'continuing units' away from the site of composition. The teaching of skills to enable each child to write with a fast fluent hand will free him/her to concentrate on creating meanings. As an example, spellings are learned every week in one London school, but lists are taken from the words misspelt by the children during the preceding week. The number learned by different children may vary according to their needs, and time is set aside daily for them to learn the spellings by writing, using and identifying patterns or rules which may help. The time in school for learning was felt to be particularly important in this school where not all children were supported at home, because of parents' own learning difficulties, lack of time, or where parents were not fluent English speakers. The children were tested by the teacher or other children, and if appropriate goals had been set, this was a positive experience. This approach had been developed as the learning of ten spellings for every child from one list created inevitable failure for many children, and the words were not always those the children would all want to use. Spelling was also taught outside the tests through learning rules, identifying patterns and through focusing on word origins through books such as *The Speller's Companion* (Brown and Brown, 1987). The children were fascinated by etymology – the roots of words – and morphemic units such as prefixes and suffixes kindled interest in words.

Besides enhancing children's knowledge about language structures and uses, such methods of working also provide opportunities to work on the 'Themes' and 'Dimensions' of the National Curriculum, which are so often lost in the content-led curriculum. Andrews (1994) uses the example of the word *soldier*, for example, which is used extensively within the coverage of history topics, to demonstrate how the terms used create different images, from '*hero, patriot, freedom fighter*', to '*terrorist, killer, aggressor*'. Analysis of the impact of the language used helps to deconstruct or challenge '*myths, stereotypes and misconceptions*' (National Curriculum Council, 1992) and to explore the use of propaganda through the power of language.

Assessing and recording of writing

Assessment of writing had been effectively addressed in the National Writing Project (1989), providing excellent ways of looking at text. This had led to some useful practices in schools. Unfortunately the SATs have set back practice in schools through the counting of full stops and sentences engaged in through agreement trialling, where schools tried to match children's writing to level descriptors. The annotated samples of writing kept by teachers *have* been useful, and will continue. The headings on the Primary Language Record writing sample sheets (Centre for Language in Primary Education, 1988) or the National Writing Project (1989) formats are helpful in suggesting what might need to be recorded. However, writing samples which show the full range of a child's writing soon amass, becoming bulky to store and time-consuming to administer. The SCAA advice in the 1995 Assessment Arrangements (SCAA, 1994) reiterated Dearing's call for teacher assessment to have enhanced weighting. Teachers are regaining the confidence to trust to their own, dated, observations: the 'evidence' can be the teacher's informed observations on the writing process and product, and not always or only the 'product' itself.

CONCLUSION

The revised orders, then, are an opportunity to take stock and review current practice, rejecting any practices slipped into as survival tactics during the initial introductory years of the National Curriculum. Taking stock will mean identifying resource and staff development needs for English and revising or creating policies and schemes of work for English. Jerome Harste, speaking at the United Kingdom Reading Association conference in 1992, said that he was very impressed by the wonderful books for children in the bookshops in the UK, but when he visited the schools, although they seemed to 'have every tool imaginable for cutting things in two and putting them back together', he could not see the wealth of books he would have expected. Funding has had to concentrate on the major and often costly resourcing needed to implement the full curriculum, but English co-ordinators have to set firm goals for resourcing language and literacy development. Above all, it is vital to bear in mind that the revised orders, although *in situ* until the turn of the century, must still be questioned and evaluated, so that in 2001 we can implement the changes which will inevitably be required to meet the needs of children in the twenty-first century.

REFERENCES

Alexander, R., Rose, J. and Woodhead, C. (1992) *Curriculum Organisation and Classroom Practice in Primary Schools*. London: DES.

Andrews, R. (1994) *International Dimensions in the National Curriculum*. Stoke-on-Trent: Trentham Books.

Ashley, B. (1981) *Dinner Ladies Don't Count*. Harmondsworth: Penguin.

Avon LEA (1994) *The Collaborative Reading Approach: Talking and Thinking about Reading*. Bristol: County of Avon.

Baddeley P. and Eddershaw, C. (1994) *Not So Simple Picture Books*. Stoke-on-Trent: Trentham Books.

Barrs, M. (1991) Genre theory: what's it all about?. In *Language Matters 1*. London: CLPE.

Barrs, M. *et al.*, (1988) *The Primary Language Record Handbook*. London: CLPE.

Bazalgette, C. (1991) *Media Education*. London: Hodder and Stoughton.

Briggs, R. (1978) *The Snowman*. London: Hamish Hamilton.

Brown, G. and Wragg, E.C. (1993) *Questioning*. London: Routledge.

Brown, H. and Brown, R. (1987) *The Speller's Companion*. Cumbria: Brown and Brown.

Bryce-Heath, S. (1983) *Ways With Words*. Cambridge: Cambridge University Press.

Buckingham, D. (1993) *Children Talking Television: The Making of Television Literacy*. London: Falmer Press.

Calkins, L. (1983) *Lessons from a Child*. Portsmouth, New Hampshire: Heinemann.

Carter, R. (ed.) (1990) *Knowledge about Language and the Curriculum: The LINC Reader*. London: Hodder and Stoughton.

Centre for Language in Primary Education (CLPE) (1988) *The Primary Language Record*. London: CLPE.

Chambers, A. (1993) *Tell Me: Children Reading and Talking*. Stroud: The Thimble Press.

Clark, M. (1976) *Young Fluent Readers*. London: Heinemann.

Clay, M. (1979) *Reading: The Patterning of Complex Behaviour*. London: Heinemann.

Clay, M. (1993) *Reading Recovery*. Auckland: Heinemann.

Collington, P. (1987) *The Angel and the Soldier Boy*. London: Methuen.

Collins (1987) *Bookbus*. London: Collins.

Cooper, S. (1973) *The Dark is Rising*. London: Chatto and Windus.

Cope, B. and Kalantzis, M. (1993) *The Powers of Literacy: A Genre Approach to Teaching Writing*. London: Falmer Press.

Czerniewska, P. (1992) *Learning about Writing*. London: Blackwell.

DES (1975) *A Language for Life*. London: HMSO (Bullock Report).

DES (1992) *English at Key Stages 1,2 and 3: A Report by HM Inspectorate on the Second Year, 1990–91*. London: HMSO.

DES and Welsh Office (1988) *English for Ages 5 to 11*. London: DES and Welsh Office.

DFE (1995) *Key Stages 1 and 2 of the National Curriculum*. London: HMSO.

Edwards, D. and Mercer, N. (1987) *Common Knowledge: The Development of Understanding in the Classroom*. London: Methuen.

Ferreiro, E. and Teberosky, A. (1982) *Literacy Before Schooling*. Exeter, New Hampshire: Heinemann.

Fox, C. (1993) *At the Very Edge of the Forest: The Influence of Literature on Storytelling by Children*. London: Cassell.

Gibson, H. (1994) Temporality and texts: children's lists. *Reading*, **28**. (3), November 1994.

Ginn (1994) *Flying Boot*. London: Ginn.

Goodman, Y. (1990) The development of initial literacy. In Carter, R. (ed.) (1990).

Graves, D. (1983) *Writing: Teachers and Children at Work*. London: Heinemann.

Halliday, M. (1978) *Language as Social Semiotic: The Social Interpretation of Language and Meaning.* London: Edward Arnold.

Harste, J., Woodward, V. and Burke, C. (1984) *Language Stories and Literacy Lessons.* Exeter, New Hampshire: Heinemann.

HMI (1990) *The Teaching and Learning of Language and Literacy.* London: HMSO.

HMI (1992) *The Teaching and Learning of Reading in Primary Schools 1991.* London: DES.

Hoffman, M. (1995) *Grace and Family.* London: Frances Lincoln.

Holdaway, D. (1979) *The Foundations of Literacy.* Sydney: Ashton Scholastic.

Howe, A. (1992) *Making Talk Work.* London: Hodder and Stoughton.

Hutchins, P. (1972) *Goodnight Owl.* London: Penguin.

Kress, G. (1992) *Learning to Write.* London: Routledge.

Lewis, C. S. (1950) *The Lion, The Witch and the Wardrobe.* Harmondsworth: Puffin (Penguin).

Mallett, M. (1992) *Making Facts Matter: Reading Non-Fiction 5–11.* London: Paul Chapman.

Meek, M. (1988) *How Texts Teach What Readers Learn.* Stroud: The Thimble Press.

Meek, M. (1991) *On Being Literate.* London: The Bodley Head.

Moore, P. (1994) Authoring. *English in Education,* **28** (3), Autumn 1994.

Mortimore, P., Sammons, P., Stoll, L., Lewis, D. and Ecob, R. (1988) *School Matters: The Junior Years.* Somerset: Open Books Publishing.

National Curriculum Council (1992) *An Introduction to the National Curriculum.* York: NCC.

National Writing Project (1989) *Responding to and Assessing Writing.* Walton-on Thames: Nelson.

Neate, B. (1992) *Finding Out About Finding Out.* London: UKRA/Hodder & Stoughton.

Norman, K. (1990) *Teaching Talking and Learning at Key Stage One.* York: National Curriculum Council/National Oracy Project.

Norman, K. (1992) *Thinking Voices.* London: Hodder & Stoughton.

Ormerod, J. (1981) *Sunshine.* London: Penguin.

Ormerod, J. (1982) *Moonlight.* Harmondsworth: Penguin.

Phinney, M. (1988) *Reading with the Troubled Reader.* Ontario: Ashton Scholastic.

Rosen, M. (1989) *Did I Hear You Write?* London: Andre Deutsch.

School Curriculum and Assessment Authority (SCAA) (1994) *Key Stage 1 Assessment Arrangements 1995.* London: SCAA.

School Curriculum and Assessment Authority (SCAA) (1995) *Planning the Curriculum At Key Stages 1 and 2.* London: SCAA.

Shortland (1983) *Storychest.* Auckland, New Zealand: Shortland.

Shortland (1993) *Literacy Links.* Auckland, New Zealand: Shortland.

Smith F. (1988) *Joining the Literacy Club.* London: Heinemann.

Swann, J. (1992) *Girls, Boys and Language.* Oxford: Blackwell.

Tizard, B. and Hughes, J. (1984) *Young Children Learning.* London: Fontana.

Turner, M. (1992) *Sponsored Reading Failure: An Object Lesson.* Warlingham: IPSET Education Unit.

Webb, K. (1986) *I Like This Story.* Harmondsworth: Penguin.

Wells, G. (1986) *The Meaning Makers.* London: Hodder and Stoughton.

Wells, R. (1978) *Noisy Nora.* Harmondsworth: Puffin.

Westall, R. (1975) *The Machine Gunners.* London: Macmillan.

Westall, R. (1990) *The Kingdom by the Sea.* London: Methuen.

Wiltshire LEA (1993) *From Policy to Practice.* Trowbridge: Wiltshire LEA.

Wilson, J. (1992) *The Suitcase Kid.* London: Transworld.

Chapter 7

Implementing Mathematics in the National Curriculum

Ruth Barrington

INTRODUCTION

Since the introduction of the National Curriculum for mathematics, primary schools have developed their mathematics curriculum in a variety of different ways. This chapter examines how two schools have implemented the National Curriculum for mathematics at Key Stage 1 and Key Stage 2: the policies they have derived for planning, teaching, progression, assessment and record-keeping.

The schools used as case-studies are Abbotswood Infants School, Yate, near Bristol, and Bleakhouse Junior School, Oldbury, Warley, West Midlands. Both schools have a two-form entry. In the infant school there are six class teachers and five general assistants in addition to the head teacher. The junior school has eight class teachers, and a special needs teacher and a deputy head who provide group and class-based support in addition to the headteacher. The infants school provides three distinct contexts in which mathematics is taught and the children are grouped according to the demands of the activity. In the junior school children are set across the year group and an additional teacher is available so that three separate mathematics classes are formed. In both the case-study schools the organization varies according to the activity and the needs of the children and includes whole-class teaching, group work and individual work.

A mathematics policy should indicate the overall aims identified by the staff for the teaching of mathematics. In order to be an effective policy the views identified within it must be reflected in classroom practice throughout the school. Where all staff have been involved in discussions leading to the writing and reviewing of the policy, they will have ownership of the policy and will therefore be in a stronger position to understand the intentions and implement the policy in the classroom. An effective policy will therefore have a major influence upon the way mathematics is taught in the school. It will need to be reviewed and updated regularly. In both case-study schools the mathematics policy was written prior to the National Curriculum and was subsequently reviewed by the staff and updated in the light of the 1995 orders.

AIMS FOR TEACHING MATHEMATICS

The first point to be considered is the overall purpose for teaching mathematics. Chapter 3 in this book identifies three main reasons:

Mathematics offers life skills which are essential within education, employment and everyday life.

The subject is a prominent part of the culture and helps us understand and describe the world we live in.

Mathematics trains the mind by offering an approach to problem-solving.

The importance attributed to each of the above differs between different interest groups, but the priority which a school gives to a particular reason will have an influence on approaches to teaching and on the content of the curriculum in the classroom.

CHILDREN'S ATTITUDES TO MATHEMATICS AND SELF-ESTEEM

Children need a positive attitude and a confident approach towards mathematics. Their early experiences will have a major effect on their attitude towards the subject throughout their lives. Each time a child is involved in mathematics it will have a cumulative effect on his or her view of mathematics. This in turn will have a major effect on motivation and the ability to think mathematically both in the classroom and outside. The teacher needs to be aware of this, not only in the planning of activities, but also in the creation of an appropriate classroom atmosphere.

The policy for mathematics at Key Stage 2 in the junior school pays particular attention to the child's self-esteem, stating that

to enable children to learn effectively there needs to be an atmosphere which inspires interest and confidence, for with confidence will come the ability to think independently and logically whilst retaining flexibility of approach.
(Bleakhouse Junior School, 1995)

Adults and children learn most effectively in an atmosphere where they are confident that they can say what they think without fear of criticism or ridicule. When children feel safe within the classroom environment they will be more ready to test out and share their thinking without fear of being reprimanded.

Children's attitude towards the subject is determined by how they perceive themselves working in the subject area. The teacher is in a position to have an effect on children's attitude by securing a suitable learning environment and by providing a variety of stimulating work presented to the child at an appropriate level. This is set out in the junior school's policy:

An enthusiastic attitude can be achieved through a varied diet. Well structured schemes of work, which offer a wide range of experiences and clear stages of progression, whilst enabling children to enquire, experiment and investigate should result in a clearer understanding of mathematics.
(Bleakhouse Junior School, 1995)

The teacher needs to be aware that it is not just the planning and presenting of activities that can have such an effect. It is also how the teacher responds to work the child produces which effects his/her attitude. The teacher is in a position to be able to communicate to the child how much the child's contribution is valued, in written or oral work.

The range of experience that children should receive is recommended in the Cockcroft Report:

Mathematics teaching at all levels should include opportunities for

- exposition by the teacher;
- discussion between teacher and pupils and between pupils themselves;
- appropriate practical work;
- consolidation and practice of fundamental skills and routines;
- problem solving, including the application of mathematics to everyday situations;
- investigational work.

(Committee of Inquiry into the Teaching of Mathematics in Schools, 1982, para. 243)

EXPOSITION BY THE TEACHER

Exposition refers to the teacher's explanations and commentary in guiding understanding. This will not be a one-way process as the teacher needs to elicit responses from the children in order to check that the child has understood. Discussion between teacher and pupils and between pupils themselves is a sharing process involving verbal exchange of ideas with others. For the child in the classroom this will involve discussion with his/her peers and discussion with the teacher. The teacher should pay attention to the classroom atmosphere and create a safe environment for children to exchange ideas. He/she will need to encourage the children to respect and to support each other and to plan strategies to create the desired environment. One strategy is to create situations which encourage children to support each other, such as asking a child to provide positive comment on another child's contribution. A further example would be for the teacher to lead discussion with the children focusing on how they like to be treated by others.

Discussion between children is an important tool with which children can clarify their own thinking, perhaps putting forward newly formed ideas to check that perceptions are accurate and make sense. It also provides a forum for listening to other children's ideas and views in order to gain a different perspective. Through discussion a child may gain a clearer understanding of a particular concept. A child's explanation in the child's words can sometimes make more sense to another child than an adult commentary.

Where children are set a task that involves them working collaboratively and sharing ideas they are likely to reach a more effective solution than working individually, as they will be able to build upon the ideas of others as well as their own ideas. Also the teacher will be able to use discussion as a means of interjecting new terminology and at times will want to provide situations which will encourage the use of certain terminology.

> By the careful introduction and development of mathematical language and the recognition that this plays an essential part in the formulation and expression of mathematical ideas and problems.
> (Abbotswood Infants School, 1995)

Sometimes the vocabulary that is being introduced may be familiar to the child, but it may have a different meaning in everyday usage compared with its mathematical meaning. For instance, an understanding of *difference* in everyday usage may lead a child to respond to a question such as *What is the difference between 4 and 6?* by replying that one of the numbers is odd and the other one is even, or that the 4 is made up of straight lines and the 6 is made up of curved lines. In mathematics *difference* refers to a comparison between the value of two numbers.

Through listening to discussion between children, the teacher will be able to assess a child's understanding, intervening if appropriate, as well as using it as an opportunity to assess the effectiveness of the activity. In the example below, children are encouraged to use the term *difference* by providing an opportunity for pairs of children to talk in a mathematical context. It is important that children experience using mathematical language through speaking mathematically and that the concept is clarified by the child.

> *A game for four children working as two pairs*
>
> You need: Four sets of number cards containing numbers 1 to 8.
>
> All cards are laid on the table face down.
>
> Each player takes it in turns to turn over two cards.
>
> Where the two revealed cards has a difference of 4, then the player keeps the pair and turns over a further pair of cards.
>
> Where the two cards do not give a difference of 4 the next player has their turn.

The above activity encourages discussion between children as they are asked to work together in pairs. Through listening to the ensuing discussion from the children the teacher is able to see whether the activity has been effective in encouraging the children to use the mathematical term *difference* in an appropriate context. In addition it gives the teacher the opportunity to assess their knowledge of subtraction and also to note any change in their speed of recall through carrying out the activity.

The teacher needs to be aware of adjustments that can be made to activities which can have a significant effect upon the amount of mathematical talk required from the children. For instance, if the activity had been a game for two children working individually it would not encourage the same amount of mathematical talk, but it would have involved quiet contemplation by the individuals concerned.

PRACTICAL WORK

Cockcroft (1982) emphasizes that it is essential to draw on practical work throughout the primary years. In order to help a child to think mathematically a teacher will need to encourage the child to draw upon practical work as one of a number of tools that are available to help simplify a problem, or to assist understanding. Practical work needs to be built into the policy and reflected in the planning of the mathematics curriculum at both Key Stages. For instance, the junior school policy states that:

> Practical work in all areas of mathematics, both in initial stages in understanding concepts and later in their application, is vital.
> (Bleak House Junior School, 1995)

There may be some reticence about the use of practical resources among children at the upper end of Key Stage 2. Where there is such resistance it is usually because the pupils associate the use of apparatus with play in the younger age-ranges. It is important that these associations are challenged by teachers and that children are encouraged to use apparatus when required. At any age it is important when any new piece of apparatus is introduced that there is some opportunity for children to play with and explore the property of the apparatus. Reference has already been made to what the teacher communicates to the child as being of value. One way that the teacher can support the status of practical work is by example, drawing upon practical apparatus in order to solve mathematical problems herself. Another way is to ensure that all children are encouraged to draw upon apparatus where appropriate, rather than allowing it to be perceived as for the lower attainers only.

CONSOLIDATION AND PRACTICE

Activities can be presented in a range of different ways in order to allow children to consolidate their mathematics. Consolidation and practice refer to all aspects of the mathematics curriculum. At Key Stage 1, for number, children will need to focus on 'developing and reinforcing skills of both written and mental calculations' (Abbotswood Infants School, 1995). This is supported by the non-statutory guidance which was given with the original National Curriculum Mathematics Order of 1989 (National Curriculum Council, 1989) which refers to the teacher providing a balance between drawing upon children's own methods of calculating, using the calculator and applying more formal methods as well as supporting children's idiosyncratic written methods.

In order to give children such opportunities there can be a place for drawing on materials within a commercial scheme or using a worksheet, but there is often greater potential within other contexts. One particularly effective way of practising skills that a child has newly learned, and of strengthening those that they already possess, is through the use of mathematical games. For example, number games focusing on number bonds would provide an opportunity for children to increase the speed at which they can recall these number bonds. A game provides a motivating context which can often encourage the children to carry out far more calculations than might have been achieved through being given a worksheet of 'sums' to complete.

PROBLEM-SOLVING: THE APPLICATION OF MATHEMATICS TO EVERYDAY SITUATIONS

Problem-solving provides a mathematical context and gives children the opportunity to apply their mathematical skills and concepts to a new situation. It is important to consider what is meant by problem-solving as it can be portrayed in different ways. In some commercial mathematics books it is often presented in the form of verbal problems. These incorporate computations hidden in sentences, such as: 'John has 5 sweets and Sarah gives him 3 more sweets. How many sweets does John have altogether?' In order to be successful a child would need to make a correct choice of operations (addition) before carrying out the calculation. This type of activity requires much support from the teacher, particularly in the early stages. The activity places more demands on the children's reading and understanding than on their ability to calculate accurately. As the purpose of such an activity is really to select the correct operation rather than to work out a computation, it is appropriate for children to work together to encourage them to talk about the problem and to have a calculator available. It is particularly frustrating to children to have carried out a calculation only to find that they have selected the wrong operation.

It is helpful if the child can relate to the problem that is being posed. In order to be a valuable exercise the problem would need to be solved in practice rather than just be an abstract problem. An example which would not be particularly relevant to most primary-aged children would be if they were asked to work out how much wallpaper they would need to decorate a room. This is irrelevant to most children of this age, since it is unlikely to be a problem that they will be expected to carry out and therefore lacks a satisfactory conclusion. The starting-point for the most effective problems to be solved will come from the children identifying the problem. There are many aspects of the school day and school environment which might provide a useful focus for a problem-solving activity. These could include how the tuck shop is organized, how children move around the school, the organization of resources, the school disco. The playground and the school field can often be improved to the benefit of children and staff through giving children time to focus on the problem and to suggest changes and follow these through into practice.

These examples will be carried out most effectively by a group and the context will provide them with meaningful opportunity to discuss and co-operate. Children will require sufficient time to think through the problem, talk through solutions and carry out the task, so problem-solving is rarely a short activity. The teacher's role is crucial in deciding when to intervene, depending upon individual children's participation in the group and on their prior experience. Problem-solving gives children the opportunity to experience mathematics in an everyday context and to use appropriate skills and strategies such as those identified within the 'Using and Applying' Programme of Study in the National Curriculum.

One of the roles of the teacher is to give children the opportunity to gain the necessary tools which will equip them to be able to tackle problems effectively in everyday life as an adult. This view is reflected at Key Stage 1 where the school's policy states that

> children should be encouraged to develop concepts and skills which help them to understand and solve the many mathematical problems which present themselves in everyday life.
>
> (Abbotswood Infants School, 1994)

In addition to stressing the importance of preparing children to be able to tackle mathematical problems in everyday life, the policy also indicates the place that mathematics fulfils in supporting other subjects. This aspect will be discussed more fully later in this chapter.

INVESTIGATIONAL WORK

Chapter 3 in this book cites Papert's (1972) view that children should learn how to be mathematicians rather than be taught mathematics. Through an investigation a child has such an opportunity to experience *being a mathematician* rather than merely learning about mathematics. The Programme of Study section, Using and Applying Mathematics, in the National Curriculum gives an indication of the strategies and process skills which a mathematician would need to draw upon in order to be doing mathematics. It is interacting with mathematics which enables the child to experience *being a mathematician*. It is an active process of learning about mathematics through exploration which is essential for a child to experience.

An investigation gives children the opportunity to apply the knowledge that they have gained. The focus of an investigation is likely to be related to a question about mathematics itself. An investigation may be short, or it may be an extended piece of work, but its focus is based upon encouraging children's fascination with mathematics, the puzzling over mathematics for its own sake and the development of mathematical strategies. The teacher's role will need to include careful monitoring of the children's progress.

Many publishers produce a range of investigational ideas for the teacher, but there are plenty of opportunities for the teacher or the child to formulate an open question which can be used as an initial stimulus for an investigation. Such comments as 'What would happen if . . . ?' or 'How many other ways are there?' could be the starting-point of such an investigation. For instance, a closed task would be 'Make a cube by drawing and cutting out its net on card.' If the task was altered to ask whether there were a number of different ways a net of a cube could be produced it would give the children greater opportunity to explore their spatial awareness as well as giving greater scope for developing skills and strategies associated with mathematical thinking, such as encouraging them to work systematically.

GAMES

Both case-study schools emphasize the important role which games can play:

> By providing pupils with opportunities to select specific games from a library of resources which are intended to develop skills, strategies and logical thinking, as well as practising number facts with speed and accuracy.
> (Abbotswood Infants School, 1995)

Mathematical games should be used to assist children's learning at all ages and at all levels of attainment. It is vital that mathematics is seen in a context rather than in a detached and disembedded way (Donaldson, 1978). Games provide a context for mathematics which, if appropriately introduced, do encourage the interest and motivation required by children. They are particularly helpful for encouraging speed of recall of number facts. They give children the opportunity to practise and consolidate with a purpose. For example the following board layout can be used by a pair of children:

5	7	4	11	9
7	12	18	3	7
13	10	3	6	5
8	12	14	16	1
5	15	2	13	18
11	9	6	14	8
9	1	15	18	10

A game for 2 players

You need: one base board as above, three dice and two differently coloured counters.

Three dice are thrown by the first player.

The player must use the numbers which are uppermost on the dice to compute a number, which is on the board. Any of the operations ($+ - \times \div$) can be used.

This number must be explained to the other player. The number can then be covered by the player's counter.

The game is complete when one player has 4 counters in a vertical, horizontal or diagonal line.

Through examples such as this children can increase their speed of mental recall. In order to carry out the above activity the pair would be involved in many calculations prior to selecting the optimum one for themselves. This particular example also gives the opportunity for children to play with numbers and provides a context for discovering how numbers relate to each other. For instance they may discover that $2 + 3 + 4 = 9$ and so does $3 + 2 + 4$, which could later support their broader understanding of the associative law. The use of the computer can provide a further context for development of mathematically based games.

PLANNING METHODS: INTEGRATED THEMES OR DISCRETE SUBJECTS

It is valuable to consider how different parts of the mathematics curriculum can be most effectively presented to children. There is much debate concerning teaching mathematics through using a thematic approach or by teaching it as a discrete subject. In terms of mathematics there are advantages and disadvantages in each approach. It would seem more appropriate to plan by drawing upon the strengths of each option rather than limiting the potential of either possibility. Either approach could provide the starting-point for planning purposes, but both approaches will need to be drawn upon if mathematics is to be taught effectively.

The topic or thematic approach encourages a more holistic view of the curriculum rather than compartmentalizing subject areas. This can provide a more relevant curriculum for the child (see Chapter 5). However, the chosen themes are often selected to be based upon a history, geography or science focus rather than mathematics and as a result it is unlikely that sufficient mathematics would be covered by teaching it through topic alone. It can also result in a rather tenuous link between mathematics and the topic.

Starting from a thematic approach seems to lend itself more easily to mathematics at Key Stage 1. The thematic approach does assist with placing mathematics in context, although often the context can be in terms of providing the setting for a game or investigation. For instance, a topic on Transport could lend itself to a range of opportunities to focus on early number work, such as making collections of a certain number of cars, lorries, cycles, buses on the road between certain times. It would also lend itself to measuring how far different toy cars travelled. Various stories could also be drawn upon with a transport theme as a starting-point for mathematical activity. In most cases it will be the presentation which relates to the theme rather than the concept itself. It is unlikely that it will be possible to attribute all the mathematics taught within a given term to one particular topic without extremely tenuous links. It would be appropriate to plan parts of the mathematics curriculum which most realistically relate to the term's theme. However, in order to ensure complete coverage of the mathematics curriculum, there needs to be a place for planning mathematics as a discrete subject as well.

The change of emphasis to an initial focus on mathematics as a discrete subject can assist with a focus on the mathematical skills and concepts which need to be taught and the planning can concentrate on ensuring that links between different aspects of mathematics are considered. It is important to bear in mind that mathematics requires a child to make these links between different aspects of the subject and that this can be supported with carefully focused planning. Where mathematics is planned through a topic there can be a tendency to skim the surface of the subject rather than focusing upon a particular concept or skill in sufficient detail. Although some mathematics will be taught through links with topic, the focus should be on providing adequate coverage of the mathematical concepts.

The National Curriculum is organized into Programmes of Study sections which can lead to an apparent compartmentalizing of the subject. This form of planning supports the integration of these sections. There is a rationale for the selection of topic mathematics chosen for each year group. The amalgamation of the two approaches is supported in the guidance on long-term planning which is provided by SCAA (1995). The document focuses upon overall planning of the whole curriculum and identifies two broad categories in terms of planning. The first refers to 'continuing work' which

- requires regular and frequent teaching and assessment to be planned across a year or key stage to ensure progression;
- contains a progressive sequence of learning objectives;
- requires time for the systematic and gradual acquisition, practice and consolidation of skills, knowledge and understanding.
  (SCAA, 1995, p.40)

The second broad category is termed 'blocked work' which

- can be taught within a specific amount of time, not exceeding a term;
- focuses on a distinct and cohesive body of knowledge, understanding and skills;
- can be taught alone or have the potential for linking with units of work in other subjects or aspects of the curriculum.
  (SCAA, 1995, p.15)

In both cases the work can be taken from one subject or one part of the curriculum and it is recommended that, where possible, links should be planned between different parts of the curriculum and between different subjects. In terms of planning, the links between subject areas are emphasized through considering the thematic approach. These aspects were clearly identified as continuing units of work. Where appropriate, the decision as to when to teach a particular part of number (including algebra) and time are planned by the teacher, drawing on his/her own judgement of the children's needs and comprehensive record-keeping.

A block of work in terms of mathematics is taken to mean a mathematical focus which can be taken and taught in isolation for a set period of time. It is a distinct body of knowledge for the purpose of planning work. It must, however, be remembered that any aspect of mathematics is actually part of a whole picture of mathematics. One example would be that of symmetry where there is an element of completeness within a symmetry topic, but it contributes to a broader understanding of shape and space.

In terms of planning, both case study schools recognize the importance of planning across the curriculum. The focus in each school is to provide thorough coverage of the mathematics curriculum and to plan the most appropriate means to ensure that this occurs. In both schools during any term there will be a link between mathematics and a topic teaching mathematics, as well as discrete subject teaching where appropriate. But the infant school begins its planning from a topic and the junior school focuses upon the discrete subject as the starting-point.

PLANNING METHODS: KEY STAGE 1

Within the infants school the staff initially focus on the topic and produce a topic web. From here the mathematics which would come from the topic can be clearly identified. Each topic lasts for one term. The key stage topic planning encompasses Years 1 and 2, so six topics are planned overall. The mathematics is then considered in terms of the National Curriculum. To ensure coverage of all aspects of the programme of study within the key stage a thorough matching exercise is pursued. This incorporates a 'cut and paste' method in which the staff literally cut up a copy of relevant elements of the National Curriculum programmes of study and place them within the planned topics. Through this process it is possible to see if any part of the programme of study is missing. These can then be planned for separately, and in addition to, the mathematics planned through the topic.

This method is most appropriate for 'blocked work' (SCAA, 1995). However, there are some elements which are not limited to being placed within one particular topic or term as they require 'continuing work' (SCAA, 1995). For instance, the references to the opportunities that all children need to gain within the key stage do not lend themselves to such a approach but indicate the experiences that the child requires.

The example shows planning for one of the six topics and is planned for Year 2 children. Table 7.1 indicates the other headings which are appropriate to the school's planning. By working through the mathematics contained within the six topics the average child should fulfil all the requirements of the National Curriculum Key Stage 1 by the end of Year 2.

Within one term, there are some parts of the mathematics programme of study which are addressed through a topic and there are other aspects of mathematics which are planned to be taught during the term but which do not relate to the topic. From here, the specific activities can be identified for all subject areas, thus providing detailed topic planning. The children are taught mathematics in three different ways on a weekly basis. The core of practice and reinforcement is covered during regular morning sessions with the class teacher. These sessions focus on basic mathematical skills. The second way encompasses mathematics through topic and involves the mathematics co-ordinator, Jenny Shaw. The children are presented with mathematics through investigations or games on a two-weekly cycle. The third way is *Hall Mathematics* and

Table 7.1 *Planning for a topic for Year 2 children*

Cross-curricular topic	Mathematics from the topic	Core of practice and reinforcement	Discrete mathematics topics	Incidental mathematics
Pattern	**Section 2:** Multiplication and division patterns	**Section 2:** More complex + and -	Hall Maths*: Number lines, Patterns to 50, Number bond games. Shape games.	Models
				Large and small construction
	Halving squares	Half and quarter		
				Art work
	Secret codes	Introduce multiply and divide	Practical division	
	Weather charts, handling data	Whole number problems	Sand	
	Domino patterns		Water	
	Section 3: Symmetry	More complex money work		
	Tessellation	**Section 3:** More 2D and 3D work		
	Rotational patterns			

Note: * = Mathematics activities taking place in the hall

involves the whole class in mathematical activities in a large space. The children move around in the hall doing mathematics with large apparatus. It is one way of taking mathematics out of the classroom and making it an exciting activity. In addition, the 'incidental mathematics', referred to in Table 7.1 takes into account the other types of activity that the children will be doing at this time. These are the activities which involve mathematics incidentally, such as play in the home corner, or work with construction kits.

In addition to this the infants school uses a series of lists which were produced prior to the National Curriculum. These lists identify the key learning experiences that the staff felt were important. These have been categorized and listed under certain headings such as sets, shape, number. The lists were found to correspond with the requirements of the National Curriculum and are still seen by staff as an invaluable planning guide within the school. As an example, the sets list is provided below:

- General sorting, e.g. all lego in this box, all cars in another box.
- Sorting for different attributes, e.g. colour, size, function, like/unlike.
- Sorting using two attributes using more complex apparatus.
- Sorting and finding their own criteria.
- Identifying criteria set by someone else.
- Partitioning of sets into subsets, e.g. story of numbers, sorting for negatives.
- More complex sorting for two attributes, three attributes.
- Venn diagrams, tree diagrams, Carroll diagrams.
- Sorting into sets for odd and even.
- Sorting by number into sets of 2, 3, 5, 10.
- Sorting into 10s and odd ones or units.
- Sets of 2s, 3s etc leading to work on equal addition and multiplication.
- Sets for sharing (practically).

The value in such a list is that it arose from discussion and the sharing of ideas amongst colleagues and therefore the staff involved have ownership and thus commitment to it.

PLANNING METHODS: KEY STAGE 2

The junior school does acknowledge that some mathematics will come from a topic, but for planning purposes it considers mathematics separately from the class topic across the four years of Key Stage 2. Shape and space, data-handling and most aspects of measurement are planned so that different year groups focus on different parts of the programme of study to ensure that, by the end of Key Stage 2, they will have had the opportunity to experience the complete programme of study. This could be seen to be aligned with 'blocked work' (SCAA, 1995). Aspects of each section identified above have a certain completeness about them, although it is recognized that within any block of work links will be made to other parts of the curriculum and within the mathematics curriculum itself where it supports understanding. These are illustrated in the four examples of mathematics topics below.

Mathematics topic: measurement

Measurement provides an example of 'blocked work'. The focus encompasses a number of different forms of measurement and this can be overwhelming in that there can appear to be too much to teach. If each form of measurement is covered by each year group then the quantity of work demanded could undermine the teaching of skills and concepts associated with measurement.

Rather than planning to cover all aspects of measurement within one year, the junior school confines each year group to a more limited emphasis, involving two forms of practical measurement only. Where there are links which can be made between different sections of the mathematics programme of study these are taken into account in planning. The focus is on exploring the two forms of practical measurement in greater depth, giving children sufficient opportunity to estimate and to carry out practical activity and to ensure progression. As the mathematics co-ordinator, Pauline Hancock, said: 'Although they are measuring all through the four years what they are concentrating on is different things and hopefully one idea is hooked onto another.'

As the children revisit measurement each year it allows the teacher opportunity to reinforce the same concept through different forms of measurement. This is of greater benefit in terms of the children's learning than attempting to cover a wide range of forms of measurement: 'being fed the same sort of experience ... over and over again ... finally the penny drops and ... Eureka!'

This approach does reinforce the idea of blocks of work. Below is an example to indicate with Year 3 how the different parts of mathematics support each other.

Year 3:

Measurement: Length, area.
Shape: 2D shape/right angles/perimeters/area.

a. *choose appropriate standard units ... and make sensible estimates with them in everyday situations;*
b. *choose and use appropriate measuring instruments; interpret numbers and read scales to an increasing degree of accuracy;*
c. *find perimeters of simple shapes; ... finding areas by counting methods.*
   (DFE, 1995, Key Stage 2 Shape, Space and Measures)

The teacher begins by establishing the children's understanding of using non-standard measures, and moves on to establish the need for standard units. Children are taught to use the instruments and to measure with standard units through focusing on length and area. The focus is of a practical nature and estimation is an important part of the process.

The work on length in Year 3 is supported by a 'shape and space' focus on recognizing squares, rectangles, circles, hexagons, pentagons and work on two-dimensional shape, including their construction. As a result of needing to be able to measure accurately, they will need to learn to use a ruler. From here they can progress to finding perimeters of simple shapes, thus reinforcing length through shape work. In addition, as they will have experienced non-standard measures in area, it is not problematic to move on to finding areas by counting the squares.

It is inappropriate to designate some parts of the curriculum to certain year groups as they need to be focused upon on a more regular basis to ensure adequate progression. In the junior school they are identified as time and number (including algebra and money).

Mathematics topic: money

Money is an important element of the curriculum in its own right. A suitable context, such as a class shop, can be provided for children to learn about money. The vast majority of children do relate well to money and can draw upon experience that they have gained outside the classroom. During the previous key stage a focus on money will have concentrated upon the different value of coins and equivalence. It can support work on the four rules of number as well as support other aspects of the curriculum, such as measurement and decimals within Key Stage 2.

The co-ordinator, working with Year 4 children, observes that they

> can actually multiply money to 2 decimal places and know that their answer is right or wrong from what they get. They seem to know instinctively where the decimal point goes because they've had a lot of experience and this then links on to addition, decimals, subtraction decimals etc.

Building the money into the planning in this way supports work in other areas as well.

> in length they could add decimals so we did actually do conversion of one metric unit to another ... things like 136cm is 1.36m, 143cm is 1.43m ... How many metres is that altogether? They could actually convert, add up and get the answer right.

In the National Curriculum, shape, space and measures at Key Stage 2 'convert one metric unit to another ... extend their understanding of the number system to ... decimals no more than two decimal places in the context of measurement and money' (DFE, 1995, p.29).

Mathematics topic: time

Although time is a form of measurement, it can be most effectively taught as a separate element. It encompasses not only telling the time but also the concept of the passing of time. Children's understanding of the passing of time is often limited and difficult for them to grasp. In order for children to understand the concept of the passing of time they need to experience it. This can be most effectively achieved by focusing the children's attention on to time as they carry out everyday activities. It is preferable not to limit the experience of time to mathematics lessons; for instance, the passing of time can be experienced while carrying out a scientific investigation. The emphasis should be on children gaining a range of experience related to the passing of time rather than being expected to memorize times on a clock face without the underlying conceptual understanding.

In the junior school, time is taught as a separate mini-topic at some point in the year to be determined by the year group teachers. One or two learning objectives are focused upon rather than aiming for a broader coverage and the focus is on giving the children a breadth of experience related to it. The mathematics co-ordinator explained that

> it was agreed that each year group would spend a set period developing children's concept of time in the sense of duration and not simply telling it.

Every classroom has a working clock and every teacher in every class is encouraged to refer to the time as they carry out everyday activities. For example:

> The teacher asks the children various questions to bring Time to the attention of the children, such as 'What time is it?', 'How long is it before assembly?', 'What can I do before then?', 'You've got 15 minutes to do this.'

In the National Curriculum, Shape, Space and Measures at Key Stage 2 'make sensible estimates with them in everyday situations' (DFE, 1995, p.29). Through this type of activity children are likely to become more aware of the passing of time. It is the passage of time which it is particularly important to focus upon sufficiently rather than placing too great an emphasis on the telling of the time alone.

Mathematics topic: number

It is important that all four rules are focused upon within a year. The level will vary according to the needs of the children concerned. At any one time there is likely to be a particular focus on one of the four rules; however this should not be to the exclusion of any other rule. It must be remembered that each rule relates to the others and does not exist in isolation.

There are a number of benefits in focusing on one particular aspect of number work at a time. It gives the child sufficient time to focus on a particular concept, but it does not prevent children from feeling that they are progressing, as all children will change their focus on a regular basis. Because of the relationship between the number operations, these changes of emphasis may also assist a child's understanding of other rules of number. For instance, a child may come to understand concepts associated with addition at a time where the focus of work is actually on subtraction. The number operations reinforce each other and therefore help to support children making links between different rules of number.

The infants school offers a particular focus at certain times of the year. In the autumn term the focus is on addition and subtraction and in the spring term it is on multiplication and division. This is not to the exclusion of making links with other operations, such as acknowledging that through tackling subtraction an understanding of addition is required and can be supported. During the summer term the class teacher decides which of the four rules of number need developing and consolidating further.

Within certain aspects of number there are certain elements which fit together better than others and thus aid the learning process. For example in the National Curriculum for number at Key Stage 2 the child needs to

> know the multiplication facts to 10 x 10; develop a range of mental methods for finding quickly from known facts those that they cannot recall.
> (DFE, 1995, p.27, para. 3c)

Although this statement does emphasize the importance of recall it also implies that the child would need an underlying understanding of the process involved in order to be able to use appropriate strategies to find out facts that cannot be instantly recalled.

Mental mathematics is an important and integral part of number work and needs to be emphasized throughout the school. An emphasis on number pattern and relationships between numbers can assist with this development. It is important to consider the relationship between different multiplication tables as they can be grouped together and strategies can be developed to support the learning process and assist recall of number facts. For instance, in order to work out the multiplication tables for 4s and 8s the child can be encouraged to build upon their knowledge of 2s and use a doubling strategy. The links between multiplication and division also need to be reinforced. For instance, $3 \times 6 = 18$ is made up of three numbers which can be grouped together in different ways, incorporating multiplication or division ($18 \div 6 = 3$), to help the child to build up the links between them. The understanding of multiplication and being able to develop strategies is essential and needs to be encouraged in conjunction with recalling number facts. The junior school plans to teach tables in a particular order which is broadly speaking in four stages:

Stage 1   2s, 5s 10s
Stage 2   3s, 6s, 9s
Stage 3   4s, 8s
Stage 4   7s

PROGRESSION

Termly planning by the teacher will need to pay particular attention to progression. The teacher will need to plan a range of activities which together will result in the children making progress in their mathematical understanding. This planning, or *programme of work*, will need to encompass all aspects of mathematics that will be taught during the term. It needs to include all information concerning the activities that are going to be taught, the learning objectives, the language that is going to be introduced, the resources that need to be used to support the learning. It will also need to identify where an activity will support the child in gaining experience of a particular element of a programme of study within the National Curriculum and whether it provides the teacher with an opportunity for assessment. Where possible teachers should be encouraged to work together on the programme of work as this is likely to encourage the sharing of ideas which will benefit the teachers themselves and result in providing a more comprehensive plan. In both the case-study schools the teachers within one year group work collaboratively on the programme of work. The planning is a working document and it is important that the teacher monitors his/her intended planning and is sufficiently flexible to be willing to alter his/her plans according to the needs of the children, rather than rigidly maintain an inappropriate plan. In both schools as the term progresses the parts of the topic which have been covered are highlighted on the plans as a record. The teacher can also make a note of any additional work covered that was not noted on the plans. These records provide information for the termly evaluations.

In order to ensure effective coverage of the National Curriculum the co-ordinator will need to look at the plans and evaluations to check whether there are any gaps in delivery. This ensures that the co-ordinator has a good overview of how the subject is taught within the school. It also provides the opportunity to make additional suggestions if appropriate.

The co-ordinator in the infants school also produces a list of the activities to be covered during the term for topic and non-topic and ticks each part off when they are covered.

Mathematics: non-topic and core skills for the term

- Continued reinforcement of addition and subtraction
- Problems using words
- Place value activities
- Ordering of larger numbers
  e.g. Using cards. Deal one to each child, then another and ask each child to 'read' what number they have made and see who has the largest or smallest.
  Example questions: Can they change their number and make it smaller or larger? What happens with a third card?
- Continue to practise mental arithmetic – both addition and subtraction
- Continued work on money
- Telling the time – analogue. Reinforce and use quarter to and past and minutes

This gives the teacher an overall picture of the mathematics to be covered during the term and indicates in which areas the children will be expected to progress.

COMMERCIAL SCHEMES

It has already been emphasized that mathematics needs to be presented to children in a range of different ways. As far as planning is concerned this means that working through one commercial scheme is inappropriate. When teachers plan their work they will need to look at a range of materials available in school, seeing the commercial scheme as a resource rather than *the mathematics curriculum*. It is important that the emphasis is on all children seeing themselves achieving in mathematics. This requires a great deal of input by the teacher in order to provide the children with sufficient experience so that they are successful. It is appropriate to use a commercial scheme selectively. It provides guidance as to progression and, as such, is a useful tool for the teacher. Yet it cannot replace the teacher and do the teaching.

ORGANIZING THE LEARNING EXPERIENCE

Whole-class teaching enables all children to be taught together. Where it is effective it supports teacher control and it is economical in terms of teacher time. For instance, the teacher can gather all children together and explain the task or tasks at hand. This can be particularly useful if all children will be involved in the tasks during the course of the day. Another possibility is that all children will be expected to carry out a particular piece of work. For instance, the class can be introduced to an open-ended investigation. It enables the teacher to establish that all children understand the task.

Hall Maths is a class lesson undertaken on a regular basis within the infants school. At the planning stage differentiation is considered and although all children are focused on the same work the teacher differentiates in terms of the questions asked and challenges presented. Below is an example of a lesson undertaken with a Year 2 class.

Hall Maths: Number line activity

The activity involves the use of a series of large cards, each of which contain a different number.

All children are given one card. Each number is then called out in sequence by the child holding the card concerned.

This is developed into a game. The number cards are laid down on the hall floor in sequence to form a number line. Two children are used as 'counters'. Two dice are thrown, the children work out the total and then starting from zero move one of the 'counters' (child) on that number of spaces along the number line.

In the above example the activity is the same for all children. However, there is opportunity for the teacher to differentiate. She/he can ensure that the children who do not recognize numbers above 10 are given the lower number cards and spots are also included on the cards so that a child can check their number. The level of questions can vary, for instance, 'Which number comes after 6?', and 'Which number comes before 10?' assume different levels of understanding. The first question requires the child to understand the concept 'after' and to know the counting numbers up to 7. The second question requires the child to understand the concept 'before' and to have some understanding of place value. In playing the game there are different tasks which arise. One task involves working out the total value of the two dice thrown; a second task involves counting on, so that the counter knows where to stand. Within these two tasks the level of difficulty will vary and will therefore give further flexibility for the teacher to differentiate.

Activities such as this enable all pupils to have access to mathematics. It assists learning for all pupils and extends their mathematical competence. The activity can be developed further as a board game for classroom use and the game can be adapted, perhaps using subtraction dice.

Group work contains a greater range of organizational possibilities. Groups can be based on certain criteria such as level of attainment, friendship or mixed attainment. The purpose of the arrangement is to assist the teacher's organization and to enhance the pupil's learning experience. A group can be taught together and can be given the same task to carry out.

Children may be required to work together collaboratively to produce one end product. For instance, real problem-solving as a task benefits from encouraging the children to work together sharing ideas and producing a joint solution. However, children may be organized so that the teacher can explain a task to them together, but it may be an organizational tool alone, as each child may be expected to produce individual pieces of work. In order to differentiate the two styles of working the former is usually referred to as 'group work' and the latter as 'grouping'.

Planning differentiation for group activities will vary according to the criteria used to group the children. Where children are of similar attainment the planning is perceived as more straightforward in that teachers can anticipate so that they can introduce a concept which is new to all children within a particular group. In reality, it is unlikely that all children within a group will be at exactly the same stage, so some flexibility does need to be considered at the planning stage to allow for a range of responses to the teaching. This means that, whatever the criterion is for grouping the children, the teacher will need to plan for differentiation and will need to monitor their level of understanding and be willing to alter plans accordingly.

Grouping of children does need continual monitoring to ensure that it is the most effective way forward for the children concerned. There is the potential for the grouping to have an effect on children's self-esteem and the teacher needs to be particularly sensitive to the possible negative effect on children whose attainment is low (Alexander, Rose and Woodhead, 1992).

Organizing the class to allow the teacher to work with groups of children requires the teacher to plan activities that usefully occupy children who will not need teacher attention in order to create opportunity to teach a group. The example below demonstrates how the infants school tackles this form of organization.

During each afternoon the Year 2 teachers plan work across the year group. This involves a fortnightly rolling programme of ten activities representing various curriculum areas. Five activities are carried out in one classroom and these are supervised by the two general assistants who are timetabled to be with Year 2 every afternoon. The supervised activities include the more practical options. Within the second classroom there are two teacher-led activities and three other activities which do not require significant supervision. This includes activities from topic work, floor puzzles and using the computer. They are generally considered to be quieter activities. One of the teacher-led activities is always focused on mathematics investigations and games and the other is focused on science or humanities investigations and is also teacher-directed.

Each afternoon the children plan the work they are going to cover based on a planning sheet. By the end of a fortnight they should have covered all ten possibilities. Figure 7.1 gives an example of the children's planning sheet.

The reader will notice that activities 6 and 7 are not indicated on the sheet. These are the two teacher-directed activities and the children are not able to plan when they carry out these activities. The teacher ensures that all children have experienced the two teacher-led activities within the fortnight and she decides which children are going to be withdrawn at a particular time. The criterion used for grouping the children is according to how quickly the individual children pick up new concepts as this affects the pace of teaching. The teacher monitors the needs of the individuals within the group and changes the children within a group accordingly.

In the infants school the purpose of the method of organization is 'to build in quality time, and we feel that's more important than the teacher moving around and dividing her attention between all the groups'. Investigations and games are planned so that each group has a similar experience. However, on each occasion they are adapted in order to meet more accurately the needs of the individuals.

The children keep a record of the activities that they plan to carry out and this is reviewed when they are back in their own classroom, as the purpose of this particular organization is to set aside 'quality time' for the teacher to work with a group. There are many different ways of organizing the learning experiences for pupils, but the priority needs to be building up quality time for teachers and pupils.

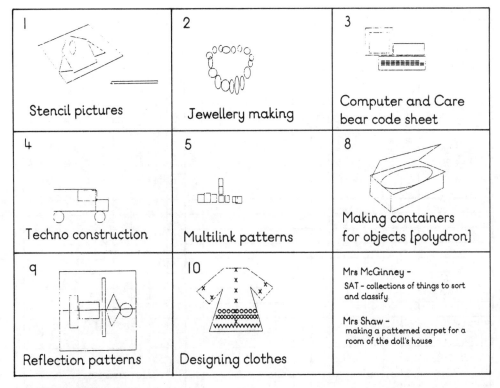

I Stencil pictures	2 Jewellery making	3 Computer and Care bear code sheet
4 Techno construction	5 Multilink patterns	8 Making containers for objects [polydron]
q Reflection patterns	10 Designing clothes	Mrs McGinney – SAT – collections of things to sort and classify Mrs Shaw – making a patterned carpet for a room of the doll's house

Figure 7.1 Children's planning sheet

ASSESSMENT AND RECORD-KEEPING

Assessment is an integral part of the teaching and learning process. It is essential that the teacher can identify what the children are expected to learn from a particular activity as this provides the main focus for assessment. There is sometimes a tendency to emphasize written work as the main means of assessing children's learning, but children can, and should, be assessed through listening to what they say and observing how each child responds in a given situation rather than relying on written work alone.

The assessment and record-keeping system therefore needs to be manageable in terms of teacher time. It must also be informative in that the information collected needs to be useful to the teacher concerned. It must give reliable information in that the assessment of a child would produce the same results on a different occasion and another teacher would give a similar assessment on a particular child.

The junior school keeps detailed individual records of children's progress which result from the teacher assessing the children in a range of different ways. Table 7.2 indicates the type of record-keeping which is kept for subtraction. It provides the teacher with an indication of the attainment of all children within the class. The relationships between different number operations are also important and are provided on a separate record sheet.

These records are a result of the teacher assessing each child. They provide a clear and informative record of progress of each child within the group and are easily and

Table 7.2 *Subtraction record sheet*

Maths record number	To 10 real objects	To 10 linear	To 10 vertical	To 10 recall	To 10 problems	Finding difficulty	To 20 linear	To 20 vertical	To 20 recall	Problems	TU no decomp.	TU decomp.	Problems	HTU no decomp.	HTU decomp. T –> U	HTU decomp. H –> T	HTU decomp. H –> T –> U	Problems	Mentally 2 digits (no decimals)	Mentally 2 digits (decimals)	Decimals	Problems

quickly accessible. It is important that the record is not made immediately to show that a child has some indication of understanding. Instead the teacher needs to wait until he/she is convinced that the child has grasped the concept securely and is regularly successful at the type of work being assessed.

These record sheets provide information which inform the National Curriculum Assessment Records and contain reference to the Level Descriptors. A highlight pen can be used to record the child's learning and if a different colour pen is used for each year group it is easy for staff to see at a glance how the child is progressing from year to year.

In terms of recording ongoing assessments, the infants school uses 'Green Books' – a green exercise book for each subject. When the teacher is working with a group, in an investigation or mathematical game, he/she writes certain standard information as the activity, the date and the names of the children, in the order they are sitting, at the beginning of the session. As the session progresses the teacher makes a note of anything that is judged to be significant in terms of the child's learning. This might include how easy or difficult a child found the task, what the child had clearly understood and what evidence indicated this to the teacher. It can also be used to provide a note to the teacher to identify particular concepts which would need revisiting in a future session. The advantage of using such a book is that notes can be made as they happen, and this can be referred to later to find out how the children reacted and to inform records and future planning. The teacher can make a mental note of any particularly significant point and this can be recorded as soon as possible after the session.

The Green Books serve two further purposes. They provide the main source of information for the audit sheet which is completed for each topic to show the work that each child has completed for each subject during that term. Contributions towards the audit sheet are made by various adults who have taught the child during the term and the record therefore benefits from a wider perspective on the child's progress.

In addition they provide an invaluable source of information for the summative National Curriculum Assessment Records. These contain not only reference to the level descriptions, but also contain reference to other selected concepts and skills that the staff have identified as key features of learning.

CONCLUSION

The successful implementation of the mathematics curriculum requires a mathematics policy which is co-operatively constructed and which underpins the development of the mathematics curriculum. The policy should allow for the organization of the curriculum into meaningful learning experiences which give children access to mathematical ideas and potential for development. There should be clear learning objectives for all learning experiences which will determine the style of the activity.

Teachers, like children, work most effectively where an atmosphere of trust and confidence has been built up with their peers. The classroom and staffroom environment need to communicate that the individual is valued. This factor alone has a major impact upon children's learning and teachers' morale and these have a significant effect on the delivery of the curriculum.

REFERENCES

Abbotswood Infants School (1995) *Mathematics policy*. Unpublished.
Alexander, R., Rose, J. and Woodhead, C. (1992) *Curriculum Organisation and Classroom Practice in Primary Schools*. London: DES.
Bleakhouse Junior School (1995) Mathematics policy. Unpublished.
Cockcroft (1982) *Mathematics Counts*. London: HMSO.
DFE (1995) *Key Stages 1 and 2 of the National Curriculum*. London: DFE.
Donaldson, M. (1978) *Children's Minds*. London: Fontana.
National Curriculum Council (1989) *Mathematics Non-Statutory Guidance*. York: NCC.
Papert, S. (1972) Teaching children to be mathematicians versus teaching about mathematics. In Floyd, A. (ed.) (1981) *Developing Mathematical Thinking*. London: Addison-Wesley.
SCAA (1995) *Planning the Curriculum at Key Stages 1 and 2*. London: SCAA.

Chapter 8

Implementing Science in the National Curriculum

Diane Ward

INTRODUCTION

Science was introduced as a core subject within the National Curriculum in England and Wales in 1989. Since that time schools have been in the process of implementing the science orders. In this chapter some of the issues which are important to this process are identified and then explored more fully. Although the focus for this chapter is the implementation of science in the primary school, it is important to view this process in the context of the whole National Curriculum.

Between 1989 and 1995, there have been several major revisions to the science orders, which have reduced the number of attainment targets, slimmed down the programmes of study, produced radical changes in layout and have resulted in the statements of attainment being replaced by level descriptions. (Details of these revisions are given in Chapter 4.)

At the same time that teachers were attempting to come to terms with the revised documentation for science, the foundation subjects were introduced and several changes were made to the mathematics and English orders. The decision to introduce the core subjects, mathematics, English and science, before the foundation subjects has possibly had the greatest impact on the subsequent implementation of science in schools. Mathematics and English were already perceived by teachers as familiar and a central part of the curriculum. Science, on the other hand, was regarded by many as a new subject in the primary curriculum. Teachers were challenged by the science order and many felt threatened by the demands it made on their own understanding of the teaching and learning of science. For many teachers, science was felt to be outside their areas of expertise, and most had received little training in the teaching of science in the primary school. They met the challenge of teaching science with a mixture of apprehension, enthusiasm and excitement, and science became a key focus for staff development in many schools. The prominence given to science at that time did much to get it under way. If the science order had been introduced later, at the same time as the foundation subjects, it is hard to imagine that the same progress in implementing science could have been made.

The period between 1989 and 1995 has been a very demanding one for primary teachers (see Chapter 1). Yet, in spite of all these difficulties, the science orders have been implemented with some success in the primary school (SCAA, 1994a; DES,1991).

One positive outcome of this period of change and revision, has been that head-teachers and their staff have needed to discuss science curriculum issues and make decisions about the implementation of the science orders in school. This has encouraged teachers to work in a collaborative way in science which was largely unknown before the National Curriculum.

Before looking at the implementation of science within the English and Welsh National Curriculum it is worth noting three salient features of the orders that are likely to have a major impact on the way in which they are implemented.

Firstly, the content of the programmes of study which specify the skills and concepts to be taught are laid down in some detail and prescribe the work that is to be carried out within the key stage. The programmes of study outline the statutory minimum entitlement for pupils. However, these concepts and skills can be developed in any context that is appropriate. For example, melting and change could be studied in a context such as ice-cream and holidays, ice and snow in a topic on winter or in a project making Easter eggs. This allows teachers to be flexible and imaginative in deciding which contexts to use for developing ideas, opening up exciting possibilities for teachers when planning for childrens' learning in science.

Secondly, the programmes of study are designed to develop both procedural knowledge – designated Experimental and Scientific Science (Sc1) – and substantive knowledge – the ideas of science (Sc2, 3 and 4). For assessment, Sc1 is weighted to almost equal Sc2, 3 and 4 combined, thus stressing the importance placed on developing children's ability to work scientifically.

Thirdly, the assessment and testing requirements at ages 7 and 11, the arrangements for reporting to parents and the production of 'league tables' of results for schools have made summative assessment a dominant feature of the science orders in the National Curriculum. Assessment and reporting were always likely to have a major impact on implementation.

These three features of the science orders are significant when implementing science in the curriculum. In the first instance it means that there are no prescribed contexts for developing ideas which need to be learned. This allows schools the freedom to organize the curriculum in the way that is the most appropriate for their situation. This flexibility in planning has been seen as a strength by many teachers, allowing a freedom that is absent in the science curricula of some other countries, especially those which have textbook-led schemes. Secondly, the requirement for children to carry out investigations and other practical activities has determined, to a great extent, how science is to be taught. Although it has been said that the science orders are 'methodologically neutral', practical, hands-on activities must be carried out by children if the programmes of study for Experimental and Investigative Science (Sc1) are to be delivered. Pupils must be doing science and not just learning about science. The third feature is controversial. The assessment requirements for the National Curriculum have been felt by many teachers to be excessive. This has now been recognized to have been the case (SCAA, 1994c). The summative assessment and reporting arrangements have often become the priority in many schools at the expense of formative teacher assessment.

The burden of trying to manage an unworkable assessment system as well as carrying out standard assessment tasks at Key Stage 1 for reporting purposes, may have negated some of the more positive developments in formative teacher assessment, which enabled teachers to plan for children's learning. Also, the pressure on pupils, teachers and schools to perform well in assessment tasks may tempt teachers, however unconsciously, to 'teach to the test' rather than to concentrate their efforts on developing the teaching of science. The assessment aspect of the science order will be explored more fully later in this chapter.

In spite of all the changes and revisions to the science orders that have taken place, the process of implementation has been going on slowly and surely in primary schools. Throughout the consultation period, prior to the Dearing Review, teachers commented that Experimental and Investigative Science (Sc1), was often motivating to pupils and although parts of the programme of study have been clarified, deferred to another key stage or removed, in total there has been little change to the programmes of study for science at Key Stage 1 and 2. This could be seen as a credit to the original curriculum working group who drew them up (see Chapter 4) or perhaps the programmes of study were overcrowded to begin with and they still are. Only when the Dearing revisions to the whole curriculum have been implemented will it be possible to say.

If one criterion for evaluating success is the enthusiasm for science which has been shown by many teachers, then implementation could be judged as going well. One example of this enthusiasm for science within the curriculum came through during the Dearing Review. There was a proposal to remove simple circuit work using bulbs, batteries and buzzers, from Key Stage 1, a part of the programmes of study with which teachers lacked confidence in the early stages of implementation. However, there was an overwhelming response from teachers who wanted simple circuit work back in Key Stage 1, a request that was met. It is a pity that controversy over national testing and the need for teachers to make assessments of children's learning against so many statements of attainment (see Chapter 4) has sapped teachers' energy which could have been more fruitfully used in the teaching of science.

Liz Thomas, Moorlands Infant School, was science co-ordinator in the infant school when the science orders were first introduced; she recalls the enthusiasm for science in her school at that time:

> When we first did science, I had just completed an in-service science course at college, the year before the National Curriculum was introduced. In my mind (science) had a very high profile then. Everyone wanted as much help as they could get, soaking it up, like a damp sponge. The course was very strong on process skills. The school was very child-centred. Everything just fitted together. It was very exciting to teach science through the process skills. There was a strong emphasis on hands on and how children learn.

ISSUES FOR IMPLEMENTATION

In the six years from 1989 to date, schools have been implementing the science orders in their own way. Every school is unique, with its own blend of teachers, pupils and resources. The teaching staff have their own individual strengths; pupil numbers and catchment will vary from school to school; the buildings and other resources will be different. Schools have implemented the National Curriculum in the way that seems most appropriate to their situation. The task of implementation of science for a small, two-teacher, mixed-age class, village school will be different from that of a large urban primary school. However, in considering the implementation of science there appear to be a number of key issues which are common to all schools concerning the organization and management of science and the way that it is to be taught. Six of these issues are listed below and then each is explored in more depth.

The following decisions have to be made at whole school level:

- What is the curriculum framework used in the school and what is the relationship between science and the other curriculum subjects?
- How is the curriculum organized for science so that continuity and progression are planned for?
- How will entitlement to science be ensured for all pupils?
- What is the role of the science co-ordinator in implementation?
- How can teachers develop their own knowledge and understanding in science?
- How will assessment of science be managed and pupil's achievements be recorded?

Few, if any, decisions about these issues can be made in isolation from the rest. However, the impact of some decisions is likely to be much greater than for others. In order to illustrate how a school might go through the implementation process three schools have been used as examples. The schools are all from within Avon; one is a medium-sized urban primary school, another is a large infant school and the third is a junior school. The three teachers interviewed have been in post since the introduction of the science orders and are able to look back over the process of implementation so far. They are all keen and experienced teachers of science and have been involved locally in a number of initiatives. Ann Orchard was previously an advisory teacher for science and Maggie Cosgrove and Liz Thomas have both been involved in in-service work, as well as being science co-ordinator in their schools.

What is the curriculum framework used in the school and what is the relationship between science and the other curriculum subjects?

Decisions about framework design will determine the pattern of almost all other planning decisions. So many variations are possible that it can take a little time to identify the framework for curriculum organization in school. Some schools plan through cross-curricular topics, where several or sometimes all subjects are planned around a topic. Others plan through a theme, usually in one subject area. There are others where subjects are taught separately as policy. Often there is a mixture of topics, themes and separate subject teaching. In many schools there is a difference in the way that the curriculum is organized for Key Stage 1 and Key Stage 2. Teachers, when asked, can also say that the curriculum is organized through cross-curricular topics, when further analysis shows there is separate subject teaching as well. When the science orders were introduced many schools incorporated science planning into the existing curriculum framework. The rationale for this decision was not always clear. The decision may have been made simply to assimilate science into the curriculum without having to alter the whole planning framework. Many schools planned science-based topics, often organized through a two-year cycle. History, art and other subjects were linked to the topic where possible. In the County of Avon LEA new guidelines (1989) were produced which suggested topics through which the programmes of study could be taught. As the foundation subjects came on stream there was a growing tension over the relationship between science and the other subjects. Some of this tension arose from simple overcrowding of the curriculum, trying to fit it all in. There was also the need to examine the extent to which the ideas and skills being taught had any relationship with each other. The important question might now be, to what extent has the relationship between science and the other subjects really been explored or has the situation just evolved without any clear rationale being offered?

The infant department in Shield Road Primary School organizes science through a theme approach. The way in which the rest of the curriculum is organized was explained as follows:

> We pick up history and geography independently. We don't think we have to glue these to our theme. You don't have to work like that; we can have a separate history theme for half a term if that's what we want to do. We have a main theme which is primarily science based and then we have a separate maths topic, some geography, child protection work, circle time, lots of bits and pieces which would not be in the science document. It's a mixture of a number of separate topics, alongside each other, fairly flexible.

At Moorlands Infants School another curriculum framework is used: the cross-curricular topic. The programmes of study which are to be taught are identified in the scheme of work for each subject and are delivered through the context of the topic.

> We plan through a cross-curricular topic. There could be a topic for the whole class and within that we would try to cover as much as we could of the National Curriculum. The teacher is free to choose the topic title, but we are basically committed to teaching the programme of study indicated in the scheme of work.

At this school there was a desire for cross-curricular links within Key Stage 1 planning wherever useful. There was a strong feeling that children learn in a holistic way and that science within Key Stage 1 fits naturally into that way of working.

At Key Stage 2 there is greater diversity in the curriculum organization used. In many schools there is a combination of topics or themes and separate subject teaching. Science is taught separately in some schools but science linked to a topic is still the preferred approach in many others. Occasionally schools have identified a specialist teacher for science, who teaches science to different classes but many teachers find this an unacceptable way forward. Teachers have developed their confidence and understanding of science teaching considerably since the introduction of the National Curriculum. Putting science into the hands of 'specialist' teachers might be a tempting solution, in the short term, but it might well lead to the de-skilling of other teachers.

The decision to teach separate subjects and the use of specialist teachers for primary science has been explored in some schools, and this approach has been promoted politically (see Chapter 5). In general there appears to be a resistance to the notion of a specialist teacher for science but a move towards separate subject teaching at Key Stage 2. The debate about children's learning in science and the relationship between learning in science and other domains has never really taken place and needs to be explored in the future. The Key Stage 2 co-ordinator highlights the apparent contradictions regarding their commitment to topic-based teaching:

We are very much cross-curricular and topic based. Some topics are science led, some are humanities led. It's always been like that. Although we are very aware of areas we have to teach separately because they are not covered by topic.
(Maggie Cosgrove, Henleaze Junior)

How is the curriculum organized for science so that continuity and progression are planned for?

Schools are required to have a policy and a scheme of work for each subject. The school policy for science will outline the school's philosophy for teaching science to all its pupils. A scheme of work is a planning framework which shows how the skills and knowledge and understanding, outlined in the programmes of study, will be covered in each year. It also shows how progression and continuity are planned for throughout the Key Stage. Examples of how the programmes of study might be developed into learning opportunities are given below and suggested activities to support children's learning are included. The scheme of work may also show links between science and the other subjects. However it may not be immediately obvious from the scheme of work what the curriculum structure is.

This is how Ann Orchard, as science co-ordinator, led the infant department at Shield Road Primary School, in drawing up their scheme of work. There are two parallel classes in Reception, Year 1 and Year 2.

When I came to the school five years ago there were already themes set, so our first task was to look at these themes and match them against the National Curriculum. We checked through all the programmes of study and highlighted them to show where we were dealing with that part of the curriculum. The next task was to go from where we were and see if the themes were sensible or if we had to change any. All staff have a planning sheet for each half term and they divided it into the main curriculum areas and wrote in the programmes of study to be taught and some activities that develop those skills and ideas. Most of the activities are cross-curricular but they identified the main area of the curriculum served by the activity and then put them in the appropriate columns on the planning sheet. As science co-ordinator I picked out the science that each teacher was doing in the half-termly topic. By the time we had done that the new National Curriculum had come out so we rechecked the whole thing again. By then we felt that most of the science curriculum was touched in Reception, in some way or other, so you have a preliminary engagement with that area. You are doing Experimental Investigative Science (Sc1) all the time. The knowledge and understanding programme of study you just deal with at an early level then pick it up in more depth in Year 1 or 2. So then I started drawing up activities teachers had identified for each half-term. For some half-terms there were many useful activities. Others were a little bare, so I took home books to refer to and identified other activities to develop those programmes of study. I tried to ensure we were giving children a good grounding in Sc1 so that they were getting opportunities for exploration and investigation. I then wrote up the scheme of work for each half term. I think we might have to cut some now (after Dearing). It's something that we have developed from what we were doing, although I wrote it up at the end. Also we were working with it for a couple of years before I wrote it up.

Ann stressed the importance of teacher involvement in developing the scheme of work and felt this sense of ownership by colleagues had been an important part of the development of science in the infant department.

At least we are trying to get good opportunities for learning into place, the children are doing active science and then we will do some further in-service when there is an opportunity. The important thing is to get the children doing science. They are working in groups. It's not worksheet orientated. The other thing we do is put in resources. We are hoping to develop topic boxes which will have books and collections. We identify the skills focus for Sc1 and links with other curriculum areas. In the final column of the scheme of work there are key questions to ask the children and where there are particularly good assessment opportunities that you might want to record. This is the first year we have been working to this scheme. It's been organic.

Ann went on to talk about the scheme of work in the junior classes.

We haven't got a scheme of work for Key Stage 2 yet, the problem is I don't get to work in the same way with Key Stage 2 staff, as I do with Key Stage 1 and as a whole staff it's too big to cope with. But we have made a start and I expect we will go through a similar process.

At Henleaze Junior School the first draft of a scheme of work was in place shortly after the science orders were introduced. The co-ordinator, Maggie Cosgrove, feels that getting the staff working with a scheme of work has been a key factor in getting science going within the school. The scheme of work has provided a focus for discussion about the implementation of science in the school. Developing the scheme of work has been an ongoing process. She commented:

We have come together very much as a professional staff and I think that was because we were quick to get the scheme of work in place, we have had something to work on, however imperfect.

The introduction of the National Curriculum has meant schools now have little freedom in terms of what is taught in science. The need for coverage in science is high on the list of priorities for many teachers, increasingly so because of the introduction of pencil and paper tests. There is likely to be a growing tension between the need for coverage of the programmes of study and the way in which they are taught. For example, will there be enough time given to allow children to carry out firsthand exploration and investigation to develop their knowledge and understanding? Or will what has been considered good practice up to now be replaced increasingly by teaching 'facts' about science ideas in Sc 2–4?

How will entitlement to science be ensured for all pupils?

The notion of entitlement is built into the National Curriculum. 'Science for all' is the phrase which has been used to express the intention that science is an entitlement for all pupils. In the school setting entitlement has several dimensions. Entitlement for all pupils can be ensured by: planning a scheme of work for science throughout the key stage, in order to teach the programmes of study; providing for differentiation of learning opportunities to meet individual learning needs; considering equal opportunities issues that are associated with gender or different cultural backgrounds.

At one level entitlement is planned for when the scheme of work is drawn up. A scheme of work specifies when the programmes of study will be covered within a key stage. It offers some examples of the sorts of learning experiences that will be used and shows how continuity and progression are planned for. In practice coverage of the 'Knowledge and Understanding' programmes of study has been found to be a problem. Evidence given by teachers about coverage of the programmes of study, that was collected for the SCAA report (1994a), identified parts of the programmes of study that were not being covered. When questioned further teachers were able to offer specific reasons for non-coverage. These included: curriculum overload with not enough time available; teachers' sense of insufficient science background knowledge, especially with physical science concepts for example forces; lack of resources, for example logic gates and sensors; the content not being amenable to a practical approach; for example the Earth's place in the universe; the extreme conceptual demand imposed on pupils by some of the ideas to be taught, for example passing on of genetic information; the requirement for time-consuming discussion sessions to support pupils in meeting the demand of the statements of attainment that they 'be able to describe, be able to explain or give account.' Many of the reasons given related to specific strands in the programmes of study, and were not simply excuses for lack of coverage. Initially the programmes of study were compiled as a best guess list of ideas drawn up by the Science Working Group, based on experience but in isolation from the other curriculum working groups. The SCAA evaluation has been the first detailed research into the coverage of the programmes of study in schools. This evidence has informed the Dearing Review and has been influential on the revised science orders.

The principle of entitlement, in terms of coverage, was commented on by Ann Orchard:

> Entitlement is not haphazard any more. It was so hit and miss (before the National Curriculum) and you felt you had a right to do what you wanted to do every year. It is the most positive outcome of implementation.

Although coverage of the programmes of study is now planned for in the scheme of work, monitoring and evaluation of what has actually been taught is still an issue for schools. SCAA (1994a) found that few schools had established systems for effectively monitoring coverage. Schools with plans to cover all the attainment targets in a year were less likely to meet those aims than schools which planned over a two-year cycle within a key stage. This was the preferred planning strategy in the schools used as examples here.

> There can no longer be classes where science no longer goes on. There may be classes where scientific process is patchily or idiosyncratically taught; nevertheless it will be taught in some form or other.
> (Liz Thomas, Moorlands Infants)

A scheme of work will go some way in making the programmes of study available to pupils throughout the key stage but planning for coverage will not on its own ensure access to appropriate science for all pupils. How will the school ensure access to science for all pupils, both girls and boys, for those who have a disability as well as the non-disabled and also for those who have different cultural backgrounds? The science policies drawn up by schools endorse the philosophy of 'science for all' but translating this philosophy into action has been difficult to achieve. Differentiation of tasks to meet the individual learning need of pupils must also to be considered during implementation. The schemes of work in the primary schools do allow scope for providing differentiated activities but research would suggest (SCAA, 1994b) that there is little differentiation in science at present. Even though science might now be going on in most classrooms, it does not necessarily follow that it is appropriate science for all pupils.

Access to the science curriculum appears to be less of a gender issue in Key Stage 1 and 2 than it is in the secondary phase. Girls and boys seem to be equally enthusiastic about doing science in the primary school. Liz Thomas commented: 'I see the girls equally participating in science and doing really well and I wonder what happens between now (Key Stage 1) and 16, because I feel that girls are getting a fair look in.'

What is the role of the science co-ordinator?

Before the introduction of the National Curriculum many schools had a teacher who was responsible for science. This teacher was usually responsible for the purchase and management of science resources; keeping staff informed of safe working practices in science; raising awareness of local and national initiatives; offering advice about science activities.

Since the introduction of the National Curriculum schools, where possible, have a co-ordinator for each subject. The role of the co-ordinator has developed considerably over the implementation period. A science co-ordinator will now usually be expected to lead the staff in writing a school policy for science and in producing a scheme of work; to be responsible for the purchase and management of science resources; to act as a consultant to colleagues for science; to keep staff informed of National Curriculum requirements and advise on implementation; to ensure that assessment and recording systems are in place; to monitor and evaluate science provision in school; to organize/lead school-based INSET; to be involved in local initiatives such as cross-phase and cluster groups.

An effective co-ordinator, supported by the headteacher, is able to lead staff in the implementation of science. The support given to a co-ordinator might include making time available for staff development activities as well as for the personal development of the science education capability of the co-ordinator. Maggie Cosgrove, science co-ordinator at Henleaze Junior School described how she had supported staff in developing science:

> I had one year when science was identified in the School Development Plan and I led a lot of workshops during that time and several areas of concern were covered, especially on teachers' knowledge and understanding of Forces, Energy and Light. One curriculum session every fortnight for two hours, four inputs over the term. The next time science is targeted in the School Development Plan is 95/96 which is perfect timing for review. I thought I might use a workshop system again. . . . What tends to happen is that anyone who isn't sure comes to me and asks for an explanation . . . much more a giver of confidence . . . more a consultant role, people come wanting subject knowledge. I have half-day non-contact time per term, I check resources. I've never used it to go into classrooms.

The importance of the science co-ordinator to the process of implementation is recognized by the government and funds have been made available by the DES and the DFE for 20-day courses for science co-ordinators. One aim of these courses is that co-ordinators have the opportunity to develop their own knowledge and understanding in science. Unfortunately these funds are drying up, reducing the availability of already scarce resources for INSET.

The science co-ordinators of schools in a locality might meet together to form a cluster group. The cluster group can be a useful forum to discuss issues such as progression and assessment, as well as age/phase transfer, if pupils tend to go onto the same secondary school. Avon LEA advisory teachers often worked with cluster groups and they proved to be valuable structures for the development of science in schools. When the funding of advisory teachers was cut, co-ordinators in a cluster group could still provide mutual support for dealing with science curriculum implementation issues.

The science co-ordinator has until now been regarded as someone to turn to in school for advice and support. There is a tension between the advice and support role of the co-ordinator and the new monitoring and evaluation role. It would seem unlikely that teachers will be willing to be open about their own areas of weakness in science to the person who is to make judgements about science provision in their class.

How can teachers develop their own knowledge and understanding in science?

The political decision to make science a core subject in the curriculum initially placed tremendous pressure on teachers who were not particularly confident with their own understanding of science (see Chapter 4). Since that time teachers have been involved in enhancing their own knowledge of science and their own professional development in the teaching of science in a number of ways. These include formal initiatives such as: DFE funded 20-day science courses and other INSET organized by higher education institutions and LEAs; in-school INSET, led by advisory teachers and increasingly by curriculum co-ordinators, focusing on specific school needs in science; the use of distance learning materials, such as those produced by the Open University and the National Curriculum Council.

Many teachers have had little access to this provision for INSET, but in spite of this, SCAA (1994a) found that teachers believed they were developing their science knowledge and skills despite the paucity of INSET provision. This increase in confidence in science, felt by teachers, may be misplaced (see Chapter 4). However, it may well be that teachers feel more confident and knowledgeable in science through personal development which may have taken place via less formal routes, such as collaborative planning and review with colleagues and through becoming increasingly autonomous learners in science. However achieved, increased understanding of science and of pedagogy by teachers is worthy of further exploration. Particularly important is the way this increased confidence in science is translated into changed behaviour during the planning, teaching and assessment cycle. The teacher's own understanding of science education will determine how well they implement science in the classroom. The five points in this cycle where scientific understanding is most needed by teachers are shown below.

Point 1:   The teacher refers to the scheme of work/programmes of study to determine concepts and skills to be taught.
Point 2:   The teacher refers to past experience, teacher and pupil resources, such as scheme of work, books, television programmes, to inform planning.
Point 3:   The teacher makes decisions about appropriate activities for children's learning.
Point 4:   The activities are carried out with children.

Point 5:   The teacher assesses children's learning outcomes, for example, utterances, children's recording, actions.

As teachers become more confident with the skills and concepts of science they behave differently within the planning, teaching and assessment cycle at each of the five points. Table 8.1 shows how the behaviour of the teacher changes as s/he grows in confidence.

Table 8.1 *Gradual change in behaviour as confidence in science increases*

	Behaviour of teacher when less confident with an area of science	Behaviour of teacher when confidence with that area of science has grown
Point 1: Interaction with scheme of work/programmes of study	Anxious, has difficulties in making sense of scientific language, poorly developed 'mental map', unable to make links between ideas, does not find programmes of study helpful to planning.	Comfortable with the scientific language, can fit ideas into own 'mental map' of science, can interpret in terms of own understanding and possibilities for children, recognizes relationships between concepts.
Point 2: Use of books, television, and other resources	Uses word association clues to select activities, has problems in analysing activities in terms of concepts and processes to be developed, has difficulties in selecting from the activities on offer, highly dependent on published resources.	Less dependent on resources, can work from own ideas and those of children, can select appropriate activities and modify context.
Point 3: Decisions about planning	Plans from resources rather than own or children's ideas, little differentiation in tasks, isolated activities, little concept of continuity and progression.	Differentiation to meet individual needs, can plan from children's and own ideas, has clear idea of purpose for activities, able to plan for progression.
Point 4: Implementation of activities in the classroom	Classroom organization and management may be good, teacher's questioning weak, problems with asking questions to help children think about concepts, problems with encouraging children to interpret experience.	Classroom skills good, can recognize purpose in activities undertaken, can elicit children's ideas, asks questions which take children's thinking forward, encourages children to make sense of their experiences and ask further questions.
Point 5: Assessment of children's learning	Finds it difficult to interpret children's naïve language in terms of science, fails to recognize significant statements, has problems in assessing children's utterances against the statements of attainment within the National Curriculum, does not use assessment evidence to inform future planning.	Can recognize the scientific significance in children's utterances, uses information to assess in terms of statements of attainment in the National Curriculum, uses assessments to inform future planning, can reflect on children's ideas to take own learning forward.

The professional development of teachers in science will be enhanced if they achieve greater independence as learners in science, in both subject knowledge and in science teaching. They will move towards gaining subject matter autonomy in science. This involves becoming conversant with the substantive knowledge of a subject and its processes and getting to know the means by which knowledge within the subject is verified. A teacher who becomes increasingly autonomous as a learner within science will go beyond knowing how to gain knowledge from appropriate sources, to making decisions about which knowledge claims are plausible and which do not hold water.

Teachers have been supported in developing their own understanding of science in a variety of ways. One of the most effective has been collaborative planning and work with colleagues, especially when linked to a scheme of work. Joint planning and evaluation were mentioned by all three co-ordinators as being powerful tools in the implementation of science. The collaborative work between teachers in planning, teaching and assessing science is in essence peer tutoring, gaining support from a more 'expert' learner in the field. One misconception about increased autonomy in a learner is that autonomy equates with working alone. That is not the case: autonomy will equip the learner so that s/he can make judgements as to when collaboration or seeking advice from a more 'expert' learner will be beneficial.

Teachers have planned together more since the introduction of the National Curriculum, a move that was initially resisted by Liz Thomas at Moorlands Infants School:

> I was quite resistant to it (joint planning) to start with. There have been so many moves to make us work together: what I was keen on was not to lose spontaneity and enthusiasm and each teacher's particular forte. But now, having done joint planning for a year, I would never, ever, want to go back to doing it on my own again. There is twice the input. You discuss things as you go along and, when it's a small group, you each see your input is important, but you are getting the benefit of all the teachers' ideas and expertise as well.

The culture of collaborative staff development that has grown since the introduction of the National Curriculum has been one of the most positive factors to arise from the implementation of the science orders.

How will assessment in science be managed and pupil's achievements be recorded?

As the implementation of science proceeded a number of initiatives were undertaken which were intended to develop teachers' skills in assessing science (Ollerenshaw *et al.*, 1991). Some of these initiatives involved working with children, focusing on what they were saying and doing. Teachers were supported in recognizing significant ideas which children held but which were expressed in naïve language. The research carried out by the SPACE Project (1990–93) showed that children held wide-ranging ideas about concepts in science. Some teachers became excited by the fact that the children in their own classes had existing ideas about the world around them. The importance of formative teacher assessment in planning for children's learning became increasingly recognized by teachers (Ollerenshaw and Ritchie, 1993). In assessing children's ideas teachers began to look at their own understanding of science in a new way.

The original statutory assessment regulations required teachers to record childrens' achievements in science against an excessive number of statements of attainment. Teachers in Key Stage 1 conscientiously grappled with the task. The obligation to carry out the SATs (standard assessment tasks) as well as teacher assessment in 1991 was for many Year 2 teachers an exhausting experience.

In schools the emphasis moved away from formative assessment linked to children's learning, towards summative assessment for reporting purposes. Assessment in science became synonymous with tick boxes against statements of attainment, record sheets and the accumulation of vast quantities of children's work as evidence for the defence of the teachers' judgements. A good deal of energy was taken up in devising recording systems and pupil profiles. The carrying out of the SATs often failed to provide any more information about a child's achievements. The requirement to report assessment levels to parents and LEAs at the end of a key stage has also meant that assessment has increasingly become summative. Liz Thomas commented:

> At the moment we are practically killing ourselves to do teacher assessment for every statement of attainment, but that is going, thankfully. At the last SAT period we had a great wad of science evidence. I know teacher assessment is ongoing but we feel we need a focus on teacher assessment at the time before filling in boxes; we must have up-to-date information. What we are doing at the moment is quite ridiculous. All the assessment we do is to enable us to fill the boxes. It is generally speaking useless for anything else. Although it did help us to draw some general conclusions. We discovered we were not doing very well with the topic Space, but I think that's why it is being moved into Key Stage 2, it's inappropriate.

Schools are putting into place their own systems for managing and recording assessment. At Shield Road, the co-ordinator, Ann Orchard, described their system:

> About recording assessment at Key Stage 1, we have record books – a page for each child for science, maths and English where we write down significant things; if we are working with an activity where we think we need to assess ... we jot down significant things they say or do. We tried having folders for children and we have a portfolio but the Key Stage 2 teachers suggested having these books and that's how it works. We're trying to develop an eye for assessment and it's something I thought we could do 'on the hoof' but I didn't find it happened. It did for some children but for others there was nothing. It's better to identify an assessment opportunity and jot down notes on everybody. At present in my class I have a collection of gloves and in the last couple of days I've started asking what they notice and I'm jotting down what the children say, to give me some idea of the sorts of observations they are making.

At Key Stage 2, national assessment has not been implemented to any extent. At Henleaze Junior School teachers have been working with a scheme of work in science for some time but Maggie Cosgrove highlighted the fact that assessment needs some input in the school:

> I've carried out a science audit to see where we are in science, but I feel the area we need to concentrate on is assessment. We take in evidence of work in Experimental and Investigative Science, but we need a system of ongoing teacher assessment that we don't really have in place. It is the time it takes to do assessment. I need to become familiar with the new Level Descriptions, I need to talk to other co-ordinators in the cluster group. It's difficult to work in isolation. Assessment so far has been summative for records, and not used in a formative way. Now that we feel comfortable with the scheme of work we can look at assessment and differentiation.

Teachers are hoping that the more general level descriptions in the new science orders will reduce the burden of summative assessment. This may prove to be the case. It will be interesting to see if the level descriptions are useful in supporting teachers in making formative assessments.

The impact of the pencil and paper tests of pupil's knowledge of science at the end of Key Stage 2 is hard to predict. Teachers in Year 6 are already talking about revision time and 'mock' tests throughout the key stage to 'prepare' children for the written tests. One outcome of testing knowledge and understanding of science at the end of Key Stage 2 will surely be to place emphasis on facts about science, and Experimental and Investigative Science (Sc1), will be marginalized. There is the suggestion that the assessment weighting of AT1 will be reduced in Key Stage 1 and 2. If this is the case the full implementation of the science orders in Key Stage 2 is even less likely to take place. It is inconceivable that the original intention of the Science Working Party, to offer children access to a broad array of science ideas, to be developed in a range of contexts, may be derailed by the imposition of 'Trivial Pursuits' like testing of facts about science at the end of Key Stage 2. Crammer texts are already with the publishers; undoubtedly more will follow. This is not to suggest that the development of subject knowledge is unimportant. What is contentious is the idea that the assessment of knowledge and understanding is easy and can be carried out simply through pencil and paper tests. As Ann Orchard commented:

> The worst outcome of implementation is the way that the government is introducing pencil and paper assessment for science and putting forward the idea that assessment is easy. The reporting aspect can be difficult and upsetting for parents and schools.

IMPLEMENTATION: HOW SUCCESSFUL HAS IT BEEN SO FAR?

The OFSTED inspections are carried out against a number of criteria for judging the quality of learning and the quality of teaching in science (OFSTED, 1993). Currently, inspectors are making judgements about the quality of learning opportunities in science against criteria which support the approaches to science promoted in Experimentel and Invesigative Science (Sc1). Part of the OFSTED guidance for inspectors includes the criterion that pupils should be developing the skills of imaginative but disciplined inquiry including systematic observation and measurement, making and testing hypotheses, planning and carrying out investigations competently and safely and drawing inferences from evidence. For children to be learning science in this way Sc1 needs to be implemented fully and children will be working scientifically using the process skills to enable them to carry out exploration and investigation.

In making judgements about the quality of teaching in science OFSTED are, furthermore, looking for evidence of clear and accurate exposition, skilful questioning to probe understanding and a balance of practical demonstration and well managed experimental work by pupils. For teachers to achieve this good practice in the teaching of science their own knowledge of science must be sound. This will enable teachers to ask probing questions and make sense of pupils' understanding, which is often expressed in naïve language. Teachers will need INSET support if they are to enhance the skills needed to become 'good quality' teachers of science against the OFSTED criteria.

The new science orders are about to be implemented in schools. This will mean that existing schemes of work will need to be reviewed in some schools, whilst in other schools they still need to be written. The development of schemes of work is an ongoing process and this will need to be the case in the future, so that they do not become stale. The new science orders are not expected to be reviewed within the next five years, following their introduction in 1995. This next five-year period will provide a space in which teachers can continue with the process of implementation without having to respond to constant change in the documentation. Hopefully this will result in pupils having quality learning opportunities in science, in the spirit of the science orders. Perhaps the sentiments of Lao Tzu are relevant here:

Governing a large country
is like frying a small fish.
You spoil it with too much poking.
(Tao Te Ching, translated Mitchell, 1988)

REFERENCES

Avon, County of (1989) *Revised Primary Science Guidelines*. Bristol: County of Avon.

DES (1985) *Science 5–16: A Statement of Policy*. London: HMSO.

DES (1991) *Science Key Stages 1 and 2: A Report by HMI on the First Year 1989–90*. London: HMSO.

Mitchell, S. (trans) (1988) *Tao Te Ching by Lao Tzu*. London: Harper Collins.

OFSTED (1993) *Inspection Handbook*. London: DFE.

Ollerenshaw, C. and Ritchie, R. (1993) *Primary Science: Making It Work*. London: David Fulton.

Ollerenshaw, C. *et al.* (1991) *Constructive Teacher Assessment*. Bristol: National Primary Centre.

SCAA (1994a) *Evaluation of the Implementation of Science in the National Curriculum. Vol 1: Executive Summary and Coverage*. London: SCAA.

SCAA (1994b) *Evaluation of the Implementation of Science in the National Curriculum. Vol 3: Differentiation*. London: SCAA.

SCAA (1994c) *The Review of the National Curriculum: A Report on the 1994 Consultation*. London: SCAA.

SPACE Project (1990-93) *Project Research Reports* (Various). Liverpool: Liverpool University Press.

Chapter 9

Information Technology in the National Curriculum

David Clemson

THE SOCIAL EFFECTS OF INFORMATION TECHNOLOGY (IT)

There can be few people in current industrial societies whose lives are not already greatly affected by the recent advances in micro-electronics. The use of increasingly intelligent domestic appliances to cashless shopping are just two commonplace examples of the effect which micro-technology is having on ordinary lives. The majority of financial transactions are now completed without the need for hard currency to touch hands. Smart cards, read in remote locations, can instantly credit or debit our accounts in central finance houses. The majority of financial transactions are already cashless operations in a *virtual* financial world. Very few people actually see, let alone handle, their salaries any more. Its passage is tracked through electronically interconnected financial systems. The social application of new technology is influencing the very nature of living. Technological innovation over the past ten years has changed, and is changing, social patterns. This is particularly obvious in the areas of distance communication and television broadcasting. Already electronic networks provide telephone and computer connections across the world. In the near future telecommunication using television receivers, fibre-optic cabling and computer technology will connect users to a much wider range of global communication facilities. Increasingly, data is stored, transmitted and manipulated digitally. This means that one common global cable network can feed digital data to and from existing telephones, televisions and computers. Though each utility has, to date, existed quite separately, there are areas of overlap that allow each utility to benefit from the other's facilities. The *convergence* of telephone communication, television transmission and computers is already being planned. The advent of global and truly interactive communication will probably become the most significant and universally far-reaching agent of change in society. Investment in systems for global communication has already been made. Multinational companies have invested vast resources in laying fibre-optic cable networks. The actual work on a cable infrastructure is nearing completion over much of the developed world. These physical land-lines of fibre-optic cables will offer most households the potential to become part of the electronically connected and interacting world. Initially the benefits will be traditional cable television and audio phone links. But the potential, available very soon, offers on-line video on demand, local community broadcasting, teleshopping and a conduit through which to communicate visually and audibly with the rest of the connected society through interlinked networks stretching across the world. Television will no longer be passive, but should become truly responsive and interactive. No longer will broadcasting companies provide a restricted diet of passive programmes from a limited range of predetermined and scheduled programmes. A personal computer agent will learn the user's interests and select items from a range of programmes world-wide which is sympathetic to the user's life patterns and desires. Popular programmes and the latest videos will cycle broadcast throughout the day, a new and complete performance starting every 5 minutes. Users will be able to log on and view when it is most convenient for them. Economically viable viewing numbers drawn from a world-wide audience will secure finance for programmes currently seen as of minority interest. Community-based subscription channels will offer a local voice to promote a regional identity and support community-based activity. The wired, communicating, interactive world is already happening around our schools. Many children are already using the Internet and chat with others across the world. It is thought that 42 million users already communicate through the Internet.

IT innovation is not just affecting the rather commonplace and mundane aspects of everyday life. In the less visible areas of research and development, IT has become an indispensable and powerful tool. For example, three-dimensional modelling inside a *cyber* world and remote sensing are two areas of discovery which owe an increased effectiveness to IT. Artists, architects and chemists alike are able to design, build and test three-dimensional structures in virtual space. Though the outcomes might be a new office block, the molecular model for a new drug or an aesthetic sculpture, the modelling software they each use is fundamentally the same. The building blocks and environment parameters are informed by known rules from the particular discipline, but, essentially, the modelling software is exactly the same for each project. IT offers the ability to build and create within a three-dimensional modelling environment in virtual space. The technology is sufficiently versatile to mimic traditional tools and duplicate the properties of materials so that an artist or craftsperson is comfortable in a 'virtual work-space'.

Advances in micro-electronics and telecommunications have allowed smaller but complex robotic devices to exist and be controlled from great distances. They are being designed to survive in hostile environments and to complete preprogrammed tasks, to broadcast data and, increasingly, to bring back samples. Such robots can either be directly driven by humans or, if the distance from the base makes real-time control unsuitable, designed to be completely self-sufficient, carrying out a preprogrammed sequence of activities. The ability to monitor both their environment and their own condition, coupled with programmed logic routines, allows machines some limited decision-making. Data from the locale and their own status is continually collected and logged. Should predetermined parameters be exceeded, routines are activated, logical options are considered and operating functions are adjusted accordingly. Already, the technology is sufficiently advanced so that there is no longer any scientific need for humans to risk life when exploring inhospitable environments. Robot drones do not need expensive life-support systems in order to survive nor would they be publicly grieved if 'lost in action'.

Improved artificial intelligence (thinking) systems are not only being developed to research extreme environments and experimental exploration. Quite commonplace domestic appliances often contain a basic logic system that senses conditions, 'thinks' and reacts appropriately. Intelligent toasters sense the thickness and moisture content of the bread and adjust the heat intensity and cooking time to produce toast of the required colour.

IT IN A 'FUTURE' CURRICULUM

Curriculum designers have a responsibility to provide an innovative education programme that recognizes an increasingly IT-dependent world. Life-skilling programmes must acknowledge the needs of today and recognize what will become normal activity in the very near future. Such programmes would help to equip learners with the necessary skills to cope with current technology and to provide future-proof skills and understandings. Such a curriculum change does not necessarily require additional content added to an already overloaded curriculum. Initially, what is required is a radical questioning of current curriculum content. Curriculum planners must be certain that every activity in the current curriculum not only has justifiable current value but also a clear and long-term future worth. Immediately this would question the usefulness, in a globally aware curriculum, of developing a predominantly nationalistic knowledge-base. The National Curriculum proposals since 1989, and particularly the revised orders (DFE, 1995a), have raised the worth of generic processes and transferable study skills at the expense of a subject knowledge base. Is it necessary to spend limited school time memorizing nuggets of nationalistic information, often in isolation, when this time could be spent developing transferable process and interrogation skills alongside a critical scepticism of 'truth'? Already technology provides pupils with the ability to browse and store information from a wide range of current national and cultural sources. The ability to see connections and make links across social and political boundaries whilst valuing all communities should, perhaps, become the agreed expectation of an educated person. In a 'content-free' and 'value-free' curriculum, IT competence would be essential. The exploration and interrogation of world-wide networks would allow informed judgements founded on current information from a wide range of sources. Such an innovative change will question not only the content of the school curriculum but also the role of teacher. A teacher's presence in the 'connected' classroom is still as crucial as ever, but the role and function will be different. S/he would be more concerned with the organization of process-developing activities and the development of high order critical thinking skills, rather than the delivery of subject knowledge. To utilize rapid changes in world situations and conflicting consensus views the curriculum content must become reactive and negotiable. The impact of the break-up of the USSR or the political developments in Northern Ireland are just two examples of the speed of change. The traditional curriculum is focused mainly upon content and established knowledge and is unable to adapt to changed circumstances quickly enough. An IT-aware curriculum would offer pupils the practice of increasingly complex applications, but always through realistic and contextualized activities. The practice scheme is underpinned and guided by a developmental map of skills. This is to establish not only the required software-dependent skills, but also to develop a confident understanding of the generic mechanics of IT. The purpose and importance of a process skills curriculum must be universally understood by subject domains and capitalized upon. The mission is to enable the current pupil (the future generation) to appreciate and harness the opportunities IT can offer now and in the future, but very much as an active participant rather than as a passive user.

Over the past 15 years computing power has consistently increased whilst relative costs have fallen. Even though software applications have become much more complex, the growth of the informal user-friendly desktops, such as Windows, has made learning easier and the piloting of utility tools largely intuitive, striving to develop *technology-users* rather than those being *technology-used*.

> Education Secretary Gillian Shephard today threw down a challenge to telecommunications, broadcasting and cable industries: 'Help us link schools and colleges to the information superhighway.'
> (DFE, 1995b)

The impact of the imminent communication revolution will have the most lasting and far-reaching effect upon the current educational provision, particularly content and delivery. Currently, children have access to a restricted amount of information from a limited range of sources: printed materials, national television, educational videos and from their teachers. Predominantly, school reference books contain watered-down and sanitized information censored by 'others' who have decreed what is useful. Due to a shortage of resources, and the need to differentiate through worksheets, teachers have further refined this information before allowing children access. Through the National Curriculum requirements some schools are developing skills of classification, interrogation, presentation and interpretation. They are the essential skills of the IT-competent learner. The choice and availability of appropriate data-sets often means explorations rarely escape from the classroom and the home country so that society's culture and beliefs are rarely challenged. The communication revolution will allow schools direct access to other schools, allowing pupils to talk to other pupils from many areas of the world. They will be able to exchange personal, social, political and environmental data without it having to pass through conventional, politically controlled gateways. Electronic mail provides an uncensored conduit, allowing pupils access to other pupils regardless of physical or political distance. The range of information holders and intelligence providers being connected throughout the world is multiplying daily. The 'connected' classroom will offer children 'real-time' information from a wide variety of sources across the world. In order to cope with what could become information overload pupils will need powerful information-handling techniques along with a firm understanding of higher order study skills. In order to engage fully and meaningfully in the debates, to understand national/political contexts and to use data effectively from a range of varied sources the need to appreciate bias and recognize propaganda becomes paramount. The confidence and competence to handle raw information from a variety of sources does not merely hinge upon the mechanical use of technology. It will also be dependent upon high level analytical and cognitive skills which are not always part of a subject/knowledge-based curriculum. For instance, can we maintain the notion of irrefutable 'fact' when, in a world context, it is more usefully defined as a personalized interpretation of events? Educators and curriculum designers have to recognize and develop strategies to cope with an information-overloaded classroom. The impact will not be just upon traditional curriculum content. The content of a world-aware curriculum will be enormously different and the teacher in the 'connected' classroom must offer a different kind of support. No longer can teachers expect to be the knowledge holders. To date this has often been an expertise in areas of the national statutory knowledge-base. The role of the teacher in a 'connected' classroom is to become a facilitator and antagonist: one who organizes experiences and challenges beliefs.

OFSTED considers a *future-proof* curriculum as one which places a competent use of information technology alongside traditional basic process skills. In the *Framework for the Inspection of Schools*:

Standards achieved by pupils are to be determined by evaluating . . .

- their competence in the key skills within reading, writing, speaking and listening, number and information technology, in the curriculum as a whole.
  (OFSTED, 1994, p. 18)

INFORMATION TECHNOLOGY IN EDUCATION

The real power of microcomputers comes from their versatility. When first switched on the computer does very little. What it has, at this point, is the potential to become a range of powerful instruments. The software or program determines what type of tool the computer will become. The range of application software available to schools is already expansive and growing in complexity and versatility almost daily. Software writers, particularly those writing for early educational machines, soon recognized the limitations of the systems and early software was often not user-friendly. As with many infant technologies there were no agreed conventions or standardized procedures. Often, children had to learn discrete key presses for each package. By contrast, the powerful personal computers available today have few hardware limitations and offer the user a common interface such as Windows. Programmers are now able to fashion programs to the needs of the users rather than to the limitations of the machinery. Simple word-processing programs have evolved into full function publishing suites with spell-checkers and thesaurus, while flat card-file index programs have become relational data-handling packages with impressive graphing capabilities. Though the power of the 'cheap' personal computer has increased in price, the associated high quality software has remained relatively affordable for all users. An increasing number of children have access to a home computer with industry standard software and, therefore, already understand the basic concepts of file-handling. It is the role of schools through an enlightened national curriculum to make sure that all children become IT competent before they complete their compulsory education. To function in an increasingly virtual world, pupils must be equipped with the necessary skills and understandings and be enabled to take full advantage of the current and future technology. Developing IT competence is fundamentally different from the acquisition of traditional subject knowledge. IT capability, in practice, concerns the selection and use of an appropriate software tool. It focuses upon a knowledge and use of a range of software tools. Underpinning and informing a knowledge of applications lies a set of high order transferable process skills. Unlike discrete and often single-purpose subject knowledge, IT offers the learner a group of interdisciplinary tools to aid and enrich tasks across the curriculum. The importance of a process skills base, though, is not exclusive to IT. In several subject orders, the developed National Curriculum recommends transferable conceptual process skills being developed alongside subject knowledge: for example, the exploration of science, investigations in mathematics and the sceptical skills of a history detective. Though they share a common notion of autonomous investigation they are still discrete to the particular subject domain. Only IT offers a truly cross-curricular set of learning and interrogation utilities: a universal panacea to aid the learner and the learning. Unlike traditional subjects, IT has no subject domain or knowledge-base in its own right. It exists only through the applications used in other curriculum areas. It exists as a means to an end and should not be seen as an end in itself. IT should never appear on a timetable but always be seen throughout the curriculum.

IT competence, therefore, should be thought of not as subject specific but rather software dependent. IT competence is the appropriate use of IT applications for good purpose and across the curriculum. IT-competent children are aware of the potential and opportunities which IT can offer in a variety of cross-curricular tasks whilst, at the same time, understanding the limitations of the specific applications. For instance, it would be expected that an IT-competent pupil would be aware of what IT can offer when handling data and understand also what individual data-handling tools are able to do. Based upon the particular task, we should expect children to choose a database or a spreadsheet as the most appropriate utility.

INFORMATION TECHNOLOGY IN A NATIONAL CURRICULUM

The evolution of IT to its current subject status has not occurred solely since the National Curriculum was established in 1988. In the early 1980s government initiatives, principally the Department of Trade and Industry's 'Micros in Schools' scheme, offered all schools part-funding to purchase a computer. The initiative boosted the British computer manufacturing industry and raised an awareness that developing pupils' knowledge of, and competence in using, computers would be essential for future generations. The result of the financial inducement was the creation of the BBC Computer and, by 1982, one primary school in five had a computer. This was hardly the 100 per cent target as originally hoped but it did signal a commitment by the government to assist, directly from central funding, the purchase of hardware and to introduce agencies to design and administer staff development programmes in computer education. At a time when IT was not universally prevalent in the world of work this was a far-reaching and ambitious project. Not only were computers to be made available in schools, but computer awareness was to become an aspiration for all children, regardless of age or social background. Following the DTI initiative, in 1980 the Microelectronics in Education Programme (MEP) was founded to help teachers to use the new technology in their teaching. This support agency has, since then, evolved through the Micro Electronics Support Unit (MESU) to emerge in 1989 as the National Council for Educational Technology (NCET). Since this time school-generated money, earmarked funding from successive governments and national teacher support projects, managed predominantly by National Council for Educational Technology (NCET), have raised the number of computers in classrooms in 1993-4 to an estimated 10 micros per school and a pupil–computer ratio of 1 micro to 18 pupils. This represents a fifty-fold increase in 11 years. As might be expected, the average expenditure on IT equipment has also increased: in primary schools some £5650 per school in 1994 compared with £2600 per school in 1991/92 and £500 in 1988. Nationally £106 million was spent on IT equipment in primary schools during 1993/4. Though centrally funded initiatives have raised the total computer numbers, much of the increased computer resources and software stock in schools has come from moneys generated by schools themselves or from other sources outside the education sector.

The importance of IT in education and a strengthening hardware base were well established when, in 1988, the architects of the National Curriculum considered the component elements that would make the statutory curriculum entitlement for all children. During the original deliberations IT was assumed to be an aspect of technology. As technology was, at this point, narrowly defined as the practical application and employment of science, technology was explicitly linked with science and was the responsibility of the Science Subject Working Group. HMI (1989) stimulated discussion on the cross-curricular use of IT and encouraged schools to devise a coherent strategy for making effective use of IT as an enrichment of the whole curriculum. There is little doubt that these discussions influenced the National Curriculum proposals and the deliberations of the subject working groups. The science working party recognized that technology touched not only science but many other subjects and should not be seen solely as the practical arm of science. While recognizing the disparate activities in design and technology (D&T) and information technology, it soon became apparent that a distinction should also be made between D&T and IT. By 1990 the statutory order for technology in the National Curriculum was published (DES, 1990). The order defined attainment targets for design and technology and a separate one (AT5) for IT. By 1993 all subject orders were in place and it became increasingly obvious that the curriculum had become overloaded (see Chapter 1). Sir Ron Dearing was commissioned to review the current orders with an intention to reduce subject content, particularly outside the core subjects, and to simplify the assessment arrangements. Even before the consultation papers were distributed, Sir Ron had announced that design and technology and information technology should be considered as distinct subjects and would be considered and presented separately. This was to enable teachers of all subjects to have separate copies of the IT requirements, and that D&T and IT be treated separately for assessment and reporting purposes. Due to the statutory definition of technology as established in the original 1988 Education Act, IT and D&T would continue to appear within the same order, but for all intents and purposes, IT and D&T should be treated as separate subjects. Though all other foundation subjects were being reviewed with the intention of reducing content, the IT requirements and its underlying philosophy would in essence remain the same. The order for information technology would provide programmes of study to develop essential skills for the future. IT competence would equip pupils with a range of skills to enhance and support their own learning and provide tools with which to enrich and develop an understanding of all other curriculum subjects. Competence in using and applying information technology is, then, a statutory entitlement for all children from 5 to 16. Developing that competence through explicit programmes of study and with appropriate hard and software is now the legal responsibility of all state schools.

Secretary of State, Shephard, in her keynote address at the British Education and Technology (BETT) Exhibition, London, in January 1995 stated that,

we have now placed IT skills at the heart of that National Curriculum. The subject orders we have published make it clear that pupils should have the opportunity to develop IT skills when studying *every* subject ... These are the everyday tools of modern society. Mastering these tools and accessing them through information technology are as crucial to cultural development as to future economic success. That mastery requires knowledge, skills and understanding – in a word, 'education'.
(Shephard, 1995)

The statutory order for IT will put pressure upon schools to prioritize their resources over a long period of time in order to achieve a realistic hardware base and software provision to enable all children to achieve their legal entitlement. The figures show that there is currently a high number of machines in schools. Hidden behind average totals is the range and age of machines currently in service. This is one reason why the order does not prescribe the actual software titles to be used. Not only would that be inappropriate due to hardware variations, but, as the orders are to be in place for five years, one can only speculate what powerful computers or software applications will be common in schools in the very near future. The statutory orders focus on the use, knowledge and understanding of generic application and content-free software. An understanding of one word-processing package should allow the user an easy transfer to another. With a firm understanding of what a word-processor is able to do we should be able easily to transfer from one package or machine to another. The differences are often different key presses and layout. Similarly, all databases function in the same way. Practice in basic operating principles and the ability to ask logical questions are required skills for any data-handling packages; they are not software dependent. The actual software package becomes of less importance. What is being established is cross-platform confidence based upon a knowledge and understanding of generic utilities. It is not useful, therefore, to measure IT competence by listing the range of software titles used by a pupil. It is more about forward planning, autonomous selection of software for a purpose and, of course, the quality of the outcome.

Progress towards IT competence will only occur when a clear whole-school developmental programme is in place and understood by all staff. The underlying principles behind such a scheme presume development and progression will be achieved by:

- experience of using an increasing variety of applications and a confident understanding of the relationship between application and purpose;
- the ability to undertake more complex tasks and to use increasingly versatile applications (with increasingly complex facilities);
- the interlinking of software packages to present information from various sources and with a recognition of audience;
- a move from teacher-dependence to personal autonomy.

The aim of the statutory orders is for the pupil to become an autonomous and competent user of IT. This goal will not be achieved unless schools plan for sufficient and appropriate long-term practice in realistic contexts and for good purpose. A developmental programme for IT would look similar to that of any other curriculum entitlement. A whole-school scheme of work would explicitly describe the IT entitlement and map the corresponding provision throughout a pupil's career. It is crucial that schools plan a long-term programme of study for IT throughout a child's career and embedded within the curriculum. Not only is the long-term development important but also the short-term immersion in an appropriate curriculum task.

The transferability of generic IT competence is best illustrated when IT skills are transparent and embedded in worthwhile activities that aim to develop subject understanding. An investigation designed to enhance subject understanding, and assuming IT competence, adds to subject knowledge and understanding while emphasizing the transferability of IT skills. Recognizing a pupil's entitlement to IT should involve innovative and imaginative subject planning.

The content for the IT order is key stage-discrete, but the constituent programmes of study follow a similar format:

Programme of Study One:
  – Establishing a critical awareness and understanding of the use of IT in everyday life.
Programme of Study Two:
  – Communicating and Handling Information.
Programme of Study Three:
  – Controlling, Modelling (and at KS2 Monitoring).
  (DFE, 1995a, pp.68–9).

What is different through the key stages, and an indication of pupil progress, are engagements with increasing challenging tasks which require the effective use of increasingly complex IT applications and the planned movement from teacher-dependence to pupil-controlled and autonomous problem-solving.

PS1 content is not hardware dependent; it involves developing a critical and sceptical awareness of the wide use of IT and its effects on everyday life.

PS2 and PS3 describe the range of IT-rich activities that pupils should be able to complete at each Key Stage. The ability to complete these tasks is the output measure of a pupil's IT competence, but their realization is dependent not only on the pupil's learning potential, but also upon schools to provide for effectively planned and appropriately resourced IT activities. To be most effective these tasks should be embedded in, and transparent to, traditional subject development. This poses schools with organizational and resourcing problems. To achieve PS2 and PS3 expectations at each key stage requires pupils' access to a range of software tools and a reliable hardware base. The orders advise that progression involves the use of more complex packages in more demanding situations. This would suggest access to more powerful programs running on more powerful and up-to-date machines. Schools should consider a long-term investment strategy to provide the hardware base to support the required software with which to enable pupils to progress. What is clear is that a few BBC Masters or early Nimbus machines in a school can no longer fulfil the pupils' statutory IT entitlement particularly at the end of KS 2.

To help teachers to plan effective and contextualized IT activities the programmes of study can more usefully be broken down into five discrete application strands:

  Strand 1 – Communication
  Strand 2 – Handling Data
  Strand 3 – Controlling
  Strand 4 – Modelling
and at Key Stage 2
  Strand 5 – Monitoring

Figure 9.1 unpacks the programmes of study into their component strands. These are further analysed to show the range of generic software applications pupils should be

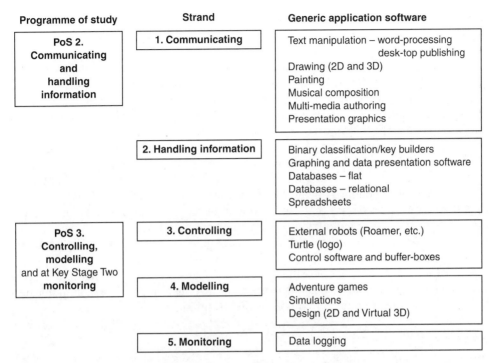

Programme of study	Strand	Generic application software
PoS 2. Communicating and handling information	**1. Communicating**	Text manipulation – word-processing desk-top publishing Drawing (2D and 3D) Painting Musical composition Multi-media authoring Presentation graphics
	2. Handling information	Binary classification/key builders Graphing and data presentation software Databases – flat Databases – relational Spreadsheets
PoS 3. Controlling, modelling and at Key Stage Two monitoring	**3. Controlling**	External robots (Roamer, etc.) Turtle (logo) Control software and buffer-boxes
	4. Modelling	Adventure games Simulations Design (2D and Virtual 3D)
	5. Monitoring	Data logging

Figure 9.1 *From programmes of study to application software*

acquainted with during their school career. The IT strands serve to highlight the separate and different tasks which application software can support. It would be useful to consider what these strands are about and what opportunities they can offer over and above traditional learning tools.

Strand 1 – using IT to communicate

This strand represents the applications which communicate ideas and meanings to others. In the early stages of hardware development the most obvious example was word-processing. This is a program that transforms the computer into an electronic typewriter. Unlike a mechanical typewriter the user has complete control over the text being written. Introductions and conclusions could be written before the main body of the text. Words, sentences and whole blocks of text can be added, altered and moved about the whole piece of writing. The work can be electronically saved and recalled at will for amendment at a future date. For the first time writers have complete control over the content, writing sequence and final presentation of the work. Desk-top publishing programs allow the writers to add pictures, charts and diagrams to their work. The style and size of lettering (font) can be chosen to give writing an ambience and prepare the reader for the content. IT allows the author complete control from an initial idea to the final published work.

Communicating ideas and emotions do not only have to be through the medium of text: sounds and pictures also convey meaning. Programs are available which provide the opportunity to compose music and record and manipulate sound samples. Musical composition and sequencer software linked to Musical Instrument Digital Interface (MIDI) keyboards are offering composers the same freedom to manipulate sounds as word-processing authors can manipulate text.

What can IT offer the artist? Painting and drawing software allows the artist to paint in light with a palette of many millions of colours, to cycle through colour-ways and repeat patterns at the touch of a button. Sculptors and designers can create three-dimensional structures which are impossible in the real world. Virtual buildings can be created in cyber space, explored and tested even before the first real brick is laid.

As computer power has increased and relative costs have fallen, the opportunity now exists to merge all the media above into an exciting and revolutionary mode of communication: text, sound and motion video combined in multimedia presentations. This is not science fiction. The latest systems in schools are multimedia capable.

The order for IT advised that pupils should, in their communications, be aware of and recognize a perceived audience. Communication and presentation, whether it is text, sound or pictures constructed for a target audience, add purpose to the task and value to the undertaking.

The range and quality of opportunities which IT can currently offer pupils to express themselves and to communicate to others is awe-inspiring. What communication software is just around the corner will be breath-taking.

Strand 2 – using IT to handle information

Computers can sort data from lists accurately and with great speed; so long as the data is stored in a logical manner a computer could probably locate it. This strand develops an understanding and competence in constructing and interrogating database files. Initially the data-sets will be personal to pupils and often small. As pupils' confidence increases then interrogation of large data-sets constructed by others is possible.

Applications that allow information to be manipulated and interrogated are key building programs (Classification Trees), graphing software, databases and spreadsheets. Each tool offers a different type of data manipulation. Competent IT-users will appreciate the differences and select the package best suited to their enquiry.

Classification Trees are programs that allow classification keys to be constructed and interrogated. A hierarchical tree can be constructed from a collection of cognate items, each classified by their unique properties or attributes. The activity helps pupils to recognize what is the same and what is different about members of a cognate group, and to describe and refine a description of the variation. An understanding of, and ability to recognize similarity and difference are essential qualities for an information investigator.

Graph-drawing programs offer pupils the ability to display a discrete set of data in a variety of formats. Simple button-presses will alter the scalar factor or recalculate class-intervals to shape the graph towards a desired meaning. Pupils can easily and quickly see how different the same data looks in other graphical styles. Such an awareness will serve them well when they are presented 'pictures of data' from other sources.

Databases are programs which store data in a structured form. The mental model of a paper-based library card system will hold, but it exists in an electronic form. Once the database has been constructed, individual titles or whole sets of books can be called by asking questions about their particular attributes. Should a book on fly-fishing by an English author and written about 1940 be required, interrogating the library catalogue with a few keywords can probably locate some possibilities. Increasingly, pupils are using reference CD-Roms. These are often encyclopedias. They are in fact large databases whose individual articles are classified by keywords while the contents are conceptually cross-linked. To find a topic pupils would initiate a search for a keyword significant to the enquiry. Asking for Nelson would probably find Nelson Mandela and also Lord Nelson and any other person, animal, plant or place, with nelson somewhere in the name. Considering the initial choice and combination of significant keywords to hone down the possibilities is a crucial skill as it affects both the number and the appropriateness of the 'hits'.

Spreadsheets were originally designed as a calculating tool for accountants, but with imagination they offer rich opportunities for investigation across the curriculum. Spreadsheets are most versatile when used as a calculating and enquiry matrix. Each cell in the worksheet can contain words, numbers or formulae. In its simplest form, the spreadsheet tabularizes and sorts data. In its most imaginative form, and with a basic understanding of mathematics, pupils can construct and investigate quite complex 'what if' explorations.

Data-handling software provides pupils with a powerful investigative tool to explore connections, suggest and test hypotheses, and present the results in a range of influential images.

Strand 3 – using IT to control

It is increasingly common for everyday household devices to be controlled by a microchip. Washing machines, toasters, microwave ovens and televisions with a snooze option are just a few of the ordinary machines that contain a control microchip. The chip has a dedicated function or job to do and it sits in the machine waiting for the user to decide what colour the toast should be or what washing cycle is needed. Children can get a feel for the dedicated devices by programming and driving an external robot. These devices, such as Roamer, can be connected to the computer or be free-running. Even the connected variety do not need to be physically joined by a cable. The connection and transfer of program from computer to robot is by an infrared beam. The most common programming language is Logo as it uses commands and phrases derived from physical movements. Pupils soon learn that the Roamer will do only what the program says: no matter how much you talk to it cannot make decisions for itself.

Strand 4 – using IT to model and to simulate

There are three aspects to this strand: adventure gaming, virtual modelling and simulation. Each capitalize upon the computer's ability to create virtual environments inside the computer's memory: environments which can be programmed to act and react to predefined rules. These conditions could mirror real life, or they could be alien environments with different but consistent limits.

Adventure gaming. Computers have the ability to create virtual adventure worlds. These are lands where new rules apply and have to be learned, often to survive. As the explorer roams through this virtual environment, perils are encountered or tasks are to be performed. In their simplest form these are probably objects to be collected from one location in order to be used an another. The outcomes can be as varied as reuniting Granny with her cat or finding the Holy Grail.

Modelling packages allow users to construct objects and structures in a three-dimensional virtual environment. The structures usually follow the real laws of physics and act like concrete objects. The computer gives designers, architects and artists the ability to explore and alter their virtual creations as it they were real objects.

Simulations. The virtual environment can be used to create interactive models of real systems for teaching and research purposes. Learners can grasp more readily quite difficult ideas if they can see and control a phenomenon in operation. An interactive model of the water cycle where the height of mountains or the evaporation rate can be altered, or the propagation of seeds where light, water and heat can be adjusted and the effects logged, are just two examples of systems that are difficult, if not impossible, to manipulate in the real world.

Strand 5 – using IT to monitor external events

Data-logging software allows the gathering of data from the physical world over a very short or long period of time. Data is collected through sensors attached to the computer. These monitor characteristics from the physical world such as light, temperature, sound, humidity. The samples are taken at predetermined times and recorded, usually on a time/characteristic graph. The time intervals are determined by the investigation. To log the temperature change from night to day would have readings every 10 minutes over the 24-hour period. Monitoring light increase when a light bulb is switched on would require readings every millisecond. Read-outs from data-logging investigations allow pupils to see a graphical representation of real-time change.

IMPLEMENTING THE ORDERS FOR IT: THE ROLE OF THE IT CO-ORDINATOR

In order to plan, provide for and maintain the programme of study, there is now a strong case for the appointment of an IT co-ordinator in all schools: someone who has a more specialist knowledge of the computer systems in use, an understanding of whole school issues and curriculum goals and the influence to initiate change. Not only will their role involve curriculum planning and long-term programming, but they are also responsible for the management of IT resources, hard, soft and human. There is a variety of machines current in schools. Newer, more powerful systems have the access advantages of a hard-disk drives, but require regular file management. The range of computers in schools means software is likely not to be compatible between computer types and would require clear labelling and sympathetically written documentation. Increasingly, due to the demise of LEA purchasing agreements, software in teachers' toolboxes would need to be licensed and separately registered.

For an effective long-term provision staff should be both aware and competent in developing pupils' IT and in utilizing IT to enrich the learning experience. IT is a new subject for many teachers and was probably not a part of their training. One crucial factor in assuring curriculum quality is a recognition of staff strengths and the provision of a programme of support to alleviate areas of weakness. An important aspect of curriculum co-ordination is to identify staff development needs and offer support programmes in the specialist subject. An IT co-ordinator should audit staff IT competence and awareness and devise sympathetic programmes of staff development.

As one would expect of all curriculum subjects, staff should be equipped and capable of providing for the statutory requirements, and aware of long-term curriculum goals. The difference with IT as a subject is that its development is application-driven and critically context-dependent. Teachers should be competent with the software their pupils will need to use and innovative in placing the IT exercise into realistic and worthwhile settings. It should not be expected that IT co-ordinators have subject knowledge in all areas of the curriculum, rather that they are aware of the transferable skills and the sort of investigations IT can enable and enrich. Staff support and curriculum integration are just two of a co-ordinator's responsibilities. Someone also needs to consider the resources base required to support the statutory requirements for IT. Due to the widespread decrease of LEA support schools are increasingly having to provide for themselves. The chart adapted from Gibbon and Reid (1992) (see Table 9.1) lists some of the tasks and responsibilities that need to be assigned if a school is to become IT-effective. It is a useful exercise for schools to consider who, if anybody, is currently responsible for these activities.

As already stated, IT competence is about using a variety of IT-based utilities appropriately, and for good purpose, and ensuring that complete competence is demonstrated by the autonomous use of IT. There are aspects of children's autonomy in IT which are not specifically mentioned in the statutory orders, but these are essential attributes of a self-sufficient IT-user. In order that pupils use IT unsupported they will need to be confident in the use of the technology itself. This means that pupils should be competent to use the machinery by themselves. This involves understanding hard-disk structures, formatting disks, saving work and, in integrated environments, cutting, pasting and switching from one application to another. Such practical skills should not be left for children to pick up unaided. They must also become a part of the long-term development plan. Table 9.2 describes some of the machine skills which must be mastered to become a truly autonomous user of IT. Therefore, a whole-school progression map for IT would chart three discrete areas of development: one which denotes opportunities for integration, another which defines an increasing application knowledge and a third which describes the development of machine-handling skills. The map would show points in the pupils career when:

- realistic tasks and contextualized activities will introduce or develop an IT strand;
- the application skills base would need to be increased;
- it would it be necessary to introduce new, and practise existing, machine skills.

Table 9.1 *Allocation of roles and responsibilities in an IT-effective school*

TASK	SMT	Head	ITCo	Staff	Everyone	Others
Organize and manage groups to write IT policy						
Alert others to the IT support services offered regionally and nationally						
Alert others to the IT support available for pupils with SEN						
Assist in the design of IT development plans						
Responsible for ordering and distributing IT equipment around the school						
Create opportunities for teacher training and development in school						
Ensure equality of opportunity with IT						
Ensure that the school guidelines for assessment include IT as an element						
Identify needs and formulate policies for IT across the curriculum						
Plan and provide IT INSET for other teachers						
Keep abreast of current philosophies in the use of IT						
Advise staff and parents about the current 'best buy' for home use						
Alert others to the nature of IT capability as defined in the NC						
Alert others to the uses of IT as a tool to enhance learning						
Attend all the courses offered by the LEA						
Be responsible for the software and hardware policy of the school						
Chair the school IT development group						
Co-ordinate the support provided by LEA advisers and other agencies						
Compile staff 'toolbox'						
Compile and produce timetables for IT equipment						
Deliver training to other teachers						
Diagnose equipment faults (simple)						
Oversee and ensure the balanced delivery of IT across the curriculum						
Evaluate classroom practice involving the use of IT						
Inform other staff of good, bad and interesting practice using IT						
Keep a catalogue of hardware and software available in school						
Keep others aware of the IT opportunities in all subjects of the NC						
Liaise with outside agencies in industry and commerce						
Make 'toolbox' copies of hardware						
Manage and maintain hard disks on all machines						
Monitor and assess the uses of IT made by pupils						
Negotiate the purchase of site licences for key pieces of software						
Provide classroom-based IT support for staff in all curriculum areas						
Recommend IT activities for different curriculum situations						
Recommend appropriate software for pupil and teacher needs						
Regularly discuss IT provision with Head and curriculum co-ordinators						
Repair computer equipment (simple)						
Represent the school at LEA meetings for IT co-ordinators						
Set up displays showing a range and uses of IT in school						
Liaise cross-phase to ensure continuity of experience in IT						
Build and program concept keyboard overlays for all staff						
Deliver IT skills to all pupils in the school						
Keep records of pupils' progress through levels of attainment in IT						
Prepare reports on individual pupils' progress in IT						
Alert others to the uses and importance of IT in society at large						
Manage the school information system, support and train admin. staff						
Produce school publications using desk-top publishing equipment						
Take minutes for the school IT development group						
Diagnose equipment faults (complex)						
Make and repair cables for computer equipment						
Repair computer equipment (complex)						
Supervise the IT technician (joke)						

Source: Based on an original idea by MITAC (see Gibbon and Reid, 1992)

Table 9.2 *Developing machine-handling skills*

	Nur	Rec	K.S. One		K.S. Two			
			Y1	Y2	Y3	Y4	Y5	Y6
Turning on the machine								
Loading a disk								
Starting a program								
Printing a file								
Switching/logging off								
Taking care of disks								
Mouse skills								
Return/enter key								
Saving to disk – same disk								
Recovering from disk – same disk								
Operating the printer								
Selecting appropriate software								
Saving to disk – work disk								
Recovering from disk – work disk								
Using integrated programs								
Formatting a disk								
Copying disks								
Copying files								

The machine-handling skills base is not a part of the statutory orders, but without competent handling of the technology pupils can never become completely autonomous. Table 9.2 lists the range of machine-handling skills needed just to complete key stage tasks. Schools might consider when, if ever, these skills are currently being introduced.

Developing competence requires pupils to experience and become competent in an increasing variety of more versatile and complex software applications. For this to happen, schools need to be sure that they have sufficient software not just to cater for the strands, but also to provide for the necessary progression: to use software of increasing complexity and versatility. The co-ordinator should audit, categorize and catalogue titles alongside the strands. Application software which builds IT competence should be evaluated and designated to a phase so that staff and pupils are clear which software applications best support each strand and each particular stage in the pupil's development. For example, the text-manipulation programs should be evaluated by their facilities, spell-checkers, thesaurus, ability to import pictures, tables and their ease of use. These are allocated a place on the development matrix. If this was done for all National Curriculum strands the co-ordinator would be aware of the gaps, both in software applications and in age phases. Individual staff would have a reduced set of titles with which to become familiar and competent. As a starting-point, co-ordinators could focus staff-development sessions upon specific titles and, if necessary, cater for individual staff needs. Table 9.3 offers schools an empty software/strand matrix to complete.

IMPLEMENTING THE ORDERS FOR IT IN THE CLASSROOM

Implementation at the class level requires of teachers an understanding of the opportunities IT can offer to other curriculum activities, while remaining mindful of the need to support pupils' ongoing IT skills development programme. IT proficiency is about employing a range of process and technical skills which do not exist in a vacuum and without a context. Teachers should devise imaginative and worthwhile tasks which are embedded in the subject curriculum, but also be conscious of the school's long-term IT programme.

The example activity described in Table 9.4 illustrates the need for teachers to recognize a pupil's previous IT experiences in order to inform their planning. This activity presents pupils with an understanding of a collection and experience in sorting and classifying items by their individual physical attributes. The activity can mark a crucial stage in a pupil's understanding of similarity and difference and an introduction to the logic of IT data handling.

It is a practical floor activity based upon concrete items. The concrete experience and an introductory understanding of logical structuring should allow the movement to an abstract computer-based programme much more easily. It is planned for Key Stage 1 pupils, assuming that a long-term programme for IT development is established in school. If this were not the case then the concrete-to-abstract progression should still be recognized as a crucial process. Making the activity applicable for older children would simply require:

- the use of a different collection more meaningful to the age range such as recorded music, books or a mini-beast collection;
- teachers to have a higher expectation of the quality of questions being formed;
- an assumption that pupils use more sophisticated classification criteria, rather than just visual attributes, such as by accurate measurement or scientific experiment.

The planning chart in Table 9.4 describes the educational intentions for the sessions and highlights the cross-curricular connections which are possible.

EXAMPLE OF AN IT ACTIVITY: SOFT TOYS

Session One

The initial activity is a floor-based discussion and the building of a classification tree with the real items. The pupils will initially be seated in a circle around an open carpet space, each child holding a member of the soft toy collection.

Introduce the collection of soft toys by name and allow pupils to handle each member.

Table 9.3 *Developing IT competence – software/strand progression*

Developing IT competance – Software/Strand progression

	Communicating information and handling information					Controlling, modelling and monitoring		
	Text manipulation	Drawing/painting	Musical composition	Sorting/databases	Spreadsheets	Controling	Modelling	Monitioring
Rec Y1								
Y2								
Y3								
Y4								
Y5								
Y6								

Table 9.4 *Implementing the IT Orders – Information Technology: Key Stage 1*

IT Stand: 2 (handling information) Sessions: 3 (sequential) Time: 3 x 40 minutes			
Cross-curricular support : Mathematics – number; English – speaking and listening; Science – experimental and investigative science, variation and classification, materials and their properties; Art – investigating and making			
Programme of study : (questions/concepts/skills/knowledge to develop) *What do I want the children to learn?*	**Activities:** (teaching and learning experiences) *What do I want the children to do?*	**Resources:** *What resources will the children need access to?*	**Assessment :** (nature of evidence) *What evidence will I have?*
General aims: *Introducing generic skills for handling information and developing an understanding of classification structures and interrogation (questioning) techniques – a pre-database activity.*	**1. Classify items from a cognate group by their individual and significant physical attributes.** i.e. build a concrete binary sorting tree.	**A collection of soft-toys (approx. 8 initially); each toy has a name badge.** For this age select toys which have several obvious common attributes; e.g. eyes, legs, ears.	**Completed tree (physical) as a floor activity or an interactive wall display.**
Specific aims: **1. What is a collection?** Notion of a cognate group/collection as an early introduction to a sample group.	**2. Apply consistency to the sorting criteria.** Test their ability to add more items to the tree by acknowledging their existing question in relation to the new items attributes.	**10 blank yes/no question templates.** These can be laminated to enable instant wipe-off question refinement.	**Observation of collaborations and records of questions formed, defined and refined.**
2. How are members of a collection different or the same? Develop a recognition of similarity and difference by obvious attributes – Physical. At this age and with this collection this will involve observable differences only.	**2. Test out their tree/questions for robustness.** Put name tags back on to toys by questioning their way through the tree.	**Labels matching names on badges.**	**Computer-based tree.**
3. What are good (robust) questions? Introduce an understanding that 'good' questions are those not based upon value 'personal' judgements. They are based upon actual physical/visual properties; not opinion.	**3. Create an electronic classification key for the soft-toy collection.** Use a computer-based tree building program.	**Application software – Binary sorting tree.** E.g. information tree – IBM, tree – Archimedes, branch – BBC, Nimbus.	**Hard copy from the computer-based tree in the form of a usable classification key.**
4. What is meant by classification? Introduce notion of classification by attribute and practical experience of constructing and interrogating classification keys.			**Observational evidence of ability to trial completed tree and with the introduction of another member to apply consistency.**
5. Computers can only answer yes/no questions This is a crucial understanding particularly when pupils begin to frame questions with which to interrogate a computer database.			

Teaching point: Will each child look carefully at their soft toy. I want you to describe it to everyone else.

Look at ways to divide the collection into two groups by some attribute. The teacher would provide the first few examples and pupils would be asked to guess the attribute selected.

Teaching point: Can anyone work out how I have sorted the toys out?

Later individual pupils would do the sorting and the rest of the group would try to guess the criteria used.

Teaching point: Can anyone work out how Meena has sorted?

The blank question sheets are introduced and discussed.

Teaching point: Look at these question sheets. When you have answered the question there are arrows pointing to which way to go next. If the answer to the question is 'yes' you go this way, while if the answer is 'no', this is the route to be taken.

Pupils are asked to invent a question that divides the group into two smaller groups. The question is such that the answer can only be yes or no for each toy.

Teaching point: Let's try that question out on each toy. Has Jenny got any white fur on her body?

Continue to subdivide the items by questions until each toy is at the end of its own twig. The route from the start to the item describes the toy's unique properties.

Teaching point: Sarah is the only toy who does not wear ribbons, has eyelashes, is naked and has white fur on her body.

At this point it would be useful to add a few more toys to see if the children can apply consistency. Can they work through the tree and then add another question to differentiate the new item from the one already at that twig end?

Teaching point: I have just found Blue, can we see where it will fit on our tree?

Replace the toys at the twig ends with the name badges and put the toys at the start of the tree. If the questions chosen are 'robust', then it should be possible to take a toy through the questions and, by following the yes/no route, name the soft toy.

Teaching point: Can we see if we can name this toy!

Robust questions are those which anyone can answer by looking carefully at the item. They are not value judgements, such as, 'Is it cuddly?', 'Is it nice?' The physical tree can be transferred to a wall display for other children to test out. The same collection of items can be used for different groups of children. If the questions are robust then every completed tree is correct. The completed tree in figure 9.2 shows just one possibility.

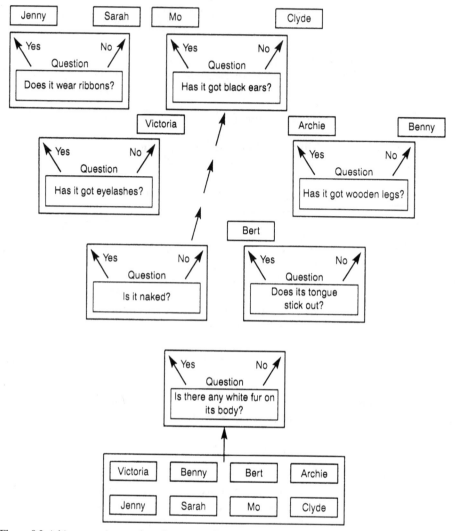

Figure 9.2 *A binary sorting tree based upon a collection of soft toys*

Session Two

This session allows pupils to copy and refine their questions while entering them onto an appropriate computer-based classification program. When this has been completed the naming of toys activity can be done again, this time using the virtual version. It is useful for children to interrogate other groups' 'answers' in order to value others' work and to refine their own questioning techniques.

Session Three

For assessment purposes it would be useful for children to examine physically and classify another collection, but this time with little teacher intervention. This would allow the teacher an opportunity to observe children making decisions, take notes on the quality of each child's contribution and make a judgement about their skills of collaboration. IT competence is not just having an established IT skills-bank, but also being capable of using these skills autonomously.

This pre-computer activity develops skills and understandings necessary before embarking on database projects in cyber space. Learners of all ages need concrete models with which both to visualize and to conceptualize what is going on in an abstract system (inside the computer). This activity is not key stage-dependent, but illustrates the need to recognize progression and long-term development. The context (the collection) and the examination technique (the questions) can easily be altered to suit other age-ranges. It is essential to follow a concrete to abstract progression at whatever age.

CONCLUSION

There can be little doubt that the usefulness of knowledge will diminish while information-gathering processes, communication and presentation will become increasingly evident in the 'connected' world. One deduction might be to consider what value there is in bringing pupils together to learn nationalistic 'detail' when these facts, plus others, will increasingly be available in their own homes. An information centre in most homes must have an effect upon what is done in schools and raises the question of the validity of much of the current activity in local institutions. It is evident that there is a need to justify what currently goes on when pupils come together in a school. What can be better done at home and what exactly is gained by pupils coming together? Is there a future in the corporate act of learning when the home environment is information-rich?

Underpinning the ideas in this chapter is the belief that IT competence is both desirable and necessary for all pupils. Children who have not developed an understanding of IT-application and an ability to utilize the technology for their own purposes will be severely disadvantaged in the future. This will not just limit their ability to assume a valued role in an increasingly technological world of work, but will also dramatically affect the variety and quality of leisure opportunities available. There is a growing fear that already there are two cultures developing in the world: those who have a grasp, an understanding of and, most importantly, access to, the new technology and those who do not. Schools are a key force in ensuring that children do have this access and the skills and knowledge to use it.

REFERENCES

DES (1990) *Technology in the National Curriculum*. London: HMSO.
DFE (1995a) *Key Stages 1 and 2 of the National Curriculum*. London: HMSO.
DFE (1995b) *Department of Education News Bulletin*, 002/95, 11 January 1995. London: DFE.
Gibbon, W. and Reid, I. (1992) *Management of Information Technology across the Curriculum* (MITAC Project). Newcastle upon Tyne: NORIC Centre.
HMI (1989) *Curriculum Matters 15: Information Technology 5 – 16*. London: HMSO.
OFSTED (1994) *Framework for Inspection of Schools*. London: OFSTED.
Shephard, G. (1995) Keynote speech at BETT exhibition, London. Reported in *Department for Education News Bulletin* 002/95, January 1995. London: DFE.

Index

Abbotswood Infants School   120, 122, 125, 126
ABSLU   39
ACACE   39
adventure games   170
Aldrich, R.   12, 14
Alexander, R.   48, 74, 83, 84, 85, 102, 138
Andrews, R.   99, 116
Ashley, B.   109
assessment   49–50, 54, 60, 62, 63, 65, 67, 104, 105,
    111, 112, 115, 117, 123, 135, 139–41
assessment in science   54, 60, 62, 63, 65, 67, 144,
    155–6
Assessment of Performance Unit (APU)   54
Association of Science Education (ASE)   55, 67
Ausubel, D.   58
Avon LEA   55, 101, 147

Baddeley, P.   109
Baker, K.   28, 41
Barrs, M.   20, 26, 105, 106, 111, 113
Bash, L.   3, 14
Bazalgette, C.   104
Beano   107
Bennett, S.N.   63
bilingualism   99, 110
Black, P.   20
Bleakhouse Junior School   120, 121, 123
Blenkin, G.M.   75, 78
Blin-Stoyle, R.   41
Bolton, E.   20
Briggs, R.   107
Brown, G.   100
Bryce-Heath, S.   30, 100
Buckingham, D.   114
Bullock Report   15, 100
Burnett, F.B.   114
Burton, N.   68

Calkins, L.   114
Carey, J.   21
Carre, C.G.   63
Carter, R.   26, 32, 97
Chambers, A.   110
Children's Learning in Science (CLIS) Project   57
Clanchy, J.   19
Clark, M.   106
Clarke, K.   18, 43, 83
classification trees   168
Clay, M.   106, 111, 112
Cockroft, W.   40, 122, 123
collaborative working   152
Collington, P.   107
computers   98, 105, 107, 110, 111, 115
connected classroom   160
constructivist approaches   57
control using IT   169
convergence   158
Cooper, S.   109
co-ordinator   170, 171
co-ordinator, role of science   151
Cope, B.   113
Coulby, D.   3, 4, 5, 14, 78
Cox, B.   7, 8, 14, 15, 20, 25, 29, 75, 78
Croll, P.   74
cross-curricular links   48, 71–95, 97, 100, 103–4,
    105, 111, 112, 116
Crowley, T.   32
Curriculum Council for Wales (CCW)   56
Czerniewska, P.   112

data-handling using IT   168
databases   168
Dearing, R.   x, 44, 145, 148
Delamont, S.   74

Department of Education and Science (DES) 39, 41, 47, 53, 54, 56, 60, 61, 63, 64, 67, 71, 73, 75, 79, 94, 96, 99, 151
Department for Education (DFE) 50, 53, 65, 66, 81, 87, 97, 99, 102, 106, 108, 111, 113, 114, 116, 120, 133, 134, 152
DES and Welsh Office 76, 78–81
desk-top publishing 167
Dixon, A. 24
Dombey, H. 20, 25, 26
Donaldson, M. 126
Dowling, P. 47
Duckworth, E. 69
Dyson, A.E. 75

Eddershaw, C. 109
Edwards, D. 100
Egglestone, J. 72
Emmerson, C. 2, 14
equal opportunities 49, 149
Ernest, P. 38
Evans, N. 68
experimental and investigative science 65, 66, 67

Ferreiro, E. 105
Fox, C. 114
Frater, G. 20
Fullan, M. 72

Galton, M. 74, 84
games 123, 124, 126–7, 137
gender 101
Gibson, H. 112
Gipps, C. 49
Goddard, I. 2, 14
Goodman, Y. 105
Gorman, T. 18
Graham, D. 20, 42, 78
graph-drawing 168
Graves, D. 114
Gretton, J. 75
Gunning, S. 72

Halliday, M. 100, 103, 113
Halsey, P. 9, 14
Hargreaves, A. 72
Harlen, W. 54, 58, 60
Harste, J. 105, 112, 117
Her Majesty's Inspectorate (HMI) 16–17, 38, 39, 48, 58, 74, 75, 85, 86, 98, 99, 107, 108, 111, 112
Hoffman, M. 114
Holdaway, D. 106
Howe, A. 103
Huey, E.H. 26
Hutchins, P. 107

Initiatives in Primary Science: an Evaluation (IPSE) 55
INSET 96, 112
investigations 125–6

Jackson, M. 75
Johnson, G. 24, 25–6
Johnson, J. 20
Joseph, K. 41

Kalantzis, M. 113
Kelly, A.V. 75, 78
Kerry, T. 72
Kingman 7, 8, 14
Kingman, J. 15, 28
Kings College London 41, 47
Kress, G. 20, 113
Kruger, C. 56

Labov, W. 30
Lake, M. 17–18
Lao Tzu, 157
Lawton, D. 46
Lewis, C.S. 109
literature 97, 98, 103, 104, 105–12, 114

Mallett, M. 111
Marenbon, J. 23
McIlvanney, W. 30–1
McIntosh, A. 40
McNee, M. 31–2
Meek, M. 105, 106, 108
Mercer, N. 100
modelling using IT 169, 170
monitoring using IT 170
Moore, P. 107
Mortimore, P. 74, 102, 103
Moss, P. 29, 30
multiculturalism 49
multimedia 168

NAAE 19
Nash, I. 8, 14
NATE 19, 26
National Curriculum Council (NCC) 42, 44, 49, 56, 61, 64, 67, 79, 81, 82, 83, 84, 94, 101, 124, 143
National Oracy Project 100, 103
National Writing Project 112, 117
Neate, B. 111
Newbolt Report 15, 22, 27, 29–30, 33
Newton, L. 58
Norman, K. 100
Nuffield Primary Science 57
number 123, 124, 125, 126–7, 134, 135, 136, 137

Office for Standards in Education (OFSTED)   39,
        40, 45, 46, 63, 64, 73, 85, 86, 94, 156
Ollerenshaw, C.   57, 58, 62, 153, 154
Open University   56
organizing the learning experience   136–39
Ormerod, J.   107
Ovens, P.   60

Palacio, D.   56
Papert, S.   47, 125
Pascall, D.   23
Patten, J.   44, 84
Perera, K.   29
Phinney, M.   111
phonics   16–19, 106, 107
planning   63, 65, 67, 127–39
Plowden   73
Pole, J.   21
Primary Language Record   105, 111, 117
Prince Charles   21
Pring, R.   2, 14
problem solving   124–5
professional development   56, 62
progression   55, 61, 64, 66, 135

quangos   22–4

reading   101, 102, 105–12, 113
record-keeping   104, 105, 111–12, 117
revision   15, 26
Richards, R.   54
Ritchie, R.   57, 58, 86, 154
Rose, J.   83, 84, 85, 138
Rosen, M.   114

Sampson, G.   27
schemes of work   148
Schools Curriculum and Assessment Authority
        (SCAA)   38, 44, 45, 48, 50, 65, 82, 94, 97, 106,
        111, 112, 128, 129, 131, 144, 150, 151, 152
Science Process and Concept Exploration
        (SPACE) Project   57, 153
Science Working Group (SWG)   67

scientific exploration and investigation   61, 64
scientific skills   54, 57, 60, 63
SEAC   44
Sexton, S.   16
Shephard, G.   13, 14, 45, 84
Shuard, H.   39
Simon, B.   4, 14, 74
simulations   170
Smith, F.   105, 108
speaking and listening   99–105
Spooner, M.   78
spreadsheets   169
standard assessment tasks (SATs)   62
standard English   16, 28–31
standards of achievement   39–41
Summers, M.   56
Swann, J.   101

Tann, S.   72
Tebbit, N.   31
Teberosky, A.   105
TGAT   42, 47
Tizard, B.   30, 74, 100
Turner, M.   16, 26, 96
Tyler, D.   78

Walsh, J.P.   114
Walwayne Court Primary School   88–90
Webb, K.   110
Weir, S.   22
Wells, G.   30, 100
West, A.   24–5
West, D.   60
Westall, R.   104, 114
White, J.   4, 5, 14
Widdowson, H.   28
Wilson, J.   109
Wiltshire LEA   97
Woodhead, C.   83, 84, 85, 138
wordprocessing   167
Wragg, E.C.   63, 100
writing   98, 102, 103, 109, 112–17